Exam Ref 70-411: Administering Windows Server 2012 R2

Charlie Russel

PUBLISHED BY
Microsoft Press
A Division of Microsoft Corporation
One Microsoft Way
Redmond, Washington 98052-6399

Library of Congress Control Number: 2014940584
ISBN: 978-0-7356-8479-9

Printed and bound in the United States of America.

Third Printing

Microsoft Press books are available through booksellers and distributors worldwide. If you need support related to this book, email Microsoft Press Book Support at mspinput@microsoft.com. Please tell us what you think of this book at http://www.microsoft.com/learning/booksurvey.

Microsoft and the trademarks listed at http://www.microsoft.com/en-us/legal/intellectualproperty/Trademarks/EN-US.aspx are trademarks of the Microsoft group of companies. All other marks are property of their respective owners.

The example companies, organizations, products, domain names, email addresses, logos, people, places, and events depicted herein are fictitious. No association with any real company, organization, product, domain name, email address, logo, person, place, or event is intended or should be inferred.

This book expresses the author's views and opinions. The information contained in this book is provided without any express, statutory, or implied warranties. Neither the authors, Microsoft Corporation, nor its resellers, or distributors will be held liable for any damages caused or alleged to be caused either directly or indirectly by this book.

Acquisitions Editor: Anne Hamilton
Developmental Editor: Karen Szall
Editorial Production: Box Twelve Communications
Technical Reviewer: Brian Svidergol
Cover: Twist Creative • Seattle

Contents at a glance

Contents

What do you think of this book? We want to hear from you!

Microsoft is interested in hearing your feedback so we can continually improve our books and learning resources for you. To participate in a brief online survey, please visit:

www.microsoft.com/learning/booksurvey/

What do you think of this book? We want to hear from you!

Microsoft is interested in hearing your feedback so we can continually improve our
books and learning resources for you. To participate in a brief online survey, please visit:

www.microsoft.com/learning/booksurvey/

Introduction

This book is written for IT professionals who want to earn the MCSA: Windows Server 2012 certification. This certification includes three exams:

- **70-410** Installing and Configuring Windows Server 2012
- **70-411** Administering Windows Server 2012
- **70-412** Configuring Advanced Windows Server 2012 Services

Exam 70-411, the focus of this book, serves as the middle exam in the path to the Windows Server 2012 MCSA for those who are not currently Microsoft certified in an earlier version of Windows Server. This book is therefore written specifically for IT professionals who want to demonstrate that they have the primary set of Windows Server 2012 skills, relevant across multiple solution areas in a business environment, to reduce IT costs and deliver more business value. Starting in January, 2014, this exam covers topics that include new features and capabilities introduced in Windows Server 2012 R2.

The three exams—Exam 70-410, Exam 70-411, and Exam 70-412—allow you to earn the Windows Server 2012 MCSA from scratch, without any prior certification. Together, these three exams include 18 domains of broader skills and 62 more specific objectives. Because the exams are intended for individuals who haven't yet earned Windows Server certification, the exams test new features in Windows Server 2012 as well as older features that haven't changed since Windows Server 2008 or even earlier.

The 70-411 exam tests six domains, and 22 objectives that comprise the core knowledge needed to administer a Windows Server 2012 R2 infrastructure.

In order to create a book that is a manageable study tool, we've focused on covering primarily the new features and capabilities of Windows Server 2012 R2, while not ignoring likely test subjects that were introduced in earlier versions of Windows Server.

This book covers every exam objective, but it does not cover every exam question. Only the Microsoft exam team has access to the exam questions themselves and Microsoft regularly adds new questions to the exam, making it impossible for us to cover specific questions. You should consider this book a supplement to your relevant real-world experience and other study materials. If you encounter a topic in this book that you do not feel completely comfortable with, use the links you'll find in the book to find more information—and then take the time to research and study the topic. Valuable information is available on MSDN, TechNet, and in blogs and forums.

Microsoft certifications

Microsoft certifications distinguish you by proving your command of a broad set of skills and experience with current Microsoft products and technologies. The exams and corresponding certifications are developed to validate your mastery of critical competencies as you design and develop, or implement and support, solutions with Microsoft products and technologies both on-premise and in the cloud. Certification brings a variety of benefits to the individual and to employers and organizations.

> **MORE INFO**   **ALL MICROSOFT CERTIFICATIONS**
>
> For information about Microsoft certifications, including a full list of available certifications, go to *http://www.microsoft.com/learning/en/us/certification/cert-default.aspx*.

Acknowledgments

As only writers can fully appreciate, no book ever makes it into a reader's hands without the work of many, many people, some of whom I'll never know, but all of whose efforts I greatly appreciate. Of those I do know, I'd like to sincerely thank Anne Hamilton and Karen Szall at Microsoft Press for their long-standing support and friendship. Gaby Kaplan and Dave Bishop at Microsoft for patiently taking my "bug" reports on Windows PowerShell documentation without ever once suggesting that the problem might be self-inflicted; Jeff Riley at Box Twelve Communications for his unflagging attention to keeping the project on course while working around and through whatever came our way; Rich Kershner for his excellent design and layout skills, and especially for saving me from the consequences of my own actions; Nancy Sixsmith for her light, but highly competent editing; Brian Svidergol for his meticulous technical review; and Angie Martin for creating an outstanding Index that helps you quickly find what you're looking for, no matter how obscure the topic.

I'd also like to sincerely thank two of my fellow Microsoft MVPs, Karen McCall and Jay Freedman. Their invaluable assistance with creating a Microsoft Word macro rescued me from a significant annoyance. I really, really appreciated their help. They exemplify the spirit of MVPs around the world and in every discipline, who give of their time and expertise unstintingly to make life better for the computing community.

Finally, my Research and Support Department, headed by Sharon Crawford, who came out of retirement to dig in and help when I really needed it. Her team includes Spuds Trey, Boots Khatt, and Sir William Wallace who put in especially long hours of support. I couldn't have done it without them.

Errata, updates, & book support

We've made every effort to ensure the accuracy of this book and its companion content. You can access updates to this book—in the form of a list of submitted errata and their related corrections on the Errata & Updates tab of the book page at:

http://aka.ms/ER411R2

If you discover an error that is not already listed, please submit it to us at the same page.

For additional support, email Microsoft Press Book Support at mspinput@microsoft.com.

Please note that product support for Microsoft software and hardware is not offered through the previous addresses. For help with Microsoft software or hardware, go to *http://support.microsoft.com*.

We want to hear from you

At Microsoft Press, your satisfaction is our top priority and your feedback is our most valuable asset. Please tell us what you think of this book at:

http://aka.ms/tellpress

The survey is short, and we read every one of your comments and ideas. Thanks in advance for your input!

Stay in touch

Let's keep the conversation going! We're on Twitter: *http://twitter.com/MicrosoftPress*.

Preparing for the exam

Microsoft certification exams are a great way to build your resume and let the world know about your level of expertise. Certification exams validate your on-the-job experience and product knowledge. Although there is no substitute for on-the-job experience, preparation through study and hands-on practice can help you prepare for the exam. We recommend that you augment your exam preparation plan by using a combination of available study materials and courses. For example, you might use the Exam Ref and another study guide for your "at home" preparation, and take a Microsoft Official Curriculum course for the classroom experience. Choose the combination that you think works best for you.

CHAPTER 1

Deploy, manage, and maintain servers

Installing servers implies a unitary operation, but deploying servers is something you do often, not just once in a while. You have to install servers reliably and repeatedly, without major user intervention. After the server is deployed, you have to keep it up to date with the latest security, critical, and important updates while minimizing the amount of intervention required. And you have to be able to monitor the server to ensure that it is running efficiently and without major failure events.

This chapter discusses the deployment of Windows Server 2012 R2 by using Windows Deployment Services (WDS) to automate the deployment of standard or custom images to servers. It also discusses implementing Windows Server Update Services (WSUS) to automate and customize patch management on the network. Finally, the chapter covers monitoring servers with Windows Performance Monitor (perfmon) and Windows Event Viewer.

> **IMPORTANT**
> ### Have you read page xvii?
> It contains valuable information regarding the skills you need to pass the exam.

A major change in Windows Server 2012 R2 is the nearly complete coverage of all server tasks with Windows PowerShell. This is a significant change over earlier versions of Windows Server, and this chapter covers Windows PowerShell ways to deploy, update, and monitor Windows Server.

Objectives in this chapter:
- Objective 1.1: Deploy and manage server images
- Objective 1.2: Implement patch management
- Objective 1.3: Monitor servers

EXAM TIP
Exams are written to a very demanding specification, and exam question writers must not only justify their correct answers but their wrong answers as well. If you're unsure of the correct answer to a simple multiple choice question, start by eliminating any answer that you know to be wrong. If there is more than one answer that appears to be correct, it's likely that you missed an important clue in the description of the question. Go back and carefully read the question to see if there's a clue you overlooked.

Objective 1.1: Deploy and manage server images

Automating the deployment of servers has become an important part of what information technology professionals (IT Pros) are expected to do, and this exam description recognizes it with an objective focused on deployment and image management. The key role that Windows Server 2012 R2 uses to manage and deploy server images is Windows Deployment Service (WDS). The new WDS features in Windows Server 2012 and Windows Server 2012 R2 are likely to be the primary focus of the exam questions, especially because WDS in Windows Server 2012 R2 introduces full support for Windows PowerShell, with 33 cmdlets to manage WDS.

> **This objective covers how to:**
> - Install the Windows Deployment Services role
> - Configure and manage boot, install, and discover images
> - Update images with security updates, hotfixes, and drivers
> - Install features for offline images
> - Configure driver groups and packages

Installing the Windows Deployment Services role

Before you can use WDS, you have to install the Windows Deployment Services role on a server. That server can be in an Active Directory Domain Services (AD DS) domain or it can be a stand-alone server. The minimum prerequisites for installing WDS are these:

- **AD DS** An AD DS server is required if WDS is integrated into Active Directory. The deployment server can be either a member server or a domain controller. WDS imposes no minimum AD DS domain or forest versions, and a standalone WDS doesn't require AD DS.
- **DHCP** An active DHCP server on the network is required to support Preboot eXecution Environment (PXE).
- **DNS** A working and reachable Domain Name Service (DNS) server is required.
- **NTFS** The image store must reside on an NTFS volume.
- **Credentials** You must be a member of the Local Administrators group on the server to install the Windows Deployment Services role.

The Windows Deployment Services role can be installed and managed only on a server running the GUI Windows Server installation. WDS is not supported on Windows Server Core installations.

Installing WDS by using Server Manager

Windows Server Manager is the GUI way to install and configure the Windows Deployment Services role on a server, whether running stand-alone or integrated with Active Directory. Use the Add Roles And Features Wizard to install the Windows Deployment Services role. You'll use the Role-based Or Feature-based option. Server Manager can be used to insert roles and features into virtual hard disks or to manage multiple servers from a single console, as shown in Figure 1-1.

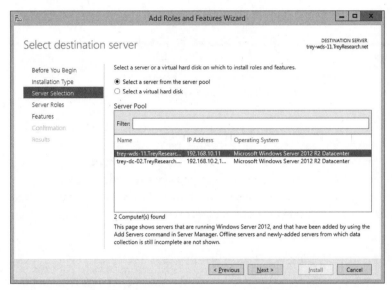

FIGURE 1-1 The Select Destination Server page of the Add Roles And Features Wizard

When you install the Windows Deployment Services role using Server Manager, it automatically prompts you to install the necessary management tools. WDS can be deployed with the combined Deployment Server role service and Transport Server role service, as shown in Figure 1-2, or (less commonly) with the Transport Server role service only.

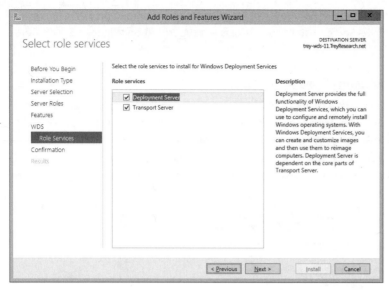

FIGURE 1-2 The Select Role Services page of the Add Roles And Features Wizard

Installing WDS by using Windows PowerShell

An important change in Windows Server 2012 R2 is the new Windows PowerShell WDS module, which provides virtually 100 percent Windows PowerShell coverage. Existing command-line tools are deprecated, and all tasks can be performed with Windows PowerShell.

Use the Install-WindowsFeature cmdlet to install the Windows Deployment Services role on a server. The Install-WindowsFeature cmdlet accepts parameters of –Name for the feature name, -ComputerName for the name (or IP address) of the target server or –Vhd for the name

of the virtual hard disk, and a –Credential parameter that enables you to provide credentials as a <PSCredential> object. Additionally, you can specify flags of –IncludeAllSubFeature and –IncludeManagementTools. By default, the Install-WindowsFeature cmdlet installs only the specific feature or role specified; it does not install any subfeatures or management tools for the feature.

To install the Windows Deployment Services role, including the management tools on the trey-wds-11 server, open an elevated Windows PowerShell window and use the following Windows PowerShell command:

```
Install-WindowsFeature –Name WDS –ComputerName "trey-wds-11" -IncludeManagementTools
```

> **NOTE USING AND ELEVATED WINDOWS POWERSHELL PROMPT**
>
> Many management tasks require administrative privileges. You can either pass in a PSCredential object, created by using the Get-Credential cmdlet, or open an elevated Windows PowerShell window with the following command (which prompts you for credentials and then opens up a new elevated Windows PowerShell window):
>
> ```
> Start-Process PowerShell.exe -Verb RunAs
> ```

EXAM TIP

Windows PowerShell commands that require elevation typically support a -Credential parameter. Exam answers that leave this parameter off typically fail. If the answer includes a -Credential parameter as a string in the form "DOMAIN\User", it will also fail because the parameter expects a PSCredential object. Use the Get-Credential cmdlet to generate a PSCredential object.

Configuring WDS

Before you can actually use WDS, you have to configure some basic information from Server Manager or directly in the Wdsmgmt.msc console. You have to make several configuration decisions, including the following:

- AD DS integrated or stand-alone server
- Location of the Remote Installation folder
- Initial PXE server settings

The AD DS integrated option is available only in an AD DS domain environment. The location for the remote installation folder should be on an NTFS-formatted volume with sufficient free space to hold several images, applications, and driver packages. It is not usually installed on the system volume; it is installed on its own dedicated volume.

Initial PXE settings control which client computers are allowed to download images. You can set this to none, only prestaged clients, or any PXE client that requests an image.

After the initial configuration is complete, you can choose to continue to install the initial images to the server, as shown in Figure 1-3.

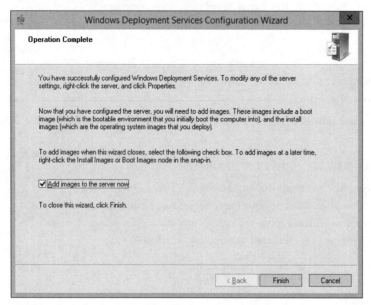

FIGURE 1-3 The Operation Complete page of the Windows Deployment Services Configuration Wizard

Configuring and managing boot, install, and discover images

There are four types of images used by WDS: boot images, install images, capture images, and discover images. The minimum requirements to boot to the WDS server and deploy an image to a client computer are a boot image and an install image.

Boot images

Boot images are Windows PE images that reside in the \Sources folder on the Windows installation media as \Sources\Boot.wim. The Boot.wim file includes both Windows PE and the WDS client.

Install images

Install images are the actual operating system images that are deployed to the client computer. You can use the default image in the \Sources folder of the installation media (\Sources\Install.wim), or you can create a custom image by using a capture image or other tool.

Capture images

Capture images are used to create a custom install image from an existing template computer. You must prepare the template computer with Sysprep and then boot by using the capture image. You have to have sufficient spare disk space on the template computer to save the captured image to a local volume.

Discover images

Discover images are used by WDS client computers that don't support PXE boot. You use the Boot.wim file from the Windows installation media, and you also need the tools in the Windows Assessment and Deployment Kit (Windows ADK) for Windows 8.1, which is available at *http://www.microsoft.com/en-us/download/details.aspx?id=39982*.

Managing images in the WDS image store

You can copy, disable, enable, import, export, remove, and set the properties of images within a WDS image store by using either the GUI or the Windows PowerShell WDS module.

EXAM TIP

The Import-WDS* cmdlets lend themselves well to exam questions. The unqualified candidate will likely choose the Copy or Set verb, rather than Import.

Use the Add Image Wizard in the Windows Deployment Services console or the Import-WDS* cmdlets in Windows PowerShell to add images to the WDS image store. WDS organizes install images into an image group to enable them to share common file resources and security. You must create at least one image group.

To add an install image to the WDS image store, use the following Windows PowerShell command:

```
Import-WdsInstallImage -Path "<WIM or VHD Location>" -ImageGroup "<GroupName>"
```

The command for adding a WDS boot image is essentially the same, but without the -ImageGroup parameter:

```
Import-WdsBootImage -Path "<WIM or VHD Location>"
```

Both cmdlets support a wealth of additional parameters, allowing you to set various properties of the images. Use the Get-Help cmdlet with the -Full parameter to get complete details on a particular Windows PowerShell cmdlet.

EXAM TIP

To copy an image from one image group to another, use the Export-WdsInstallImage and Import-WdsInstallImage cmdlets. The Copy-WdsInstallImage cmdlet allows you to copy an image only within the same image group.

Updating images with security updates, hotfixes, and drivers

You can use a capture image to create an updated install image that includes current hotfixes and updates, or you can use the Deployment Image Servicing and Management (DISM) platform commands and the Windows PowerShell Dism module to mount an offline image and update it directly.

You can directly modify an offline image (.wim) or virtual hard disk (.vhd or .vhdx) with the Dism cmdlets. To modify an image or virtual hard disk by inserting an update into it, follow these steps:

1. Set the image to read-write by clearing any read-only attributes with attrib -r.

2. Mount the image on an empty mount point using the Mount-WindowsImage cmdlet.

3. Extract the contents of the update (.msu file) using WinRAR or another third-party tool.

4. Inject the .cab file into the mounted image by using the Add-WindowsPackage cmdlet.

5. Commit the changes and unmount the install image by using the Save-WindowsImage and Dismount-WindowsImage cmdlets.

Installing or removing features in offline images

You can add or remove Windows features in an existing image or virtual hard disk by using the Enable-WindowsOptionalFeature cmdlet or the Disable-WindowsOptionalFeature cmdlet, respectively. You can modify the currently running image with the -online parameter, or modify an offline image or virtual hard disk by mounting it and modifying the mounted image. To modify an offline image or virtual hard disk, follow these steps:

1. Set the image to read-write by clearing any read-only attributes with attrib -r.

2. Mount the image on an empty mount point using the Mount-WindowsImage cmdlet.

3. Modify the image with the Enable-WindowsOptionalFeature cmdlet or the Disable-WindowsOptionalFeature cmdlet, as appropriate.

4. Commit the changes and unmount the install image by using the Save-WindowsImage and Dismount-WindowsImage cmdlets.

Capturing a new template image

For many changes, it's easiest to modify an existing image by updating an offline image or virtual hard disk. When more substantial changes are required, however, or when there is a change in the underlying hardware or core software suite, it is often easier to create a new template computer and then capture an image from it. To do this, follow these steps:

1. Create a capture image in the Windows Deployment Services console by right-clicking a boot image and selecting Create Capture Image to start the Create Capture Image Wizard, as shown in Figure 1-4.

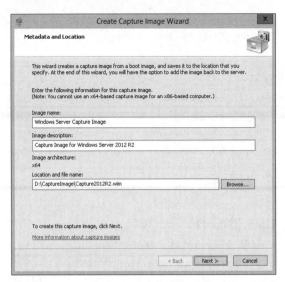

FIGURE 1-4 The Create Capture Image Wizard

2. Add the capture image to the WDS image store.

3. Deploy Windows to the computer that will act as the source for the template image. This computer's hardware should be as similar to the intended target computers that the captured image will support as is practical.

4. Install roles and features that will be part of the template.

> **NOTE SUPPORTED ROLES FOR SYSPREP ON WINDOWS SERVER**
>
> Not all roles that can be enabled on Windows Server are supported as a template image. All Active Directory roles, for example, are not supported. To see a list of roles that are supported by Sysprep, see *http://technet.microsoft.com/en-us/library/hh824835.aspx*.

5. Install any additional software that you want to be part of the template.

6. Apply all updates and hotfixes that you want to be part of the template. Add all drivers that the template needs.

7. Disable or remove any packages that should not be deployed on target computers.

8. Run Sysprep on the template computer using the following command from the %windir%\system32\sysprep directory:

```
Sysprep /oobe /generalize /reboot
```

9. Restart the computer and boot from the network.

10. Select the capture boot image you created and follow the steps of the Windows Deployment Services Image Capture Wizard to save the image.

> **NOTE SAVING IMAGES LOCALLY**
>
> Ensure that you have sufficient room on the template computer to save a local copy of the image you are capturing. You can automatically upload the image to your WDS server as well, but you must always save a copy on a locally mounted drive. It can be a Server Message Block (SMB) share from a network computer, as long as the share has an assigned drive letter.

Configuring driver groups and packages

WDS enables you to add hardware-specific drivers to your deployment images and to allow images to request a specific set of images from the available driver store. You can create driver groups to host and organize collections of drivers. The initial configuration of WDS creates a default driver group called "DriverGroup1". You can use the Windows Deployment Services console to add or remove driver groups, rename or duplicate driver groups, and modify the properties of driver groups.

In addition to the Windows Deployment Services console, you can use the Windows PowerShell *-WdsDriverPackage cmdlets to manage your drivers and driver packages. The cmdlets available include these:

- **Add-WdsDriverPackage** Adds a driver package from the WDS driver store into a driver group or injects it directly into a boot image.
- **Disable-WdsDriverPackage** Makes a driver package in the WDS driver store unavailable to clients without removing it from the driver store.
- **Enable-WdsDriverPackage** Makes a driver package in the WDS driver store available to clients. Packages are enabled by default when added to the WDS driver store.
- **Get-WdsDriverPackage** Gets the properties of all the driver packages in the WDS driver store, or the properties of a specific package if you specify the name or ID (GUID) of the package.
- **Import-WdsDriverPackage** Imports a driver package into the WDS driver store and optionally adds it to a driver group.
- **Remove-WdsDriverPackage** Removes a driver package from a WDS driver group, or removes it from all driver groups and deletes it completely from the driver store.

The WDS Windows PowerShell cmdlets do not allow you to create or directly manage the properties of driver groups. You can manipulate the contents of driver groups, but not create new driver groups.

You can inject drivers into an existing image or virtual hard disk by using the Add-WdsDriverPackage cmdlet. After you add a driver package to an existing image, WDS can't remove the driver package. You would have to re-create the image without the driver installed.

Thought experiment
Upgrading hardware

In this thought experiment, apply what you've learned about this objective. You can find answers to these questions in the "Answers" section at the end of this chapter.

You are the network administrator for TreyResearch.net. Your current server hardware specification is no longer available, and the company has chosen a new vendor and has upgraded hardware from that new vendor. The current custom WDS images that support the older hardware contain all the required software, but fail to boot with the new hardware.

In discussions with management about future directions, it is revealed that in the near- to mid-term, the new servers will be rolled out to support all the Finance, Accounting, and Human Resources users who use thin clients to connect to Remote Desktop Session Host servers that will be replaced. At the same time, a new version of a key line of business applications used by these departments is to be rolled out with the new hardware.

1. You have to come up with an immediate solution for the new hardware to support the new users coming on board this week. What's the best way to support the new hardware?

2. What should you do to support the move to new software and hardware for the Finance, Accounting, and Human Resources departments?

Objective summary

- The Windows Deployment Services role can be installed only on a full (GUI) installation of Windows Server. It isn't supported on a Windows Server Core installation.
- Before installing and configuring the Windows Deployment Services role, ensure that your network infrastructure is in place and reachable. DNS and DHCP are required for WDS, as is AD DS if you are using an Active Directory integrated WDS deployment.
- When you install the Windows Deployment Services role with the Install-WindowsFeature cmdlet, use the -IncludeManagementTools parameter.
- Initial configuration of the Windows Deployment Services role is required after installation and includes setting the location of the WDS image store. The image store must reside on an NTFS volume and is typically installed on a volume other than the system volume.

- There are four different types of images used by the WDS server: boot, install, capture, and discover images.

- Capture images are used to capture a custom install image from a template computer. Discover images are used to deploy by using physical media rather than PXE boot.

- Use the Dism module of Windows PowerShell to update images. You have to mount an offline image on the local file system in read-write mode and use the Add-WindowsPackage or Enable-WindowsOptionalFeature cmdlets to update the mounted image.

- Before you can use the updated image, you have to commit the changes and unmount the image.

- You must use the Windows Deployment Service console to create WDS driver groups or change the properties of existing driver groups.

- You can use the WDS cmdlets to manage drivers and driver packages in existing WDS driver groups.

Objective review

Answer the following questions to test your knowledge of the information in this objective. You can find the answers to these questions and explanations of why each answer choice is correct or incorrect in the "Answers" section at the end of the chapter.

1. Which of the following are required to install the Windows Deployment Services role on Windows Server 2012 R2? (Choose all that apply.)

   A. An active DHCP server

   B. A working and reachable DNS server

   C. A local volume with a Resilient File System (ReFS)

   D. An AD DS server

2. Which types of images are required to create a custom image from a template computer? (Choose all that apply.)

   A. Boot images

   B. Install images

   C. Capture images

   D. Discover images

3. Which Windows PowerShell cmdlet is used to update an offline boot file with a new driver?

   A. Import-WdsBootImage

   B. Import-WdsDriverPackage

   C. Set-WdsBootImage

   D. Add-WdsDriverPackage

Objective 1.2: Implement patch management

Centralizing your patch management is an important server function and one that can't be entirely managed with Windows PowerShell. You need a combination of tools to fully manage your network's updates.

Windows Server Update Services (WSUS) is the primary technology for deploying updates.

This objective covers how to:

- Install and configure the Windows Server Update Services role
- Configure Group Policy Objects (GPOs) for updates
- Configure WSUS groups
- Configure WSUS synchronization
- Configure client-side targeting
- Manage patch management in mixed environments

Install and configure the Windows Server Update Services role

You can install and configure the Windows Server Update Services role and its supporting services by using Server Manager, the command line, or a mixture of the two. If you choose the command line, use a combination of Windows PowerShell and the Wsusutil.exe utility for configuration. The Windows Server Update Services role is supported on a Windows Server Core installation.

Installing and configuring by using GUI

Windows Server Manager is the GUI way to install and configure the Windows Server Update Services role on a server. Use the Add Roles And Features Wizard with the role-based or feature-based option to install the Windows Server Update Services role. Server Manager can be used to insert roles and features into virtual hard disks or to manage multiple servers from a single console.

When you install the Windows Server Update Services role using Server Manager, it automatically prompts you to install the necessary management tools and the other features and roles that are required (see Figure 1-5).

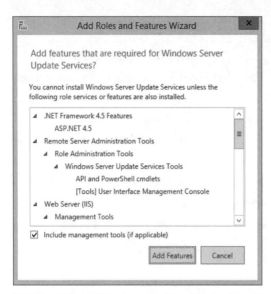

FIGURE 1-5 The Add Features That Are Required For Windows Server Update Services page

The WSUS installation defaults to using the Windows Internal Database (WID) as the WSUS repository. Alternately, you can choose to use SQL Server as the repository by selecting Database instead of WID Database on the Select Role Services page of the Add Roles And Features Wizard. You can't install both on the same server, however. If you intend to have only a single WSUS server at a site, the default is generally a good choice. But if you need a shared database across multiple WSUS servers, need SQL query access to the database, or already have a SQL Server infrastructure in place, choose SQL Server instead.

The WSUS content can be stored on Windows Update, keeping the disk footprint smaller, or it can be stored on a locally accessible volume or share for reduced wide area network (WAN) utilization and faster access. The default is to use a locally accessible location. This location must be an NTFS-formatted volume and needs to have at least 6 GB of free disk space (and a good deal more for most networks.)

When the installation of the Windows Server Update Services role is complete, you'll see the WSUS node in Server Manager. If you click the Configuration Required For Windows Server Update Services yellow bar in the Servers pane (see Figure 1-6), the configuration will complete with the settings you made during the Add Roles And Features Wizard.

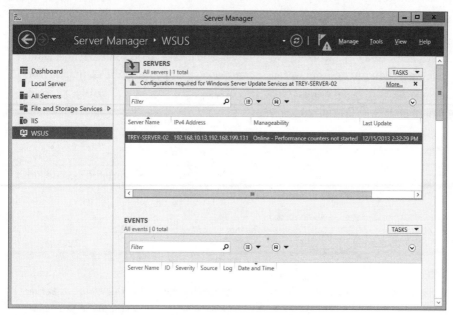

FIGURE 1-6 The WSUS pane of Server Manager

Installing and configuring by using the command line

You can install WSUS by using Windows PowerShell. The basic command is this:

```
Install-WindowsFeature -Name UpdateServices -IncludeManagementTools
```

This command installs WSUS in the default configuration and uses the WID database. To install WSUS to use a SQL Server database, use this command:

```
Install-WindowsFeature -Name UpdateServices,UpdateServices-DB -IncludeManagementTools
```

EXAM TIP

The expected command line to install the Windows Server Update Services role would include an -IncludeAllSubFeatures parameter, but this will fail. You can't install both the WID database and a SQL Server database for WSUS. It is an easily overlooked conflict that can cause you to choose an incorrect answer to an exam question.

Windows PowerShell can't be used for all WSUS configuration and management; you have to rely on the Wsusutil.exe utility for at least some of the command-line configuration.

Postinstallation configuration

Installing the Windows Server Update Services role and supporting services and features is only the first step of creating a working WSUS server. You'll have to do some postinstallation tasks as well, which you can do from within Server Manager or by using the command line.

To configure WSUS to use the WID database and a content directory of D:\WSUS, use the following commands from an elevated prompt:

```
cd "C:\Program Files\Update Services\Tools"
.\wsusutil postinstall content_dir=D:\WSUS
```

To configure WSUS to use a SQL Server instance on the local server with the update files stored on D:\WSUS, use these commands:

```
cd "C:\Program Files\Update Services\Tools"
.\wsusutil postinstall SQL_INSTANCE_NAME=localhost content_dir=D:\WSUS
```

EXAM TIP

A potential exam question scenario might be the following: You install the Windows Server Update Services role with a **SQL database**. However, after successfully completing the command, you notice that the database wasn't created. What should you do next? The answer: **Run wsusutil.exe and point to the SQL server and instance.**

To configure the location from which WSUS synchronizes updates, use the Set-WsusServerSynchronization cmdlet. To configure the local WSUS server to sync with Microsoft Update, use this command:

```
Set-WsusServerSynchronization -SyncFromMU
```

You can also configure WSUS to sync with an upstream WSUS server. You can specify the server name, port number, whether to use SSL, and whether the WSUS server is a replica. To configure the local WSUS server to sync with an upstream server, SRV2, over port 8530, use this command:

```
Set-WsusServerSynchronization -UssServerName SRV2 -PortNumber 8530
```

You can use the WSUS cmdlets to manage remote WSUS servers. Use the Get-WsusServer cmdlet to generate an IUpdateServer object and then pass the object to Set-WsusServerSynchronization on the command line:

```
Get-WsusServer -Name SRV2 -PortNumber 8530 | Set-WsusServerSynchronization -SyncFromMU
```

You can use Windows PowerShell to manage which updates are approved or denied, and which classifications and products are synchronized. To approve a single update, use this command:

```
Get-WsusUpdate -UpdateID <GUID> | `
  Approve-WsusUpdate -Action Install -TargetGroupName "All Computers"
```

Use the following commands to get all the security updates that are needed and that have either failed or have not been approved, and then set them to be installed on the "Servers" group:

```
Get-WsusUpdate -Classification Security -Status FailedorNeeded | `
  Approve-WsusUpdate -Action Install -TargetGroupName "Servers"
```

> **MORE INFO** **COMMAND-LINE REFERENCES**
>
> For more information on the WSUS cmdlets in Windows Server 2012 R2, see
> *http://technet.microsoft.com/en-us/library/hh826166.aspx*. For help using Wsusutil.exe,
> type **Wsusutil.exe /?**.

Configuring Group Policy Objects for updates

You can configure Group Policy Objects (GPOs) to enforce organizational standards for applying Windows Updates by using the Group Policy Management Editor, as shown in Figure 1-7.

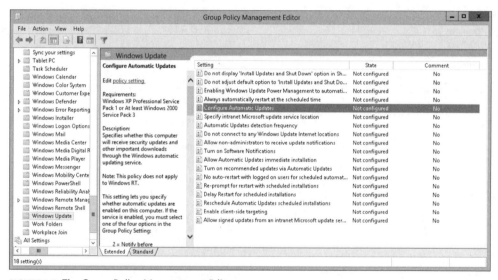

FIGURE 1-7 The Group Policy Management Editor

By using the WSUS GPO settings, you can enforce the location that domain-joined client computers use for updates, which updates are installed automatically, whether updates that require a reboot enforce that reboot, and so on. The available WSUS settings are shown in Table 1-1.

TABLE 1-1 WSUS GPO settings

setting	Applies to Versions
Do not display 'Install Updates and Shut Down' option in Shut Down Windows dialog box	Windows 7, Windows Server 2008 R2, Windows Vista, Windows XP Service Pack 2 (SP2)
Do not adjust default option to 'Install Updates and Shut Down' in Shut Down Windows dialog box	Windows 7, Windows Server 2008 R2, Windows Vista, Windows XP SP2
Enabling Windows Update Power Management to automatically wake up the system to install scheduled updates	Windows Server 2008, Windows 7, Windows Vista
Always automatically restart at the scheduled time	At least Windows Server 2012, Windows 8, or Windows RT
Configure Automatic Updates	Windows XP SP1 or at least Windows 2000 SP3
Specify intranet Microsoft update service location	At least Windows XP SP1 or Windows 2000 SP3. Excluding Windows RT
Automatic Updates detection frequency	At least Windows XP SP1 or Windows 2000 SP3, excluding Windows RT
Do not connect to any Windows Update Internet locations	At least Windows Server 2012 R2, Windows 8.1, or Windows RT 8.1
Allow nonadministrators to receive update notifications	Windows XP SP1 or at least Windows 2000 SP3
Turn on Software Notifications	Windows Server 2008, Windows 7, Windows Vista
Allow Automatic Updates immediate installation	At least Windows XP SP1 or Windows 2000 SP3, excluding Windows RT
Turn on recommended updates via Automatic Updates	At least Windows Vista
No auto-restart with logged-on users for scheduled automatic updates installations	Windows XP SP1 or at least Windows 2000 SP3
Re-prompt for restart with scheduled installations	Windows 7, Windows Server 2008 R2, Windows Vista, Windows Server 2003, Windows XP SP2, Windows XP SP1 , Windows 2000 SP4, Windows 2000 SP3
Delay Restart for scheduled installations	Windows 7, Windows Server 2008 R2, Windows Vista, Windows Server 2003, Windows XP SP2, Windows XP SP1 , Windows 2000 SP4, Windows 2000 SP3
Reschedule Automatic Updates scheduled installations	Windows 7, Windows Server 2008 R2, Windows Vista, Windows Server 2003, Windows XP SP2, Windows XP SP1 , Windows 2000 SP4, Windows 2000 SP3
Enable client-side targeting	At least Windows XP Professional SP 1 or Windows 2000 SP 3, excluding Windows RT
Allow signed updates from an intranet Microsoft service location	At least Windows Server 2003 operating systems or Windows XP Professional with SP1, excluding Windows RT

Configuring WSUS groups

After the initial configuration of WSUS is complete, you can create WSUS groups to control which update policies are applied to which computers. You need to create the groups in the Windows Server Update Services console by selecting All Computers in the left pane and then clicking Add Computer Group in the Actions pane (see Figure 1-8).

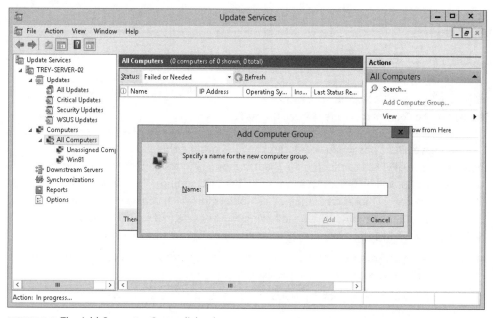

FIGURE 1-8 The Add Computer Group dialog box

You can add computers to an existing group in the Update Services console or by using the Add-WsusComputer cmdlet.

Configuring client-side targeting

The typical WSUS server uses server-side targeting with computers assigned to WSUS groups on the server. New computers are automatically assigned to the Unassigned Computers group until they are assigned to a group. This process works for small to mid-sized organizations, but it doesn't scale well in larger organizations. You can configure WSUS to use Group Policy to assign computers to WSUS groups by enabling client-side targeting.

Enable client-side targeting by selecting Computers in the Options section of the Windows Server Update Services console and selecting Use Group Policy Or Registry Settings On Computers, as shown in Figure 1-9.

FIGURE 1-9 The Computers dialog box in the Update Services console

If you have already assigned computers to WSUS groups, this choice will clear those selections. After the GPO has configured the client computers to assign them to a group, the WSUS computer groups will be repopulated based on the GPO settings. You can also manually set it in the registry for any non-domain-joined computers for which you want to manage the updates for by setting the values for the following registry keys in the HKEY_LOCAL_MACHINE\ Software\Policies\Microsoft\Windows\CurrentVersionWindowsUpdate subkey:

- **ElevateNonAdmins** If 1, non-administrators can approve or disapprove updates. If 0, only administrators can approve or disapprove updates.
- **TargetGroup** Name of the WSUS computer group to use if client-side targeting is enabled.
- **TargetGroupEnabled** If 1, client-side targeting is enabled; if 0, it isn't.
- **WUServer** URL of the WSUS server used by Automatic Updates.
- **WUStatusServer** URL of the WSUS server to which to send reporting information. Both WUServer and WUStatusServer must be set to the same value.

To configure Group Policy to work with client-side targeting, you need to edit the GPOs for your domain. You can create an overall GPO that you link at the domain level that turns Automatic Updates on; then sets the location of the WSUS server and additional GPOs that assign computers to specific WSUS groups based on their organizational unit (OU) or other criteria. To enable Automatic Updates and set the location of the WSUS server, you have to edit two policy settings:

- Configure Automatic Updates
- Specify Intranet Microsoft Update Service Location

The Configure Automatic Updates setting can be set to notify, download and notify, automatically download and install, or allow local administrators to control the setting. The Specify Intranet Microsoft Update Service Location setting requires you to specify the server name and port for detecting updates and the update statistics server (see Figure 1-10).

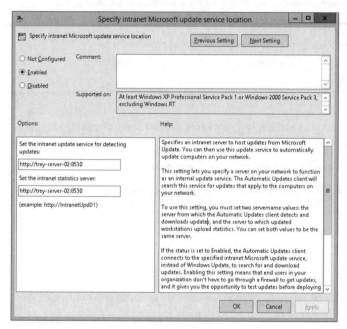

FIGURE 1-10 The Specify Intranet Microsoft Update Service Location Group Policy edit dialog box

To specify the specific WSUS groups that are used, edit the Enable Client-Side Targeting setting.

After the GPOs have propagated and clients have connected to check for updates, the groups in the Windows Server Update Services console will repopulate and show the computers that are assigned to the WSUS groups by Group Policy.

Thought experiment

Setting up new deployments and patching services

In this thought experiment, apply what you've learned about this objective. You can find answers to these questions in the "Answers" section at the end of this chapter.

You are the network administrator for TreyResearch.net. Trey Research has added a new building and is hiring, and you've been tasked to set up new deployment and patching services in the new building, which will be on a separate subdomain and subnet. Updates will be synchronized to the existing company WSUS server.

Company policy dictates a minimum number of physical servers and a minimum security and patching footprint for servers on the network, with no unnecessary roles or features installed.

With these requirements, answer the following questions:

1. Can you install your patching and deployment servers to the same physical server while minimizing the security footprint?

2. What is the minimum number of physical servers required?

3. What virtualized servers can you group together while meeting the requirements?

Objective summary

- The Windows Server Update Services role can be installed on both a Windows Server full installation and a Windows Server Core installation.

- WSUS supports either the WID or a SQL Server database, but you have to make a choice at install time.

- The installation of the Windows Deployment Services role can't use the -InstallAllSubFeatures parameter to the Install-WindowsFeature cmdlet because both databases can't be installed at the same time.

- The postinstallation tasks normally handled by the Server Manager Add Roles And Features Wizard can be done on the command line by using a combination of the wsusutil.exe utility and Windows PowerShell.

- Managing remote WSUS servers using Windows PowerShell uses the Get-WsusServer cmdlet to generate an IUpdateServer object.

- You can use the Group Policy Management console (gpmc.msc) and Group Policy Management Editor (gpedit.msc) to create and edit GPOs that control how WSUS is used in your organization.

- Use WSUS groups to aggregate subsets of client computers that need to have the same set of updates applied. WSUS groups can be created only in the Windows Server Update Services console (wsus.msc).
- The default installation of WSUS is configured to use server-side control of what computers are in which WSUS groups. This default requires that each computer be explicitly assigned to a specific WSUS group. You can change WSUS to use client-side targeting, which sets WSUS to have client computers assign themselves to a WSUS group based on GPO settings or individual registry entries.

Objective review

Answer the following questions to test your knowledge of the information in this objective. You can find the answers to these questions and explanations of why each answer choice is correct or incorrect in the "Answers" section at the end of the chapter.

1. What is the Windows PowerShell command to install the Windows Server Update Services role and supporting features for use with the WID database?

   A. Install-WindowsFeature -Name UpdateServices -IncludeAllSubFeatures

   B. Install-WindowsFeature -Name UpdateServices -IncludeAllSubFeatures -IncludeManagementTools

   C. Install-WindowsFeature -Name UpdateServices -IncludeManagementTools

   D. Install-WindowsFeature -Name UpdateServices,UpdateServices-DB -IncludeManagementTools

2. What are the required GPOs to assign computers to WSUS groups? (Choose all that apply.)

   A. Configure Automatic Updates

   B. Specify intranet Microsoft update service location

   C. Turn on recommended updates via Automatic Updates

   D. Enable client-side targeting

3. What are the required postinstallation commands to configure WSUS to connect to a SQL Server database? (Choose all that apply.)

   A. wsusutil postinstall content_dir=D:\WSUS

   B. wsusutil postinstall SQL_INSTANCE_NAME=localhost content_dir=D:\WSUS

   C. Set-WsusServerSynchronization -SyncFromMU

   D. Invoke-WsusServerCleanup

Objective 1.3: Monitor servers

An important part of managing and maintaining servers is to monitor of faults, alerts, and events; and performance and bottlenecks.

> **This objective covers how to:**
> - Configure Data Collector Sets (DCSs)
> - Configure alerts
> - Schedule performance monitoring
> - Monitor real-time performance
> - Monitor virtual machines (VMs)
> - Monitor events
> - Configure event subscriptions
> - Configure network monitoring

Configuring Data Collector Sets

A Data Collector Set (DCS) is the foundation of building performance monitoring and re-porting that fits your environment and needs. A DCS organizes multiple data points from Windows Performance Monitor into a single collection.

You can create a DCS from an active Windows Performance Monitor view, from a tem-plate, manually by adding a custom combination of data logs, or by configuring performance counter alerts to monitor performance counters.

Creating DCS from Performance Monitor

To create a DCS from a Windows Performance Monitor view, first create the view by adding the counters to the Performance Monitor that you want to include in the DCS. Right-click Performance Monitor; then select New, Data Collection Set (see Figure 1-11).

New DCS are displayed in the User Defined section of the Performance Monitor console. You can modify the properties of the DCS to add a schedule, change storage details, con-figure start and restart conditions, and add tasks to run when the DCS stops.

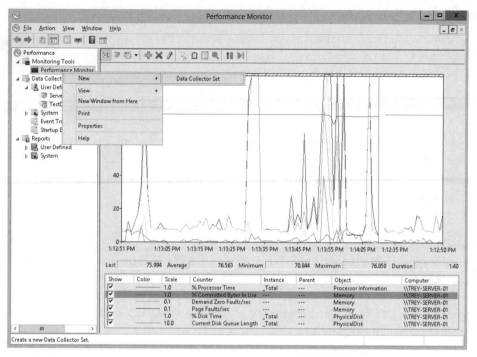

FIGURE 1-11 Creating a DCS from an existing Performance Monitor

Creating a DCS from a template

You can create a DCS from a template. There are four default templates, or you can browse to open additional templates if you have them. The four default templates are these:

- **Basic**   Creates an empty DCS to which you can add counters.

- **System Diagnostics**   Generates a report on hardware resources, response times, and processes. Includes configuration data and suggestions for ways to improve performance

- **System Performance**   Generates a report on hardware resources, response times, and processes.

- **WDAC Diagnostics**   Provides detailed debug information for Windows Data Access Components (DACs).

After you create the DCS, you can modify its properties as described previously. You can save any user-defined DCS as a template to use as the basis for future DCS creation.

Creating a DCS manually

Rather than start from a DCS template, you can create the DCS manually. When you create a DCS manually, you can choose from two types of data to include the following:

- Data logs, which include a combination of the following:
    - Performance counters, which include any set of performance counters
    - Event trace data, which includes any set of system or application events
    - System configuration information, which includes the value and changes to specified registry keys
- Performance counter alerts, which enable you to configure actions to take based on a threshold value of a performance counter

Configuring alerts

Performance counter alerts enable you to trigger actions and events based on the value of a performance counter. You specify the counter or counters to add to the DCS, whether your threshold value is a floor or ceiling threshold, and the limit for that threshold. You can also change where the DCS stores data, what action to take when the threshold is reached, and under which account the DCS runs.

To configure alerts, create a new manual DCS by using the steps described in the "Create a DCS Manually" section, and then use these steps:

1. In the Create new Data Collector Set Wizard, on the What Type Of Data Do You Want To Include page, select Performance Counter Alert.

2. Click Next and then click Add to add one or more Performance counters. On the Add performance counter dialog, shown in Figure 1-12, select one or more counters to add and then click the Add button to move them to the Added Counters field. Click OK when you've finished adding counters.

3. On the Which Performance Counters Would You Like To Monitor page, select a counter that you've added and in the Alert When box, select Above or Below from the drop-down list.

4. Enter the limit for the counter.

5. Repeat steps 4 and 5 for each counter you've added.

6. Click Next, and specify the account which the DCS should run, and then select Open Properties For This Data Collector Set.

7. Click Finish to open the properties for the DCS.

8. In the Properties for the DCS, set a schedule as described in "Scheduling performance monitoring" and set any additional properties needed.

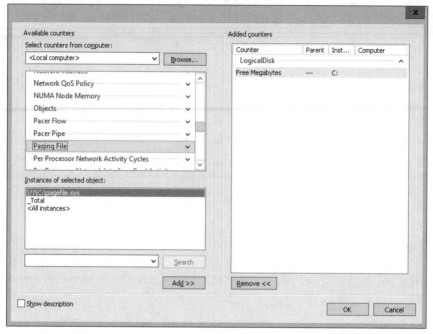

FIGURE 1-12 Adding counters

Scheduling performance monitoring

Beginning in Windows Server 2012, you can determine when a DCS runs, so you can schedule regular performance monitoring. To schedule a DCS to run as a scheduled job, you have to configure the DCS.

The DCS can be set as a scheduled task during initial creation or after it is created by right-clicking on the DCS and selecting Properties to open the Properties dialog box for the DCS. Click the Schedule tab and click Add to add a schedule to the DCS, as shown in Figure 1-13.

> **NOTE** **MANAGING PERMISSIONS AND RIGHTS REQUIRED**
>
> To allow a scheduled DCS to run, it must be scheduled to run as a user with Log On As A Batch User rights. Members of the Performance Log Users and Administrators groups have this permission, or it can be assigned directly to a specified account by using a GPO.

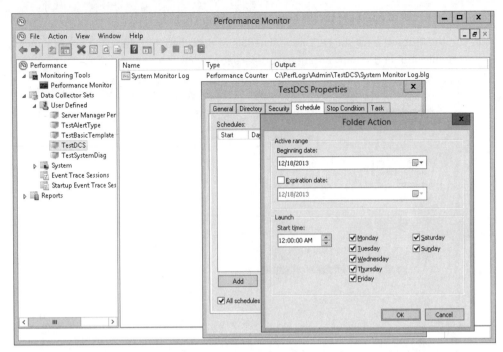

FIGURE 1-13 The Folder Action dialog box of the DCS Properties dialog box in Performance Monitor

Monitoring real-time performance

You can monitor real-time performance by using the Resource Monitor view of the Windows Performance Monitor. Start the Resource Monitor by using the shortcut in Administrative Tools by clicking the link in the Overview Of Performance Monitor pane of Windows Performance Monitor. You can also type **perfmon /res** from a command shell.

The Resource Monitor provides detailed real–time process monitoring, CPU usage, memory, logical and physical disk, and network usage. You can end a problem process or the entire tree of a problem process. You can also suspend a process (and resume previously suspended processes). When a process appears to be a problem, you can analyze the wait chain for the process to see whether it is a problem and what it is waiting for, as shown in Figure 1-14.

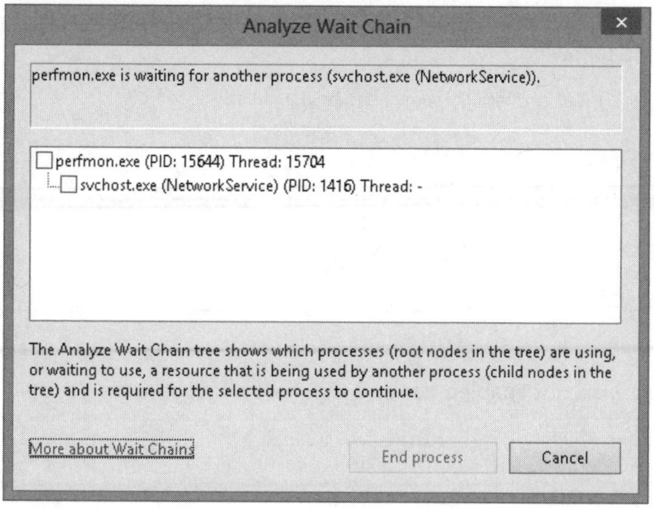

FIGURE 1-14 The Analyze Wait Chain dialog box

Monitoring virtual machines

All Hyper-V hosts include virtual machine (VM) resource pools that align with the resources that the host provides to guest VMs. These resource pools include processor, Ethernet, memory, and Virtual Hard Disk (VHD). By monitoring these resource pools, you can also monitor the aggregate usage of the resource by the guest VMs. You can also create new resource pools that measure a subset of a resource, such as the VHDs on a specific volume. To get a list of the resource pools, use the Get-VMResourcePool cmdlet. The default output on a Hyper-V host that hasn't had any configuration done is the following:

```
Name        ResourcePoolType         ParentName ResourceMeteringEnabled
----        ----------------         ---------- -----------------------
Primordial  FibreChannelConnection              False
Primordial  FibreChannelPort                    False
Primordial  VFD                                 False
Primordial  ISO                                 False
Primordial  VHD                                 False
Primordial  Memory                              False
Primordial  Ethernet                            False
Primordial  Processor                           False
```

The predefined resource pools are named Primordial to indicate that they represent the resources of the entire host machine. To enable a pool, use the Enable-VMResourcePool cmdlet. To enable resource metering on all available pools, use this command:

```
Enable-VMResourceMetering *
```

The preceding command enables all resource pools on the host that have a resource to enable. On my host, it yielded the following:

```
Name        ResourcePoolType         ParentName  ResourceMeteringEnabled
----        ----------------         ----------  -----------------------
Primordial  FibreChannelConnection               False
Primordial  VFD                                  False
Primordial  ISO                                  False
Primordial  VHD                                  True
Primordial  Ethernet                             True
Primordial  Memory                               True
Primordial  FibreChannelPort                     False
Primordial  Processor                            True
```

The pools that still show False were not enabled because there are no resources associated with them.

Creating new VM resource pools

You can create new VM resource pools that monitor subsets of the primordial pool. For example, to create a new resource pool to monitor the resources used by the VHDs on the E drive, create a new VM resource pool with the following command:

```
New-VMResourcePool "E-Drive" VHD -Paths "E:\"
```

```
Name         ResourcePoolType  ParentName   ResourceMeteringEnabled
----         ----------------  ----------   -----------------------
E Drive Pool VHD               {Primordial} False
```

Monitoring resource usage by VMs

You can use VM resource pools to monitor the resource usage of specific VMs. To enable resource metering on the VM trey-dc-02, use the following command:

```
Enable-VMResourceMetering -VMName trey-dc-02
```

To see the resource usage of trey-dc-02, use this command:

```
Measure-VM -VMName trey-dc-02
```

VMName	AvgCPU (MHz)	AvgRAM (M)	MaxRAM (M)	MinRAM (M)	TotalDisk (M)	Network Inbound(M)	Network Outbound(M)
trey-dc-02	20	1358	1358	1358	130048	7	2

Because Measure-VM supports lists of VMs, you can quickly get the resource usage of all the VMs running on the local machine:

```
Get-VM | Measure-VM
```

VMName	AvgCPU (MHz)	AvgRAM (M)	MaxRAM (M)	MinRAM (M)	TotalDisk (M)	Network Inbound(M)	Network Outbound(M)
charlie-monster	0	0	0	0	0	0	0
trey-dc-02	20	1382	1420	1342	130048	79	16
trey-server-01	102	1010	1044	972	334848	16	5
trey-Server-02	45	5803	5838	5682	260096	4	3
trey-wds-11	16	1688	1744	1638	348862	14	73
vm-ts-05	73	1287	1401	1248	130048	113	14
Win7-DRM	0	0	0	0	0	0	0

This is useful, but the VM cmdlets also support remoting, so you can easily get the status of a remote machine as well:

```
Enable-VMResourceMetering * -ComputerName hp350-srv8-7
Get-VM -ComputerName hp350-srv8-7 | Measure-VM
```

VMName	AvgCPU (MHz)	AvgRAM (M)	MaxRAM (M)	MinRAM (M)	TotalDisk (M)	Network Inbound(M)	Network Outbound(M)
HP350-TS-05	20	2703	2703	2703	539648	2	2
srv2	290	16384	16384	16384	614401	3	3

Monitoring events

Event monitoring has not materially changed in Windows Server 2012 or Windows Server 2012 R2 over the behavior and tools available in Windows Server 2008—with the exception of a limited number of Windows PowerShell cmdlets. The exam questions will likely focus on that one area that is new while retaining some legacy questions such as how to create a custom event view.

Creating custom views

You can create custom Event Viewer views by opening the Event Viewer console (eventvwr.msc) and clicking Create Custom View in the Actions pane. Specify the time period for the view in the Logged drop-down list, and set the Event Level to View. Continue configuring what you want to see in the custom view. As shown in Figure 1-15, you can track by log or by source, and specify Event IDs, task categories, keywords, and the user and computer that generated the event.

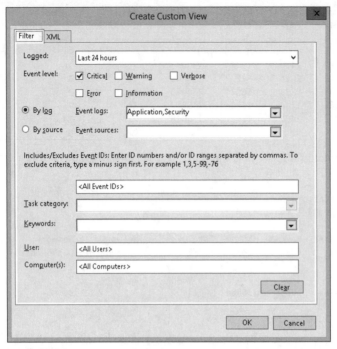

FIGURE 1-15 The Create Custom View dialog box of the Event Viewer console

Using Windows PowerShell to monitor events

You can use Windows PowerShell to monitor events. A quick way to get a list of all available event–related Windows PowerShell cmdlets, organized to make it easier to find what you need, is to use this command:

```
Get-Command *event*,*counter* | sort noun,verb | Format-Table -auto Verb,Noun,Module
```

This command gives you a list of all the Windows PowerShell cmdlets on the current computer that have "event" or "counter" in their name, sorted by noun.

Some of the common Windows PowerShell cmdlets used for server monitoring are shown in Table 1-2.

TABLE 1-2 Popular Windows PowerShell cmdlets for server monitoring

Cmdlet	Description
Get-Counter	Returns an object with performance counter data from the specified computer(s).
Export-Counter	Exports performance data to log files in .blg, .csv, or .tsv format. The data exported comes from the Get-Counter or Import-Counter cmdlets.

Cmdlet	Description
Import-Counter	Imports performance counter data from log files and converts each counter sample to a PerformanceCounterSampleSet object.
Get-Event	Returns events from the Windows PowerShell event queue for the current session.
New-Event	Creates a new custom event from the current Windows PowerShell session. To subscribe to an event, use the Register-EngineEvent.
Get-WinEvent	Returns events from event logs, including both classic logs and the new Windows event log technology introduced in Windows Server 2008 R2 and Windows Vista.
New-WinEvent	Creates an Event Tracking for Windows (ETW) event.
Clear-EventLog	Clears (empties) the specified event log. Valid only for classic Windows event logs, not the new Windows event log technology introduced in Windows Server 2008 R2 and Windows Vista.
Get-EventLog	Returns events and event logs that match the specified parameters. Valid only for classic Windows event logs, not the new Windows event log technology introduced in Windows Server 2008 R2 and Windows Vista.
Write-EventLog	Writes an event to the specified event log. Valid only for classic Windows event logs, not the new Windows event log technology introduced in Windows Server 2008 R2 and Windows Vista.

Using event subscriptions

Event Viewer allows you to connect to a remote computer, but only one at a time. This limitation can make it difficult to collect events that span multiple computers, and it is positively tedious to try to capture the event health of your entire network. However, beginning in Windows Server 2008, you can create subscriptions to enable multiple computers to forward events from multiple logs to a single computer for evaluation.

When you create an event subscription, you specify exactly which events are forwarded and in which log they are stored locally. When you have the subscription events in a local log, you can view and process them in the same way you would a local event.

Configuring for event subscriptions

Before you can use event subscriptions, both the event sender (forwarder) and event receiver (collector) have to be configured to support the subscription. On each source (forwarding) computer, you have to enable and configure Windows Remote Management (WinRM) with this command:

```
WinRM quickconfig
```

You have to run the same WinRM command on the collector computer if you need to configure event delivery optimization. In addition, you have to run the wecutil qc command on the collector computer from an elevated prompt.

Finally, add the collector computer's account to the local Administrators group on each of the source computers. This is sufficient configuration on domain-joined computers that are all part of the same (or a trusted) domain. Additional configuration is required for workgroup computers:

- Only pull subscriptions are supported.

- A Windows Firewall exception is required.

- A local administrative account must be added to the Event Log Readers group on each source computer.

- Each source computer must be a trusted host for WinRM on the collector computer:

```
WinRM set winrm/config/client @{TrustedHosts="<source1>,<source2>,..."}
```

Creating a new event subscription

After you configure the source and collector computers to support event subscriptions, you can create a new subscription in Event Viewer by following these steps:

1. Select Subscriptions in the left pane and click Create Subscription in the Actions pane.

2. Configure the subscription properties, including name, destination log, and source computers.

3. Select the events to collect, as shown in Figure 1-16. Click OK.

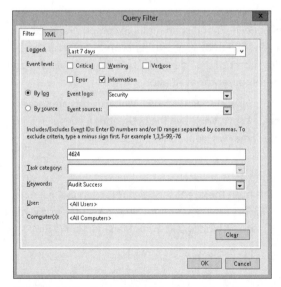

FIGURE 1-16 The Query Filter dialog box of Event Viewer

4. To optimize event delivery, click the Advanced button. You can configure event delivery optimization to the following:

- **Normal** Uses pull delivery mode and batches 5 items at a time with a timeout of 15 minutes
- **Minimize Bandwidth** Uses push delivery with a batch timeout of six hours and a heartbeat interval of six hours
- **Minimize Latency** Uses push delivery mode with a batch timeout of 30 seconds

Configuring network monitoring

Windows Server 2012 R2 provides a new module of Windows PowerShell cmdlets to enable network packet capturing. The NetEventPacketCapture module includes the cmdlets shown in Table 1-3.

TABLE 1-3 NetEventPacketCapture cmdlets

Cmdlet	Description
Add-NetEventNetworkAdapter	Adds a network adapter as a filter on a remote packet capture provider.
Get-NetEventNetworkAdapter	Returns the network adapters associated with a remote packet capture.
Remove-NetEventNetworkAdapter	Removes a network adapter associated with a remote packet capture.
Add-NetEventPacketCaptureProvider	Adds a new remote packet capture provider. Only one remote packet capture provider can be active at a time.
Get-NetEventPacketCaptureProvider	Displays a remote capture provider.
Remove-NetEventPacketCaptureProvider	Removes a remote packet capture provider, allowing you to add a new one.
Set-NetEventPacketCaptureProvider	Alters the configuration of a remote packet capture provider.
Add-NetEventProvider	Adds an ETW provider to a session.
Get-NetEventProvider	Returns the ETW providers that are present on the computer, or those associated with an event or packet capture session.
Remove-NetEventProvider	Removes an ETW provider from a session.
Set-NetEventProvider	Modifies the configuration of an ETW provider.
Get-NetEventSession	Returns an object describing the network event sessions.
New-NetEventSession	Creates a new network event session.
Remove-NetEventSession	Removes an existing network event session.
Set-NetEventSession	Modifies the configuration of a network event session.
Start-NetEventSession	Starts the event and packet capture for a network event session.
Stop-NetEventSession	Stops the event and packet capture for a network event session.

Cmdlet	Description
Add-NetEventVmNetworkAdapter	Adds a virtual network adapter as a filter on a remote packet capture provider.
Get-NetEventVmNetworkAdapter	Returns an object describing the virtual network adapters associated with a provider.
Remove-NetEventVmNetworkAdapter	Removes a virtual network adapter from a remote packet capture provider
Add-NetEventVmSwitch	Adds a Hyper-V virtual switch as a filter on a remote packet capture provider.
Get-NetEventVmSwitch	Returns an object describing the Hyper-V switches acting as filters on a remote packet capture provider.
Remove-NetEventVmSwitch	Removes a Hyper-V virtual switch as a filter on a remote packet capture provider.
Add-NetEventVMNetworkAdapter	Adds a VM network adapter as a filter on a remote packet capture provider.
Get-NetEventVMNetworkAdapter	Returns an object describing the VM network adapters acting as filters of a remote packet capture provider.
Remove-NetEventVMNetworkAdapter	Removes a Hyper-V virtual switch from a remote packet capture provider.

Thought experiment
Monitoring events remotely

In this thought experiment, apply what you've learned about this objective. You can find answers to these questions in the "Answers" section at the end of this chapter.

You are the network administrator for TreyResearch.net, and you have a mix of servers, some running Windows Server Core and some running full Windows Server installations. You have to manage these servers remotely.

1. How can you review individual System event logs across all the computers, limiting the events to the last 40 events per computer?

2. How can you clear the Applications event log on all the computers?

3. How can you get current performance counter data from individual servers?

4. How can you get an aggregate report of performance data from the servers?

Objective summary

- A data collector set (DCS) enables you to aggregate multiple event and performance data sources and types into a single view of the data to improve analysis.

- DCS can be built directly from the Performance Monitor view in the console, allowing you to interactively build the data set you want and then save the view as a DCS.

- You can build a DCS from a preconfigured template that already has the basic data you're looking for; then modify that data set and save it back out as a template for later reuse.

- You can also build a DCS manually, choosing the type and mix of data that the DCS will include. Data can be data logs, such as performance counters, event trace data, and system configuration information. Or it can be performance counter alerts, allowing you to take actions based on the value of a performance counter.

- You can schedule a DCS to run at a specific time or at regular intervals to allow you to monitor and react to changes in server performance.

- You monitor real-time performance with the Resource Monitor. You can open up the Resource Monitor from the command line with perfmon /res, but this allows you to see only the local computer. If you open up perfmon.mmc (or choose Performance Monitor from the Server Manager Tools menu), you can connect to another computer first and then open the Resource Monitor on the remote computer.

- Hyper-V VM hosts include VM resource pools that provide resources to the guest VMs. You can monitor these resources with the VMResourcePool and VMResourceMetering cmdlets.

- Event Viewer lets you see all the events on your local computer or a remote computer, but it can be difficult to identify the source of a problem if there are too many other events hiding the ones you're looking for. By creating custom views, you can focus in on a subset of events. To identify events across multiple servers, use Event Subscriptions to get events from remote computers.

Objective review

Answer the following questions to test your knowledge of the information in this objective. You can find the answers to these questions and explanations of why each answer choice is correct or incorrect in the "Answers" section at the end of the chapter.

1. How can you monitor real-time performance on a remote computer?

   A. Run Resource Monitor from the Administrative Tools folder.

   B. Run the command perfmon /res from an elevated prompt.

   C. Run Performance Monitor and connect to the remote computer. Then right-click Monitoring Tools and select Resource Monitor from the Action menu.

   D. Open a remote desktop session on the remote computer and then run Resource Monitor from the Administrative Tools folder.

   E. Create a PSSession to the remote computer with New-PSSession; then enter the session with Enter-PSSession. Run the command perfmon /res in the remote PSSession.

2. What Windows PowerShell commands can you use to measure the Hyper-V VHD resource usage of the VM trey-wms-11? (Choose all that apply.)

   A. Enable-VMResourceMonitoring -VmName trey-wms-11

   B. Enable-VMResourceMetering -VmName trey-wms-11

   C. Measure-VM -VMName *

   D. (Measure-VM -VMName trey-wms-11).HardDiskMetrics

   E. Measure-VM -ComputerName trey-wms-11 -VHD

   F. (Measure-VM -VmName trey-wms-11).Totaldisk

Answers

This section contains the solutions to the thought experiments and answers to the lesson review questions in this chapter.

Objective 1.1: Thought experiment

1. Inject the vendor–provided driver package that supports the new hardware into the existing boot image using Import-WdsDriverPackage and Add-WdsDriverPackage.

2. Create a new WDS group for the Finance, Accounting, and Human Resources department servers. Using the updated boot image created in answer #1, build a template server with the new software. After full testing of the new hardware and software together, sysprep the template server and create a capture image in the Windows Deployment Services console. You can use that image to create a new template image. Add the new hardware Media Access Control (MAC) addresses to the Active Directory Prestaged Devices folder in the Windows Deployment Services console, specifying the appropriate OU for the computer accounts.

Objective 1.1: Review

1. **Correct answers:** A, B

    A. **Correct:** An active DHCP server is required to provide an IP address for the PXE boot process.

    B. **Correct:** A working and reachable DNS server is required to allow the PXE server and PXE client to find each other.

    C. **Incorrect:** ReFS is not supported for the WDS image store. Only NTFS is required.

    D. **Incorrect:** WDS can be installed in stand-alone mode, which doesn't require Active Directory.

2. **Correct answer:** C

    A. **Incorrect:** A boot image is used by a PXE boot. In this scenario, you boot from the local hard disk.

    B. **Incorrect:** An install image is used to install a new version of Windows on a target computer. In this scenario, you boot from a running instance of Windows to capture the image for use on other computers.

    C. **Correct:** A capture image is used to capture the image of a working computer.

    D. **Incorrect:** A discover image is used when booting to a USB or DVD, not for capturing.

3. **Correct answer:** D

   A. **Incorrect:** This command adds a boot image to a WDS image store.

   B. **Incorrect:** This command adds a driver package to a WDS driver store.

   C. **Incorrect:** This command changes the properties of a WDS boot image.

   D. **Correct:** This command can be used to insert a driver package into an offline, locally mounted boot image.

Objective 1.2: Thought experiment

1. Yes, but only if you use VMs running on Hyper-V. Because WDS isn't supported on a Windows Server Core installation, you have to install WSUS on a full GUI install if they are on the same server

2. One, but by using only VMs. You need at least two virtualized Windows servers (preferably three): two running a core installation and one running a GUI installation, to provide separation of roles while minimizing the security and patching footprint. The physical server can also be a Windows Server 2012 R2 core installation with only the Hyper-V role installed.

3. You can install the infrastructure roles—DNS, DHCP and AD DS—on a single virtualized server with Windows Server 2012 R2 core installation while putting the Windows Deployment Services role on a separate Windows Server 2012 R2 full installation. It is technically possible to add the Windows Server Update Services role onto the infrastructure server, but it's a better practice to keep the patching separate from the AD DS server.

Objective 1.2: Review

1. **Correct answer:** C

   A. **Incorrect:** The -InstallAllSubFeatures parameter tries to install both the WID and SQL database, which isn't supported. No Management Tools are installed.

   B. **Incorrect:** The -InstallAllSubFeatures parameter tries to install both the WID and SQL database, which isn't supported.

   C. **Correct:** Installs the UpdateServices role with the default WID database along with the required Management Tools.

   D. **Incorrect:** Installs the SQL Server database, not the WID database.

2. **Correct answers:** A, D

   A. **Correct:** Automatic Updates must be configured before the client can connect to the WSUS server to register and be placed in a WSUS group.

   B. **Incorrect:** Client computers can connect directly to Microsoft Update to actually download updates but still register and be placed in a WSUS group.

   C. **Incorrect:** Recommended updates has nothing to do with assigning computers to groups.

   D. **Correct:** This GPO enables client-side targeting and specifies the WSUS group in which the client should be placed.

3. **Correct answers:** B, C

   A. **Incorrect:** This command sets the content directory for the WID database.

   B. **Correct:** This command sets the content directory to a local SQL Server database and the content directory.

   C. **Correct:** This command sets the WSUS Server Synchronization to download and sync updates from Microsoft Update. A synchronization source has to be set before WSUS can download updates.

   D. **Incorrect:** This command cleans up outdated or replaced updates on a working WSUS server. It doesn't do postinstallation cleanup.

Objective 1.3: Thought experiment

1. Create a simple Windows PowerShell script to poll the System event log on the servers:

   PollServers.PS1

   ```
   # Script to poll servers for recent System Event Log activity
   $Servers = @("Trey-DC-02","Trey-wds-11","Trey-Server-01","Trey-Server-02")
   ForEach ($srv in $Servers ) {
       Echo "System Event Log for Server $srv`:"
       Echo "--------------------------------"
       Get-EventLog -ComputerName $srv -LogName System -Newest 40
       Echo " "
   }
   ```

   Note that although I show this as a script, you can easily run the commands interactively from Windows PowerShell.

2. Foreach ($srv in $servers){ Clear-EventLog -LogName Application -ComputerName $srv }

3. Get-Counter -ComputerName *<computername>*

4. Create a DCS that contains the performance data you want to collect; then schedule the DCS to run at appropriate intervals on each server, forwarding the result to the server on which you're collecting the data. After each run, set a task to clear the counters.

Objective 1.3: Review

1. **Correct answer:** D

   A. **Incorrect:** This allows you to monitor real-time performance with Resource Monitor, but you can't connect to a remote computer from inside the Resource Monitor.

   B. **Incorrect:** This allows you to monitor real-time performance with Resource Monitor, but you can't connect to a remote computer from inside the Resource Monitor.

   C. **Incorrect:** Even though you're connecting to a remote computer for data collection, this still opens a local instance of Resource Monitor.

   D. **Correct:** This opens a remote session and the version of Resource Monitor will be running on the remote computer.

   E. **Incorrect:** Remote PSSessions can't interact with graphical applications to send the display back to your local computer.

2. **Correct answers:** B, F

   A. **Incorrect:** This is not a valid command.

   B. **Correct:** This is the command to start resource monitoring of a the specific Hyper-V VM.

   C. **Incorrect:** This gives you resource data on all VMs. Yes, it will include the disk usage for trey-wms-11, but mixed in with everything else, so you can't easily act on it.

   D. **Incorrect:** This gives you disk performance metrics for the virtual disk, but not the amount of disk space used.

   E. **Incorrect:** This uses the -ComputerName parameter, rather than the VMName. ComputerName is used for the Hyper-V host name, not the virtual machine guest name.

   F. **Correct:** This gives you just the hard disk usage of the VHD for trey-wms-11.

CHAPTER 2

Configure file and print services

This chapter covers the essential server functionality of file services. Despite the title, print services are not covered in this exam; they are covered in Exam 70-410. This chapter covers the advanced file services of Distributed File System (DFS), the File Server Resource Manager (FSRM), encryption, and advanced auditing policies.

Objectives in this chapter:

- Objective 2.1: Configure Distributed File System (DFS)
- Objective 2.2: Configure File Server Resource Manager (FSRM)
- Objective 2. 3: Configure file and disk encryption
- Objective 2. 4: Configure advanced audit policies

Objective 2.1: Configure Distributed File System (DFS)

Windows Server 2012 R2 Distributed File System (DFS) provides a simplified view of file resources across multiple servers and sites while enabling efficient replication of folder contents between servers. Windows PowerShell support for DFS Namespaces (DFS-N) was added in Windows Server 2012 and added for DFS Replication (DFS-R) in Windows Server 2012 R2.

> **This objective covers how to:**
> - Install and configure DFS Namespaces (DFS-N)
> - Configure DFS Replication (DFS-R) targets
> - Configure replication scheduling
> - Configure Remote Differential Compression (RDC) settings
> - Configure staging
> - Configure fault tolerance
> - Clone a DFS database
> - Recover DFS databases
> - Optimize DFS Replication

Installing and configuring DFS Namespaces (DFS-N)

Before you can use DFS-N, you need to install the role on a server. For DFS-R, you have to install it on at least two servers. These servers must be part of an Active Directory Domain Services (AD DS) domain if the DFS-N is AD-integrated, and you must be a member of the Domain Admins group to install the DFS role and role services. You can install DFS-N in Standalone mode, which is required if you want to install DFS-N on a cluster.

DFS roles can be installed on a Windows Server 2012 R2 Server Core installation. DFS-N management can then be done locally or remotely with the Windows PowerShell DFSN module; DFS-R management is done with the DFSR module. Remote administration can also be performed by using the GUI administration console, which can be run from within Server Manager or by opening Dfsmgmt.msc directly.

Windows Servers can host multiple DFS-N, depending on the version of Windows Server they run. Table 2-1 lists the Windows Server versions and the DFS-N they support.

TABLE 2-1 Windows Server versions and their DFS-N support

Version	Domain-Based Namespaces	Stand-alone Namespaces
Windows Server 2012 Datacenter and Windows Server 2012 R2 Datacenter	Multiple	Multiple
Windows Server 2012 Standard, Windows Server 2012 Enterprise, and Windows Server 2012 R2 Standard	Multiple	Multiple
Windows Server 2008 R2 Datacenter	Multiple	Multiple
Windows Server 2008 R2 Enterprise	Multiple	Multiple
Windows Server 2008 R2 Standard	Multiple	Single
Windows Server 2008 Datacenter	Multiple	Multiple
Windows Server 2008 Enterprise	Multiple	Multiple
Windows Server 2008 Standard	Multiple	Single

Here are additional notes for stand-alone namespace servers:

- They must contain an NTFS volume to host the namespace.
- They can be a standalone server, a member server or a domain controller.
- They can be hosted by a failover cluster to increase availability.

Here are additional notes for domain-based namespaces:

- They must contain an NTFS file system volume to host the namespace.
- They can be a member server or a domain controller in the same domain in which the namespace is configured.
- They can use multiple namespace servers to increase availability.

- The namespace can't be a clustered resource in a failover cluster, but can be configured on an individual cluster node as long as it uses only local resources and nonshared storage.

EXAM TIP

Most Microsoft exam questions focus on core understanding of the concepts rather than specific knowledge that can be learned by rote memory. However, the correct answer can often be constrained by very specific knowledge about which versions of Windows Server support which specific features.

Installing DFS-N by using Server Manager

You can install the DFS-N role by using the Add Roles And Features Wizard in Server Manager and following these steps:

1. Select the Role-Based Or Feature-Based Installation option.

2. On the Select Server Roles page, select DFS Namespaces. If it will be a replicated DFS-N, select DFS Replication as well, as shown in Figure 2-1.

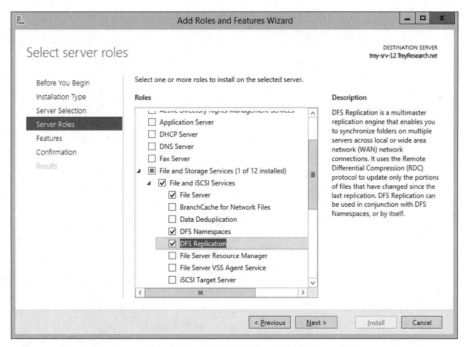

FIGURE 2-1 The Select Server Roles page of the Add Roles And Features Wizard

3. In the Add Features That Are Required For DFS Namespaces dialog box, accept the default by clicking Add Features.

4. Click Next twice and then click Install to install DFS-N (and DFS-R if you selected that role). In most cases, a reboot is not required.

Installing DFS-N by using Windows PowerShell

To install the DFS-N and DFS-R roles on a Windows Server, run the following Windows PowerShell command:

```
Install-WindowsFeature -Name FS-DFS-Namespace,FS-DFS-Replication -IncludeManagementTools
```

If you want only the DFS-N role, simply eliminate FS-DFS-Replication from the preceding command.

Creating a DFS Namespace

You create a DFS-N by using either the DFS Manager console, or the Windows PowerShell DFSN module. To create a new DFS-N using the DFS Manager console, follow these steps:

1. Select Namespaces in the DFS Management console and then click New Namespace on the Actions menu to open the New Namespace Wizard.

2. On the Namespace Server page, enter the name of the server that will host the namespace (see Figure 2-2).

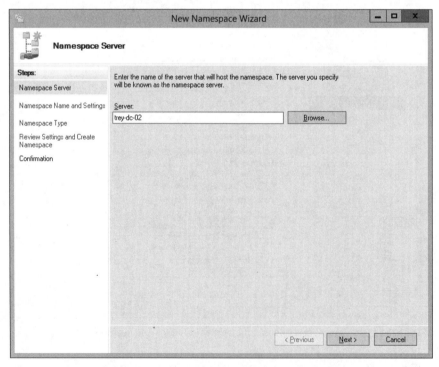

FIGURE 2-2 The Namespace Server page of the New Namespace Wizard

3. Click Next and enter a name for the new namespace.

4. Click Edit Settings to change the default local path to the namespace and to set the shared folder permissions, as shown in Figure 2-3. Click OK to close the Edit Settings box, and then click Next.

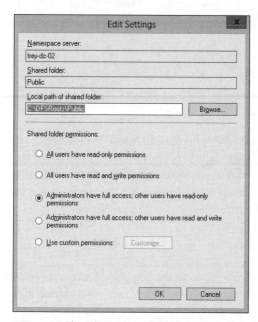

FIGURE 2-3 The Edit Settings dialog box of the New Namespace Wizard

5. On the Namespace Type page, choose whether the namespace will be a domain-based namespace or a stand-alone namespace. For domain-based namespaces, choose whether it will be Windows Server 2008 Mode.

EXAM TIP

When creating a domain-based namespace, if you don't create it in Windows Server 2008 Mode, the namespace won't support access-based enumeration. The minimum Domain functional level for Windows Server 2008 Mode DFS-N is Windows Server 2008.

6. Click Next, then click Create, and then click Close to complete creating the namespace.

To create a namespace using Windows PowerShell, use the New-DfsnRoot cmdlet. To create a new domain-based DFS-N in Windows Server 2008 Mode that has a share path of "\\TreyResearch\Download" and a target path of "\\Trey-dc-02\Download", use this command:

```
New-DfsnRoot -TargetPath \\trey-dc-02\Public `
            -Path \\TreyResearch\Public `
            -Type DomainV2 `
            -Description "Central source for Publicly visible files"
```

For a full list of DFS-N cmdlets, use the following command:

```
Get-Command –Module DFSN
```

EXAM TIP

If you look at the number of parameters available for the DFS-N and DFS-R cmdlets, you can see several ways to tweak each command, which makes them a tempting target for the exam question writer. You shouldn't attempt to memorize every possible parameter, but you should try to understand what options are available and what they mean so that you'll be able to recognize when an incorrect answer choice is leading you astray.

Adding a DFS-N folder

You can add a folder to an existing DFS-N root by using the DFS Management console or by using Windows PowerShell. To add a folder to an existing DFS-N root, follow these steps:

1. Expand the Namespaces section of the DFS Management console and select the root for the new folder.

2. Click New Folder in the Actions pane to open up the New Folder dialog box shown in Figure 2-4.

FIGURE 2-4 The New Folder dialog box of the DFS Management console

3. Enter a name for the folder and click Add to open the Add Folder Target dialog box. Enter the shared folder to use in the Path To Folder Target box or use the Browse button to open the Browse For Shared Folders dialog box shown in Figure 2-5.

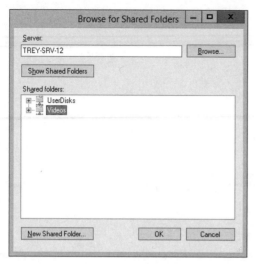

FIGURE 2-5 The Browse For Shared Folders dialog box

4. You can browse for the server or use the local server. You can create a new shared folder or use an existing one.

5. You can add multiple folder targets to an existing DFS-N root.

To create a new DFS-N folder with Windows PowerShell, use the New-DFSNFolder cmdlet. Here is an example:

```
New-DFSNFolder -Path \\TreyResearch.net\Public\Videos `
               -TargetPath \\Trey-srv-12\Videos `
               -Description "Corporate Training and Marketing Videos"
```

Changing the properties of a DFS-N

You can modify the properties of a DFS-N, including delegating management permission, changing the cache duration and cost ordering, and setting polling optimization. These properties can be changed in the DFS Management console or by using the Windows PowerShell DFSN module.

For example, you can change a DFS-N by enabling access-based enumeration. You can do this in the DFS Management console by right-clicking the namespace, and choosing Properties from the menu. Then select Enable Access-based Enumeration For This Namespace on the Advanced tab and click OK.

To set access-based enumeration for the \\TreyResearch.net\Public namespace, use the following command:

```
Set-DfsnRoot -Path \\TreyResearch.net\Public -EnableAccessBasedEnumeration $True
```

Properties that you can set include:

- Site costing
- In-site referrals
- Access-based enumeration
- Root scalability
- Target failback
- Description
- State
- Time to Live

> **IMPORTANT** **REFRESHING THE DFS MANAGEMENT CONSOLE**
>
> When working with both the Windows PowerShell DFSN cmdlets and the DFS Management console, the console does not automatically refresh. Always manually refresh before making changes in the console by right-clicking the DFS-N and choosing Refresh from the menu.

Configuring DFS-R targets

When you add multiple DFS-N targets for a DFS-N folder, you can (and in most cases should) set the targets to replicate. Doing so synchronizes the content in the targets and ensures that changes in one folder target are replicated to the other folder targets. Servers that are involved in the replication of folder targets form a replication group. The replication group name is, by default, the path of the replicated folder (see Figure 2-6).

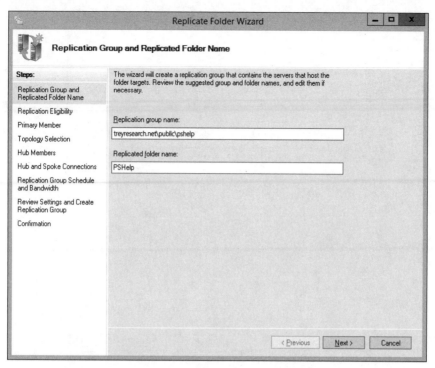

FIGURE 2-6 The Replication Group And Replicated Folder Name page of the Replicate Folder Wizard

You can configure replication directly when you add more than a single folder target to a DFS-N, or you can skip that step initially and enable replication later. When you enable replication, you need to designate which server will be the Primary Member, as shown in Figure 2-7.

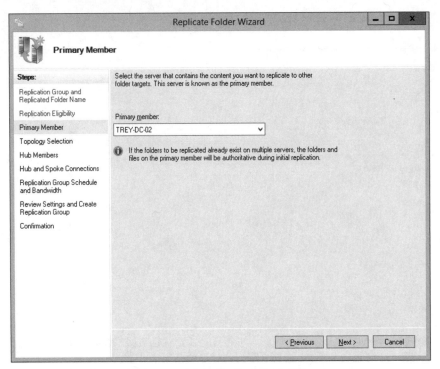

FIGURE 2-7 The Primary Member page of the Replicate Folder Wizard

The two basic replication technologies are full mesh and hub and spoke, or you can use a custom replication topology that combines some of the features of each. In a full mesh topology (see Figure 2-8), each member of the replication group replicates with every other member of the group. This works well for small replication groups, especially where new data can originate in any member of the group.

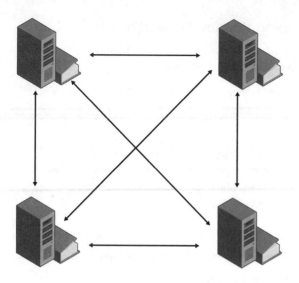

FIGURE 2-8 In a full mesh replication topology, each node replicates to every other node

In a hub and spoke technology, one or two hub servers each connect to multiple spokes, as shown in Figure 2-9. If there is more than one hub, the hubs also connect to each other. A hub and spoke topology requires a minimum of three members (a hub and two spokes), and works well in a publication or branch office scenario in which most changes originate at the hub and are replicated out to the spokes. Changes that originate at a spoke have at least two replication hops before being fully replicated to all members of the replication group.

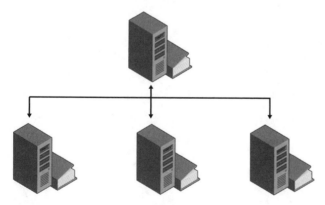

FIGURE 2-9 In a hub and spoke replication technology, the hub replicates with multiple spokes

Finally, you need to configure the replication schedule and bandwidth, as covered in the following "Configuring replication scheduling" section.

Creating new DFS-R targets by using Windows PowerShell

New in Windows Server 2012 R2 is full Windows PowerShell support for DFS-R. To see a full list of DFS-R cmdlets, sorted by noun, use the following command:

```
Get-Command -Module DFSR | Sort-Object Noun,Verb | Format-Table Verb,Noun -auto
```

> **EXAM TIP**
>
> The DFS-R Windows PowerShell cmdlets provide a rich source of possible questions and fussy syntax. Plus they are completely new in Windows Server 2012 R2. These properties make them rich fodder for exam question writers. Make sure you work through an example or two to have a clear understanding of how to use them.

To create a new DFS-R replication target, you follow a multicommand process. Create the DFS-R group, assign folders to it, and add member servers. Here is an example:

```
New-DfsReplicationGroup -GroupName "\\TreyResearch.net\Public\Build" `
    | New-DfsReplicatedFolder -FolderName "Build" `
    | Add-DfsrMember -ComputerName Trey-DC-02,Trey-Srv-13
```

Add a bidirectional connection between the two servers:

```
Add-DfsrConnection -GroupName "\\TreyResearch.net\Public\Build" `
                   -SourceComputerName Trey-DC-02 `
                   -DestinationComputerName Trey-Srv-13
```

Specify Trey-DC-02 as the primary:

```
Set-DfsrMembership -GroupName "\\TreyResearch.net\Public\Build" `
                   -FolderName "Build" `
                   -ContentPath C:\Downloads\Build `
                   -ComputerName Trey-DC-02 `
                   -PrimaryMember $True `
                   -StagingPathQuotaInMB 16384 -Force
```

Finally, specify that Trey-Srv-13 is a member server with the following:

```
Set-DfsrMembership -GroupName "\\TreyResearch.net\Public\Build" `
                   -FolderName "Build" `
                   -ContentPath C:\Downloads\Build `
                   -ComputerName Trey-Srv-13 `
                   -StagingPathQuotaInMB 16384 -Force
```

Configuring replication scheduling

DFS-R defaults to replicating 24 hours per day, 7 days per week over the full available bandwidth, as shown in Figure 2-10. This replication schedule is fine for some basic situations, but doesn't take into account specific needs.

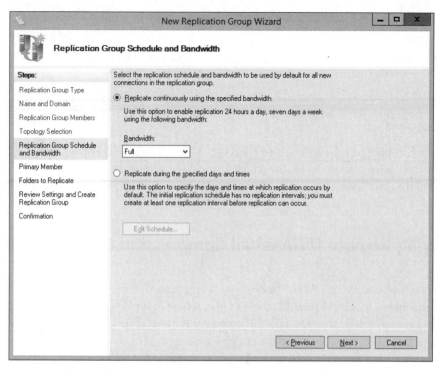

FIGURE 2-10 The Replication Group Schedule And Bandwidth page of the New Replication Group Wizard

For scenarios that require tuning this default schedule, you can set the specific times when replication should be available and the bandwidth to use for that replication, as shown in Figure 2-11. You can set different replication bandwidths in one-hour time blocks for the entire week if appropriate.

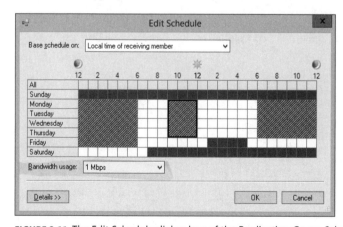

FIGURE 2-11 The Edit Schedule dialog box of the Replication Group Schedule And Bandwidth page

You can use the Set-DfsrGroupSchedule cmdlet to set replication schedule and bandwidth settings. The syntax is this:

```
Set-DfsrGroupSchedule [-GroupName] <String[]> [[-DomainName] <String>] [[-UseUTC]
<Boolean>] [[-ScheduleType]{Always | Never}] [-Confirm] [-WhatIf] [<CommonParameters>]

Set-DfsrGroupSchedule [-GroupName] <String[]> [[-DomainName] <String>] [[-UseUTC]
<Boolean>] [-Day] <DayOfWeek[]>[-BandwidthDetail] <String> [-Confirm] [-WhatIf]
[<CommonParameters>]
```

The first syntax either sets the schedule to Always (and Full) or disables it entirely. The second syntax group enables you to set the schedule and bandwidth in 15-minute intervals for each day of the week. (See Get-Help Set-DfsrGroupSchedule -Full for detailed syntax and examples.)

Configuring Remote Differential Compression (RDC) settings

Remote Differential Compression (RDC) is a client-server protocol that detects insertions, deletions, and changes in file data. With RDC enabled (the default in Windows Server 2012 R2), DFS-R copies a changed data segment only if the segment is not available on the replication partner. With cross-file RDC enabled, that data segment can be from a different file. RDC is designed to improve replication bandwidth usage of low-bandwidth connections.

By default, RDC is used only on files 64 KB or larger, but this threshold can be configured using Windows PowerShell. To change the connection from trey-dc-02 to trey-srv-13 in the Test replication group to use a threshold size of 128 KB, use the following command:

```
Set-DfsrConnection -GroupName "Test" `
                   -SourceComputerName "trey-dc-02" `
                   -DestinationComputerName "trey-srv-13" `
                   -MinimumRDCFileSizeInKB 128
```

To disable cross-file RDC and regular RDC completely on the same connection, use the following command:

```
Set-DfsrConnection -GroupName "Test" `
                   -SourceComputerName "trey-dc-02" `
                   -DestinationComputerName "trey-srv-13" `
                   -DisableRDC $True `
                   -DisableCrossFileRDC $True
```

You can enable or disable RDC for a given connection in the DFS Management console by selecting the replication group name in the console tree and clicking the Connections tab. Select a connection and then click Properties in the Actions menu for the connection, as shown in Figure 2-12.

FIGURE 2-12 The Properties dialog box of a replication group connection

Configuring staging

You can configure the size of the staging folder for a DFS-R group member. Each member of the replication group has its own staging folder, and each folder can be individually set. The default size is 4 GB (4096 MB). To change the size of the staging folder for a replication group member, select the replication group in the DFS Management console and select the member server. Right-click to open the properties and click the Staging tab, as shown in Figure 2-13. You can set the Staging Path, and the Quota (In Megabytes).

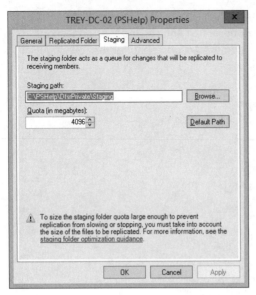

FIGURE 2-13 The Staging tab of the member server Properties dialog box

You can get the current staging size by using the Get-DfsrMembership cmdlet, and configure the staging size and path by using the Set-DfsrMembership cmdlet. To set the path and size for the server membership shown in Figure 2-13, use the following command:

```
Set-DfsrMembership -GroupName Test `
                   -ComputerName Trey-dc-02 `
                   -StagingPath "C:\PSHelp\DfsrPrivate\Staging" `
                   -StagingPathQuotaInMB 4096
```

You can also set the size and path of the Conflict and Deleted folder that caches folders and files that have been changed on two or more members or have been deleted. The default size is 4 GB (4096 MB).

Configuring fault tolerance

There are two kinds of fault tolerance available for DFS-N: multiple root targets for domain-based DFS-N and failover clusters for stand-alone DFS-N.

Domain-based DFS-N fault tolerance

When creating DFS-N root targets for domain-based DFS-N, you need a minimum of two domain controllers and two DFS-N root targets within the domain that is hosting the root. This ensures that the failure of either a domain controller or a server hosting a DFS-N root will not cause the namespace to be unavailable. Domain-based DFS roots can't be created on cluster shared storage, although they can be created on nonshared storage of cluster nodes.

So you can create a domain-based DFS-N root target on each node of a failover cluster using the local storage of each node. In the event of a node failure in the cluster, the DFS-N is still available. You can also create DFS-N roots on nonclustered servers to provide the same level of fault tolerance.

In a domain with a single domain controller, the unavailability of that domain controller also renders the DFS-N in the domain unavailable. To avoid a single point of failure for your DFS-N, you must ensure that there are at least two domain controllers for each domain that has a DFS-N root.

Stand-alone DFS-N fault tolerance

To ensure the availability of a stand-alone DFS root, you create the root on the shared cluster storage of a clustered file server by using the Cluster Administrator console. In the event of a failure of any node in the cluster, the DFS-N continues to be fully available as long as a single node of the cluster is available.

A stand-alone DFS-N is not dependent on Active Directory, so there is no specific requirement for domain controllers with a stand-alone DFS-N. If the cluster that hosts the stand-alone DFS-N is available, the DFS-N is available.

Cloning a DFS database

Windows Server 2012 R2 adds the capability to clone a DFS-R database to speed up initial synchronization time dramatically. You use preseeded files and an export/import process to quickly set up replication and synchronize the databases. Cloning a DFS-R database can be done only by using Windows PowerShell.

To clone a DFS database, first create the replication group and folders by following these steps:

1. Create and populate the folder that will be the source folder.

2. Create a replication group with New-DfsReplicationGroup.

3. Add a DFS replicated folder with New-DfsReplicatedFolder.

4. Add the source server as a DFS-R member server with Add-DfsrMember.

5. Set the source server as the PrimaryMember with Set-DfsrMembership.

After the replication folder is successfully initialized, a DFS-R event 4112 is issued, and you can export a clone of the database.

After the replicated folders are ready to clone, export the database to a clone directory with the following (where "H:\DfsrClone" is the location that will host the exported clone database):

```
New-Item -Path "H:\DfsrClone" -Type Directory
Export-DfsrClone -Volume "H:" -Path "H:\DfsrClone"
```

When cloning is complete, a set of robocopy commands are displayed by the Export-DfsrClone cmdlet. It returns Ready when the export process is complete. You can monitor the progress of the cloning by using the Get-DfsrCloneState cmdlet. When cloning is complete, DFS-R issues an Event 2402 in the DFS-R event log.

Use Robocopy to move the exported database and preseed the replication folder by using:

```
Robocopy.exe "H:\DfsrClone" "<destination path>" /B

Robocopy.exe "<source path>" "<destination path>" /E /B /COPYALL /R:6 /W:5 /MT:64 /XD
DfsrPrivate /TEE /LOG+:preseed.log
```

On the target server, verify that the replication database doesn't already exist with the following command (where H: is the drive letter of the target replicated folder):

```
Get-ChildItem -Path "H:\System Volume Information\dfsr" -hidden
```

If there is no output, there are no replicated folders on the volume. If there is a listing, you need to do cleanup to remove any residual traces from a previous replication. You can't clone into an existing DFS-R database and you have to remove traces from any previous DFS-R folders.

EXAM TIP

You can't remove residual DFS-R folders or files while the DFS-R service is running. You need to stop the DFS-R service, delete all files and folders in the "\System Volume Information\dfsr" folder and then restart the DFS-R service.

After preseeding with Robocopy is complete, you can import the cloned database and XML configuration with the following command (again H: is the target volume and \dfsrclone is the target path):

```
Import-DfsrClone -Volume H: -Path "H:\dfsrclone"
```

When Get-DfsrCloneState returns Ready, or when the DFS-R event log shows an Event 4104 (one event per replicated folder), you can complete configuring the replication by adding the target server to the replication group and setting its membership state with this:

```
$DfsrSourceComputerName = "<sourceserver>"
$DfsrDestinationComputerName = "<destinationserver>"
$DfsrReplicationGroupName = "<DFS-R Group>"
$DfsrReplicatedFolderName = "<DFS-R Folder>"
$DfsrReplicatedFolderPath = "<DFS-R Folder Path>"

Add-DfsrMember -GroupName $DfsrReplicationGroupName `
               -ComputerName $DfsrDestinationComputerName

Add-DfsrConnection -GroupName $DfsrReplicationGroupName `
                   -SourceComputerName $DfsrSourceComputerName `
                   -DestinationComputerName $DfsrDestinationComputerName

Set-DfsrMembership -GroupName $DfsrReplicationGroupName `
                   -FolderName $DfsrReplicatedFolderName `
                   -ContentPath $DfsrReplicatedFolderPath `
                   -ComputerName $DfsrDestinationComputerName
```

Use the Get-DfsrPreservedFiles cmdlet to discover any files that had conflicts during the database cloning, and use the *-DfsrPropagationTest cmdlets to validate replication.

Recovering DFS databases

You can use the database cloning technique to speed up recovery from a corrupted DFS-R database on a server. This corruption can be caused by hardware issues, such as an abrupt power loss. Rather than wait for the slow process of an automatic nonauthoritative recovery to complete, you can clone the primary database, as described previously, and use it to recover the corrupted database. You won't need to preseed the replicated folder, so you can skip that step, but you should remove the memberships of the problem server to prevent DFS-R from attempting to rebuild the database until the cloning is complete.

If the only DFS-R memberships for the server are on the same volume as the corrupted database, use Windows PowerShell to remove the member with this:

```
Remove-DfsrMember -GroupName <dfsrgroup> -ComputerName <dfsrservername>
```

If there are volumes with uncorrupted DFS-R databases, use the Dfsradmin command instead. This command enables you to specify only a single membership.

```
Dfsradmin membership delete /rgname:<dfsrgroup> /rfname:<dfsrfolder>
/memname:<dfsrservername>
```

Optimizing DFS-R

DFS-R can be optimized by tuning the file-staging sizes as appropriate on a per-server basis. Windows Server 2012 R2 adds the capability to tune the minimum staging size for files to increase performance when replicating large files.

In previous versions of Windows Server, DFS-R uses a fixed, 256 KB file size as the minimum size for staging. If a file is larger than 256 KB, it is staged before it replicates. Further, if the staging folder quota is configured too small, DFS-R consumes additional CPU and disk resources.

The staging folder quota should be large enough that replication can continue even if multiple large files are staged awaiting replication. To improve performance, the staging folder should be as close to the size of the replicated folder as possible.

Staging folder quota sizes are particularly a concern on hub members with multiple replication partners. When configuring staging folders, locate them on different physical disks from the folders that are being replicated.

Thought experiment
Configuring branch office access to corporate resources

In this thought experiment, apply what you've learned about this objective. You can find answers to these questions in the "Answers" section at the end of this chapter.

You are the network administrator for TreyResearch.net. The company has a large share of corporate training content, currently hosted on a single Windows Server 2012 R2 server in the main corporate datacenter. The share sits on a ReFS file system to provide additional resiliency.

Users in the branch offices complain of poor video performance when watching training videos, plus other users complain of slow access to other corporate resources when several users are watching training videos.

1. What would you suggest as a solution to improve the ability of branch office users to access corporate training resources? (Choose all that apply.)

    A. Copy the current corporate training share to each of the branch offices.

    B. Increase the bandwidth on the corporate wide area network (WAN).

    C. Create a root DFS-N namespace and add the training share folder to the namespace.

    D. Move the share to an NTFS file system server to improve performance.

    E. Set up DFS-R to branch office servers in a hub-spoke configuration with the corporate office at the hub.

    F. Set up DFS-R to the branch office servers in a mesh configuration.

2. All content is created in the main corporate headquarters, but the content management and creation role is being expanded to include content from all the branch offices. How does this affect the answer to question 1?

3. What steps can you take to improve the initial replication of data to the branch offices?

Objective summary

- The DFS-N and DFS-R roles can be installed on Windows Servers running full or server-core installations and on an AD DS domain controller.

- Windows Server 2012 added Windows PowerShell support for DFS-N.

- Windows Server 2012 R2 added Windows PowerShell support for DFS-R.

- Configure DFS-R scheduling and bandwidth usage to optimize WAN bandwidth while providing an appropriate replication speed.

- RDC settings can be configured to disable cross-file RDC.
- The threshold for RDC can be changed with the Set-DfsrConnection cmdlet.
- Configure the size of DFS-R staging folders to minimize thrashing and provide efficient replication of large files. Windows Server 2012 R2 enables staging folder size to be set for each member server in a replication group.
- Use failover clustering to provide fault tolerance of stand-alone DFS-N.
- Use multiple DFS-N root targets and multiple AD DS domain controllers to provide fault tolerance for domain-based DFS-N.
- Use DFS database cloning to speed up initial replication of large DFS-R folders.
- Use DFS database cloning to speed up recovery from a corrupted DFS-R database on a member server.

Objective review

1. What commands do you need to run to enable DFS-N and DFS-R on the local server?

   A. Add-WindowsPackage -online -PackagePath DFS

   B. Enable-WindowsOptionalFeature -online -PackageName DFS-N,DFS-R

   C. Install-WindowsFeature -Name FS-DFS-N,FS-DFS-R -IncludeManagementTools

   D. Add-WindowsFeature -Name DFS -IncludeAllSubFeatures

2. You need to enable remote management of DFS from your Windows 8 workstation. What commands do you need to run? (Include only the minimum that apply.)

   A. Install-WindowsFeature -name RSAT-DFS-Mgmt-Con

   B. Enable-WindowsOptionalFeature -FeatureName *DFS* -online

   C. Winrm QuickConfig

   D. Enable-PSRemoting

Objective 2.2: Configure File Server Resource Manager (FSRM)

The File Server Resource Manager (FSRM) role enables folder-level quotas, file-type screening, and comprehensive reporting of file system usage. The FSRM role also allows you to define a subset of files on a server and then schedule a task to apply simple commands to that subset of files.

This objective covers how to:

- Install the FSRM role
- Configure quotas
- Configure file screens
- Configure reports
- Configure file management tasks

Installing the FSRM role

FSRM is supported on all versions of Windows Server 2012 R2 and is supported for both full and Server Core installations. For Server Core installations, the graphical FSRM console is used remotely from another copy of Windows Server 2012, Windows Server 2012 R2, or a Windows 8 or Windows 8.1 computer with the Remote Server Administration Tools (RSAT) installed.

Installing FSRM by using Server Manager

Windows Server Manager is the GUI way to install and configure the FSRM role on a server. Windows Server Manager can be used to manage both the local server and remote servers, including those running a Server Core installation, which enables you to install FSRM graphically on Server Core without ever using the command line.

Use the Add Roles And Features Wizard to install the FSRM role. You'll use the Role-based or Feature-based option. Because Windows Server Manager can be used to insert roles and features into virtual hard disks, or to manage multiple servers from a single console, you have to select the server on which you want to install FSRM; on the Select Server Roles page, expand File And Storage Service, and then expand File And iSCSI Services and select File Server Resource Manager (see Figure 2-14). Click Next a couple of times and then Install. For most cases, installing FSRM does not require a server restart.

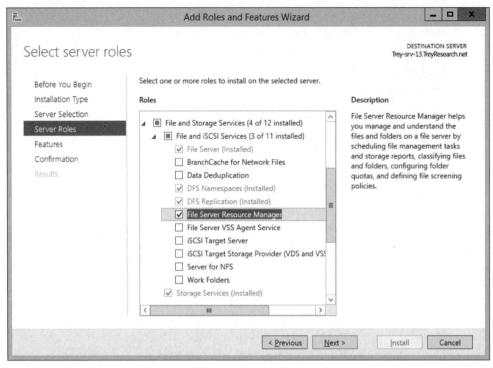

FIGURE 2-14 The Select Server Roles page of the Add Roles And Features Wizard

Installing FSRM by using Windows PowerShell

You can install FSRM by using Windows PowerShell, either locally or remotely. Windows PowerShell supports remote installation of FSRM on Windows Server 2012 R2. To install FSRM locally, use the following command:

```
Install-WindowsFeature -Name FS-Resource-Manager -IncludeManagementTools
```

To install FSRM on a remote computer that has remote management configured, use this command:

```
Install-WindowsFeature -ComputerName <ServerName> -Name FS-Resource-Manager
-IncludeManagementTools
```

The Install-WindowsFeature command requires that the user have administrator credentials to install FSRM, and the command must be run from an elevated shell.

Most management tasks that can be performed with Windows PowerShell support using a credential object. But even when providing a credential, they fail unless run from an elevated shell. To start an elevated Windows PowerShell command line, use the following:

```
Start-Process PowerShell.exe -verb RunAs
```

This command opens an elevated shell. Some commands might still require that you supply a credential object for the credentials required if the account you used to create the elevated shell doesn't have sufficient privileges for the command.

Configuring quotas

FSRM quotas allow you to limit the space that is available for a folder or volume. Quotas can be applied to new folders automatically, or retroactively to existing folders. FSRM has quota templates that can be applied, or can be used to build new quota templates.

Creating a quota

To create a quota on a folder or volume using the File Server Resource Manager, right-click Quotas in the console tree and select Create Quota from the menu. The Create Quota dialog box opens (see Figure 2-15). In this dialog box, you specify the following:

- **Quota Path**   The root of the path on which that you want to apply quotas
- **Auto Apply Template And Create Quotas On Existing And New Subfolders**   Applies the quota and enables inheritance so that subfolders can't be used to bypass the quota restrictions
- **Create Quota On Path**   Creates a quota on that path, but doesn't automatically apply the quota to existing subfolders of the path or on new subfolders created later
- **Derive Properties From This Quota Template**   Selects from a list of existing quota templates to use to define the quota
- **Define Custom Quota Properties**   Defines a custom quota with hard or soft quotas and custom notification thresholds

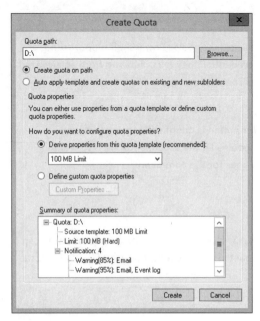

FIGURE 2-15 The Create Quota dialog box

If you choose to create a custom template, you use the Quota Properties dialog box, as shown in Figure 2-16. You can specify the following:

- **Copy Properties From Quota Template** Optionally choose from an existing template as the starting point to define the quotas for this path.

- **Quota Path** Specifies the root of the quota path. It is unavailable when already specified in the Create Quota dialog box.

- **Description** An optional description for the custom quota.

- **Limit** The space limit for the custom quota. If you used a template as the starting point, this box is filled in based on that template (but you can change the limit).

- **Hard Quota** If specified, enforces the limit on all nonadministrative users.

- **Soft Quota** If specified, the limit is used for monitoring and reporting only, but users can continue to add files to the path even when they have exceeded the limit.

- **Notification Thresholds** You can specify the percentage of the limit that will trigger a notification and also what kind of notification. You can also specify a command to run or reports to generate when the threshold is reached.

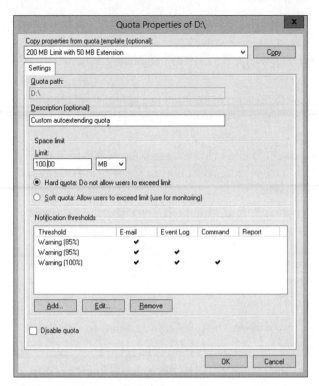

FIGURE 2-16 The Quota Properties dialog box

You can also use the Windows PowerShell FSRM module to create a quota or auto apply quota. You can create a quota on a path with the New-FsrmQuota cmdlet. The syntax is as follows:

```
New-FsrmQuota -Path <quotapath> -Size <int> -SoftLimit -Template <string>
```

To create thresholds, use the New-FsrmQuotaThreshold cmdlet. To specify an action to be taken at a threshold, use the New-FsrmAction cmdlet. The New-FsrmAction cmdlet supports the following actions:

- **Email** Sends an email to the user or administrator that the event was triggered
- **Event** Creates an event log entry
- **Command** Runs the command specified
- **Report** Runs one or more storage reports

Creating a quota template

You can create a quota template completely from scratch or by starting with one of the existing templates and modifying it for your own specific needs. Templates can have the following properties:

- **Hard or soft quotas**   A hard quota prevents a user from saving files when the limit is reached. A soft quota only warns the user (and usually the administrator) and is useful for monitoring usage.

- **Space Limits**   The space limits can be specified in kilobytes (KB), megabytes (MB), gigabytes (GB), or terabytes (TB). The limit is applied only to a specific path of a quota; it doesn't affect other volumes or paths.

- **Notification Thresholds**   You can specify as many or as few notification thresholds as you need. Each threshold is triggered when usage reaches a percentage of the space limit and can trigger email, trigger an event in the event log, run a command or script, cause one or more reports to be generated, or a combination of these actions. For more on these actions, see the following section, "Notification actions."

To create a new template, follow these steps:

1. Select Quota Templates in the console tree of the FSRM console and then click Create Quota Template in the Actions pane.

2. To start with the settings of an existing template, select the template from the Copy Properties From Quota Template (Optional) list and then click Copy.

3. Enter a Template Name and a description; and then modify the settings of Space Limit, Hard Quota Or Soft Quota, and Notification Thresholds as appropriate for your new template.

4. Click OK when you complete configuring the new quota and it is available for immediate use.

You can also create a new template by using the New-FsrmQuotaTemplate cmdlet or modify an existing template by using Set-FsrmQuotaTemplate. The process is similar to that used when creating a new quota. You first define the thresholds and actions for the quota, saving them in a variable, and then use the variables in the New-FsrmQuotaTemplate or Set-FsrmQuotaTemplate cmdlets. Alternately, you can pipe the thresholds and actions to the New-FsrmQuotaTemplate or Set-FsrmQuotaTemplate cmdlets.

Notification actions

When a quota reaches one of the thresholds set in the quota, it can trigger multiple actions, as specified in the Notification Thresholds box of the quota. There are four basic kinds of actions that can be triggered:

- **Email Message**   Sends an email to the user or administrator that the event was triggered

- **Event Log** Creates an event log entry
- **Command** Runs the command specified
- **Report** Runs one or more storage reports

The email message event is configured by the E-mail Message tab of the Add Threshold dialog box (see Figure 2-17).

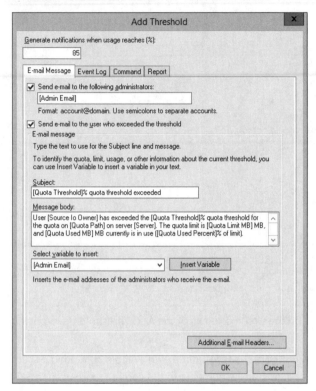

FIGURE 2-17 The E-Mail Message tab of the Add Threshold dialog box

This page allows you to set the receiver of the email and the text of the message. The text can include variables to personalize the email and add information about the quota threshold. You can also specify additional recipients of the message by clicking the Additional E-Mail Headers button.

The Event Log event is configured by the Event Log tab of the Add Threshold dialog box (see Figure 2-18).

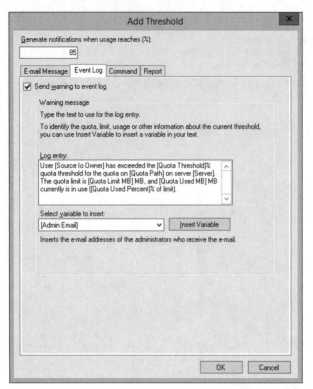

FIGURE 2-18 The Event Log tab of the Add Threshold dialog box

The Command event is configured by the Command tab of the Add Threshold dialog box (see Figure 2-19).

The Command tab enables you to configure the threshold to run a single command or script. You can specify the command or script, any arguments to the command, a working directory, and the account the command or script is run as. The available choices are:

- **Local Service** Runs the command or script with the same level of access as the user, but has access to network resources with no credentials.

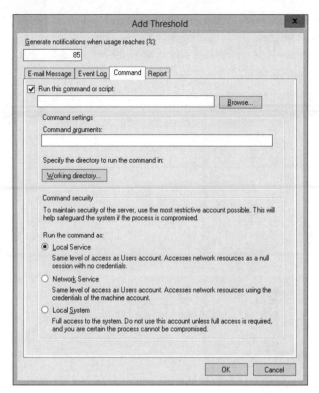

FIGURE 2-19 The Command tab of the Add Threshold dialog box

- **Network Service** Runs the command or script with the same level of access as the user and has access to network resources with the credentials of the machine account.

- **Local System** Full access to the system. This is a very powerful and very dangerous level of access and should be avoided unless you are certain that the process can't be compromised.

EXAM TIP

When reading an exam question, watch for phrases such as "using least privilege." They are a clue that one or more of the possible answers is likely to be wrong because it uses an account that has too much privilege. For example, if the action is running only locally and doesn't need to access network resources, it shouldn't be run as Network Service. And if it is specified as running as Local System, it almost certainly doesn't meet that requirement of the question.

The report event is configured by the Report tab of the Add Threshold dialog box, as shown in Figure 2-20. When a threshold limit is reached, you can automatically generate one or more of the standard reports and then optionally have the reports sent to the user or to one or more administrators. The reports are automatically saved in the default location for reports.

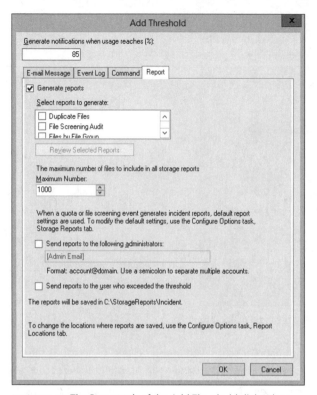

FIGURE 2-20 The Report tab of the Add Threshold dialog box

Configuring file screens

FSRM includes the capability to screen files based on a file name pattern. This screen can be an active screen, preventing the files from being saved to a specific path or volume or a passive screen that is used to monitor only. The file screen functionality of FSRM is based on the file names of the files, not on their content. Although it is traditionally used to filter by file extension, it can actually be used to filter on any portion of the file name.

> **NOTE FILE NAME PATTERNS ONLY**
>
> The file screens implemented by FSRM do not prevent users from saving files that they shouldn't; they only prevent users from saving files whose names match a pattern. Screening for audio MP3 files (for example, with a pattern of *.mp3) prevents someone from saving mymusicfile.mp3, but doesn't stop them from saving that same file renamed to mymusicfile.np3.

Creating a file screen

To create a file screen on a folder or volume using the FSRM, right-click File Screens in the console tree and select Create File Screen from the menu. The Create File Screen dialog box shown in Figure 2-21 opens. In this dialog box, you specify the following:

- **File Screen Path**   The root of the path on which you want to apply the file screen
- **Derive Properties From This File Screen Template**   Select from a list of existing file screen templates to use to define the quota
- **Define Custom File Screen Properties**   Define a custom file screen with an active or passive file screen, and notification actions

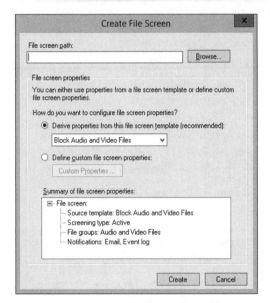

FIGURE 2-21 The Create File Screen dialog box

If you choose to create a custom template, use the File Screen Properties dialog box, as shown in Figure 2-22, which enables you to specify the following:

- **Copy Properties From Template**   Optionally choose from an existing template as the starting point to define the file screen for this path.
- **File Screen Path**   Specifies the root of the file screen path. It is unavailable when already specified in the Create File Screen dialog box.
- **Active Screening**   If specified, does not allow users to save the file type on the file screen path specified.
- **Passive Screening**   If specified, users are allowed to save the file type, but monitoring actions such as email messages are initiated.
- **File Groups**   Specifies the type of file to screen. You must select one or more types to create a screen.

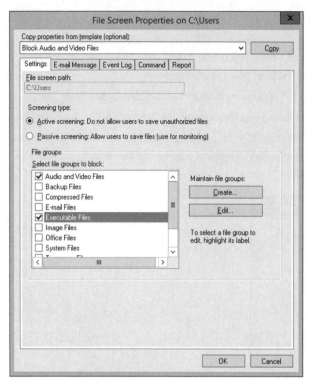

FIGURE 2-22 The File Screen Properties dialog box

You can also use the Windows PowerShell FSRM module to create a file screen. You can create a file screen on a path with the New-FsrmFileScreen cmdlet. The syntax is this:

```
New-FsrmFileScreen -Path <quotapath> -IncludeGroup <int> -Active -Template <string>
```

To specify an action to be taken on a file screen, use the New-FsrmAction cmdlet. The New-FsrmAction cmdlet supports the following actions:

- **Email** Sends an email to the user or administrator that the event was triggered
- **Event** Creates an event log entry
- **Command** Runs the command specified
- **Report** Runs one or more storage reports

Creating a file screen exception

You can create a file screen exception that allows files of a particular file group to be saved to the specified path even when there is a file screen in place. You create a file screen exception just as you would a file screen, but instead of blocking the file group, it allows the file group. A typical example has a file screen that prohibits saving any audio or video files in Public folders, but allows an exception for corporate training videos saved in the designated training folder.

Creating a file screen template

You can create a file screen template completely from scratch or by starting with one of the existing templates and modifying it for your own specific needs. Templates can have the following properties:

- **Active Or Passive Screens** An active file screen prevents a user from saving files of the specified type. A passive file screen only warns the user (and usually the adminis-trator) and is useful for monitoring usage.
- **File Groups** Define the files to be screened. File screens are based on file name patterns and can include multiple file name matches in a group.
- **Path** The root of the path in which the file screen will apply.

To create a new template, follow these steps:

1. Select File Screen Templates in the console tree of the File Server Resource Manager console and then click Create File Screen Template in the Actions pane.

2. To start with the settings of an existing template, select the template from the Copy Properties From File Screen Template (Optional) list and then click Copy.

3. Enter a Template Name, and then modify the settings of File Groups To Block, Active Screening or Passive Screening as appropriate for your new template.

4. Specify any actions to take when the file screen is triggered.

5. Click OK when you've completed configuring the new file screen and it is available for immediate use.

You can also create a new template by using the New-FsrmFileScreenTemplate cmdlet or modify an existing template by using Set-FsrmFileScreenTemplate. The process is similar to the one used when creating a new file screen. You first define the actions for the file screen, and any new file groups (using the New-FsrmFileGroup cmdlet), saving them in variables, and then use the variables in the New-FsrmFileScreenTemplate or Set-FsrmFileScreenTemplate cmdlets. Alternately, you can pipe the groups and actions to the New-FsrmFileScreenTemplate or Set-FsrmFileScreenTemplate cmdlets.

File screen notification actions

When a file screen is triggered, it can initiate multiple actions, as specified in the file screen. There are four kinds of actions that can be triggered:

- **Email Message** Sends an email to the user or administrator that the event was triggered
- **Event Log** Creates an event log entry
- **Command** Runs the command specified
- **Report** Runs one or more storage reports

The notification actions are essentially the same as for quota threshold notifications, as described earlier in the "Notification actions" section.

Creating file groups

File screens use pattern matching to describe groups of files to screen. FSRM includes 11 predefined file groups, as shown in Figure 2-23.

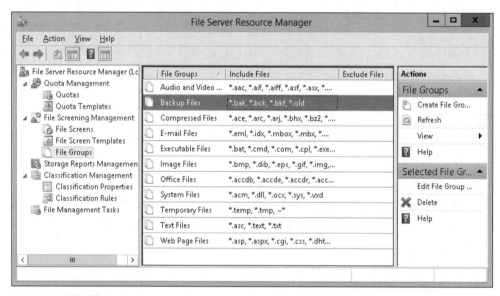

FIGURE 2-23 The File Server Resource Manager console

You can modify an existing file group or create a new file group. All the default file groups are based on pattern matching of the file extension, but file groups you create can use pattern matching against any portion of the file name. Furthermore, file groups you create have files to include in the screen, files to exclude from the screen, or both. To create a file group, select File Groups in the console tree of the File Server Resource Manager console and then click Create File Group in the Actions pane to open the Create File Group Properties dialog box (see Figure 2-24).

Because the file groups are based on whole file name pattern matching, you can use file screening to control exactly which files are allowed in a particular folder. For example, if you wanted to ensure that *only* screen captures for this chapter were allowed to be saved, you could create a file group that included the patterns "F??xx??.bmp" and "G??xx??.bmp", and excluded the pattern "F02xx??.bmp". This file group would define a file screen that screened all screen captures except those that begin with "F02".

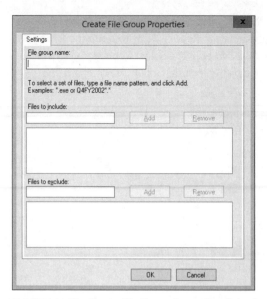

FIGURE 2-24 The Create File Group Properties dialog box

To create a file group using Windows PowerShell, use the New-FsrmFileGroup cmdlet. For example:

```
New-FsrmFileGroup -name Chp2Files -ExcludePattern "F02xx??.bmp" -IncludePattern
"F??xx??.bmp","G??xx??.bmp"
```

```
Description       :
ExcludePattern    : {F02xx??.bmp}
IncludePattern    : {F??xx??.bmp, G??xx??.bmp}
Name              : Chp2Files
PSComputerName    :
```

Notice that the -ExcludePattern and -IncludePattern parameters take a string list, which allows you to include or exclude multiple file name patterns from the group. You can modify a file group by using the Set-FsrmFileGroup cmdlet.

Configuring reports

FSRM includes 10 predefined reports. You can change the parameters of these reports, but you can't create new reports from scratch. Reports can be scheduled to run on a daily, weekly, or monthly schedule at a specific time. You can also configure the particular parameters of a report. Each report allows specific parameters relevant to the report. For example, the Files By Owner report defaults to all file owners and all files, but you can specify that you want the report to only report on specific users and only on files matching a specific pattern.

To generate a Files By Owner report of all the MP3 files on a server, select Storage Reports Management in the console tree and then click Generate Reports Now to open the Storage Reports Task Properties dialog box. Select Files By Owner in the Select Reports To Generate, and then click Edit Parameters. Enter *.mp3 into the Include Only Files Matching The Following File Name Pattern box, as shown in Figure 2-25.

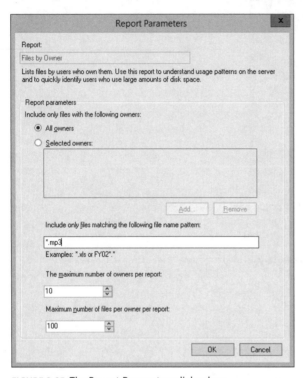

FIGURE 2-25 The Report Parameters dialog box

When you run reports interactively, as opposed to as a scheduled task, you can choose to have the report open as soon as it finishes, as shown in Figure 2-26.

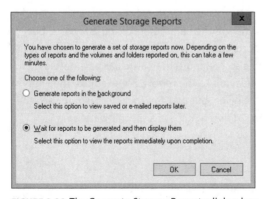

FIGURE 2-26 The Generate Storage Reports dialog box

You can use Windows PowerShell to manage Storage Reports by using the
*-FsrmStorageReport cmdlets. For details on how to create a new Storage Report, see
http://go.microsoft.com/fwlink/?LinkID=289432.

Configuring file management tasks

FSRM enables you to run file management tasks, which enable you to take actions on files
based on the file's properties. You can schedule tasks to run daily, weekly, or monthly; and to
generate reports after the task runs. You can also have the task send a warning notification to
users before it runs.

To create a file management task, select File Management Tasks in the console tree of the
File Server Resource Manager console and click Create File Management Task in the Actions
pane. The Create File Management Task dialog box shown in Figure 2-27 opens.

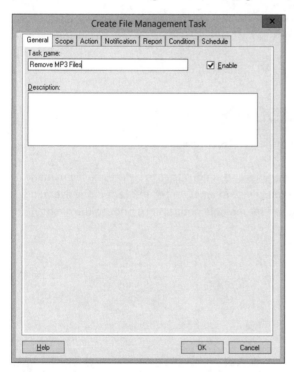

FIGURE 2-27 The Create File Management Task dialog box

Enter a name for the task and then click the Scope tab. Specify which folders the task will
run against. On the Action tab, specify what action to take, as shown in Figure 2-28. You can
set different settings depending on the action being taken.

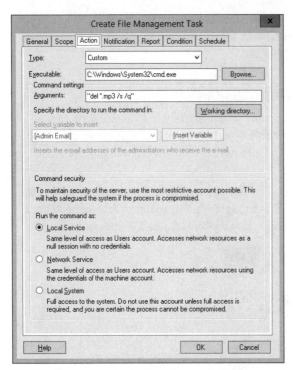

FIGURE 2-28 The Action tab of the Create File Management Task dialog box

On the Notification tab, you can set warnings and actions to take before the file management task runs, as shown in Figure 2-29. You can send email, enter an event in the event log, or run a custom command or script. You can set multiple notifications prior to the file management task to provide plenty of warning.

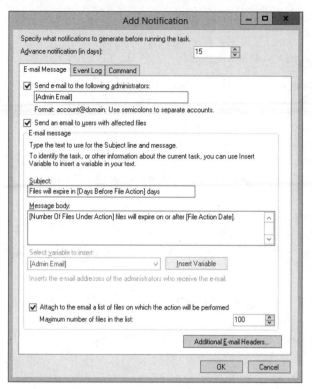

FIGURE 2-29 The Add Notification dialog box

On the Report tab, you can enable a log file, an error log file and an audit log file, along with generating a report. On the Condition tab, you can add conditions to limit the file management task to act only on files with specific property conditions. Finally, on the Schedule tab, you can specify how often a task runs. You can also set the task to run continuously against new files that match the property classifications in the condition.

You can also create file management tasks with the New-FsrmFileManagementJob cmdlet. This cmdlet uses an FsrmScheduledTask object, an FsrmFmjAction object, and an FsrmFmjNotification object. For details, see *http://go.microsoft.com/fwlink/?LinkID=289420*.

Thought experiment

Using FSRM to manage file system usage

In this thought experiment, apply what you've learned about this objective. You can find answers to these questions in the "Answers" section at the end of this chapter.

You are the network administrator for TreyResearch.net. The company uses a single main public share as a file-sharing resource to allow users to share and swap files, as well as to host shared internal corporate resources. Lately, there has been a large increase in file system usage, and adding additional disk space isn't an easy option on the hosting server.

1. What reports can you use to get a clear understanding of which files are taking up the most space and who their owners are?

2. Could you use quotas to control how much space each user is allowed to use on the share?

3. What file screens could you put in place to ensure that inappropriate files are not saved on the share?

4. How could you use file screen exceptions to allow the saving of sanctioned files even if they might violate the file screens in question 3?

Objective summary

- The FSRM role can be installed on both full installations and Server Core installations.
- Quotas, which can be hard or soft, can act on a specific path or on a path and all subfolders of the path.
- Quotas can be created from scratch or can be based on quota templates.
- Notification actions include sending an email, entering an alert in the event log, running reports, and executing a command.
- Executing commands based on a quota, file screen, or file management task should be done with the least privilege possible to accomplish the goal.
- File screens can be active or passive.
- File screens are based on file name patterns, not on file content.
- There are 10 standard storage reports,
- Storage reports can run on a schedule or can be run interactively.
- File management tasks can be set to run on a schedule, or continuously on new files.
- File management tasks can be set to notify users days before the task actually runs to prevent data loss.

Objective review

1. The company provides a public transfer share to allow users to easily share files. Without using excess privilege, you have to ensure that all files are deleted after they have been on the server for 3 days. What PowerShell command should you run as part of the file management task?

   A. get-childitem -recurse | where-object {$_.CreationTime -ge (get-date).Add(-3)}
   | remove-item

   B. get-childitem -recurse | where-object {$_.CreationTime -le (get-date).Add(-3)}
   | remove-item

   C. get-childitem -recurse | where-object {$_.CreationTime -ge (get-date).Add-Days(-3)}
   | remove-item

   D. get-childitem -recurse | where-object {$_.CreationTime -le (get-date).AddDays(-3)}
   | remove-item

2. In the scenario of question 1, what command security should the script run as?

   A. Local Service

   B. Domain Users

   C. Local System

   D. Protected Users

3. You need to allow users to store files for sharing with other users. These files are stored on the D:\UserShare folder of SRV2, which is shared as \\srv2\share. Each user's use of the space is limited to 250 MB. When users reach 200 MB, they should be warned via email and the Administrator account should also be notified by email. How can you implement this?

   A. Create an FSRM quota on the D:\UserShare folder of SRV2 based on the Monitor 500 MB Share template, but change the Limit to 250 MB.

   B. Create an FSRM quota on the D:\UserShare folder of SRV2 based on the 200 MB Limit With 50 MB Extension template.

   C. Create an FSRM quota on the \\srv2\UserShare share based on the Monitor 500 MB Share template, but change the Limit to 250 MB.

   D. Create an FSRM quota on the \\srv2\UserShare share based on the 200 MB Limit Reports To User template, but change the limit to 250 MB.

Objective 2.3: Configure file and disk encryption

Windows Server 2012 R2 supports two different types of file and disk encryption: BitLocker and the Encrypting File System (EFS). BitLocker uses a Trusted Platform Module (TPM) version 1.2 or later when available to provide whole-disk encryption, but can use a removable USB key when a TPM is not available. EFS is useful for user-level file and folder encryption on both client computers and remote file servers.

> **This objective covers how to:**
> - Configure BitLocker encryption
> - Configure the Network Unlock feature
> - Configure BitLocker policies
> - Configure the EFS recovery agent
> - Manage EFS and BitLocker certificates, including backup and restore

Configuring BitLocker encryption

To enable BitLocker encryption on Windows Server, you need to install the BitLocker feature. Furthermore, all disks encrypted with BitLocker must use the NTFS file system. To do this in Server Manager, select Add Roles And Features and then follow these steps:

1. Select Role-Based Or Feature-Based Installation.

2. On the Select Features page, select BitLocker Drive Encryption. You'll be prompted to add additional supporting features, as shown in Figure 2-30.

FIGURE 2-30 The Add Features That Are Required For BitLocker Drive Encryption? page

3. The actual supporting features that will be added will depend on which features are already installed on the server. Click Add Features and then click Next.

4. Click Install to complete the installation. At least one restart is required.

To install BitLocker using Windows PowerShell, use the following command:

```
Install-WindowsFeature -Name BitLocker -IncludeAllSubFeature `
-IncludeManagementTools -Restart
```

Enabling BitLocker protectors

When enabling BitLocker from the command line, it's a good practice to add BitLocker protectors prior to enabling BitLocker on a volume. At a minimum, you should add the recovery password protector to ensure that you have a way to recover if your hardware changes. Even very small changes can trigger a BitLocker failure. Keep a copy of the recovery password in a safe place that is accessible in an emergency, but not with the computer you're trying to protect.

The other protector you should add is the recovery key protector. This protector writes a recovery key to a USB key, allowing you to recover and boot by inserting the USB key. Keep this key in a safe place separate from the server it is protecting.

You can add a BitLocker protector with the Add-BitLockerKeyProtector cmdlet or with the manage-bde.exe command-line utility. You can add only one protector at a time. To add the recovery password protector with a default, generated, numerical key and add the recovery key protector to the operating system drive (C:), use the following Windows PowerShell commands:

```
Add-BitLockerKeyProtector -MountPoint C: -RecoveryPasswordProtector
```

```
Add-BitLockerKeyProtector -MountPoint C: -RecoveryKeyProtector -RecoveryKeyPath <string>
```

In the second of these commands, *<string>* should be replaced with the path to the USB key onto which you want to write the recovery key.

To add the same protectors by using the manage-bde command, use the following:

```
manage-bde -protectors -add C: -RecoveryPassword
```

```
manage-bde -protectors -add C: -RecoveryKey <string>
```

The available protectors are as follows:

- Recovery password
- Recovery key
- Startup key
- Certificate
- TPM (operating system drive only)
- Password (data drives only)
- TPM and pin

- TPM and startup key
- TPM and pin and startup key
- AD DS (data drives only)

Enabling BitLocker encryption of the operating system drive

You can enable BitLocker from the command line, with the manage-bde command, or with the Windows PowerShell Enable-BitLocker cmdlet.

> **NOTE USING THE BITLOCKER DRIVE ENCRYPTION CONTROL PANEL**
>
> When you install the BitLocker feature in Windows Server 2012 R2, the control panel application is not normally visible until you encrypt your first volume unless you have the Desktop Experience feature installed (you normally would not, except on a Remote Desktop Session Host computer). If you have Desktop Experience installed, you can use the BitLocker Drive Encryption control panel application for your first volume encryption.

BitLocker works best with a TPM of at least version 1.2. This hardware encryption module works with BitLocker to do full volume encryption. If the hardware changes in any significant way, BitLocker will not recognize an encrypted volume. If the encrypted volume is the operating system volume, Windows Server can't boot.

Suspending BitLocker

Whenever you need to make changes to the hardware or BIOS of a BitLocker-protected server, or install system updates, you should suspend BitLocker on the operating system drive to ensure that you can boot after the change. You can suspend BitLocker for a single restart (the default) or for more than a single restart by using the -RebootCount parameter. When BitLocker is suspended, the data on the volume is not decrypted; instead, the BitLocker encryption key is available to everyone in the clear. New data written to the volume is still encrypted, and BitLocker does not do a system integrity check on startup, allowing you to start Windows Server even though there has been a change that would have normally triggered an integrity check. To suspend BitLocker, use the BitLocker Drive Encryption control panel item or use the Suspend-BitLocker cmdlet. For a suspension on the C: drive of three restarts, use this:

```
Suspend-BitLocker -MountPoint C: -RebootCount 3
```

If you specify a RebootCount of 0, BitLocker is suspended until you resume BitLocker protection by using the Resume-BitLocker cmdlet.

Locking or unlocking BitLocker volumes

You can lock a BitLocker volume to prevent any access to the volume by using the Lock-BitLocker cmdlet. The volume remains locked until it is unlocked with the Unlock-BitLocker cmdlet. Operating system volumes can't be locked.

Enabling and disabling auto-unlock of a BitLocker volume

Data volumes and removable drives that are encrypted by BitLocker can be automatically unlocked whenever they are present in the host computer. You can't automatically unlock the operating system volume. After a user unlocks the operating system volume, BitLocker uses encrypted information in the registry and volume metadata to unlock any data volumes that have automatic unlocking enabled. To enable auto-unlock of a BitLocker volume, use the BitLocker Drive Encryption control panel item or use the Enable-BitLockerAutoUnlock cmdlet. You can disable the auto-unlock feature of one or more BitLocker volumes by using the Disable-BitLockerAutoUnlock cmdlet. You can clear all automatic unlocking keys on a server with the Clear-BitLockerAutoUnlock cmdlet. Clear BitLocker automatic unlocking keys prior to disabling BitLocker on a volume.

Disabling BitLocker encryption on a volume

When you want to remove the BitLocker encryption on a volume, you can disable BitLocker on that volume by using the BitLocker Drive Encryption control panel item or by using the Disable-BitLocker cmdlet. Disabling BitLocker encryption on a volume removes all key protectors on the volume and begins decrypting the data on the volume.

Configuring the Network Unlock feature

Beginning with Windows Server 2012 and Windows 8, BitLocker supports a new protector option for operating system volumes called Network Unlock. Network Unlock allows for automatic unlocking of operating system volumes on domain-joined servers and desktops that are connected over a wired corporate network.

Network Unlock requires the server or desktop to have a Dynamic Host Configuration Protocol (DHCP) driver implemented in Unified Extensible Firmware Interface (UEFI) firmware. Without Network Unlock, computers protected with TPM+PIN require a PIN to be entered whenever the computer restarts or resumes from hibernation. Therefore, enabling TPM+PIN without Network Unlock prevents remote updating with unattended distribution of software updates. With Network Unlock enabled, BitLocker-protected systems that use TPM+PIN can be remotely started or restarted without direct interaction at the console.

The Network Unlock feature requires the following:

- Computers running Windows 8, Windows 8.1, Windows Server 2012, or Windows Server 2012 R2 with UEFI DHCP drivers
- Windows Deployment Services (WDS) role installed on Windows Server 2012 or Windows Server 2012 R2
- BitLocker Network Unlock optional feature installed on Windows Server 2012 or Windows Server 2012 R2
- DHCP server
- Properly configured public/private key pairing
- Network Unlock Group Policy settings configured

Enabling the Windows Deployment Services (WDS) server role

If WDS is not configured on your network, install the WDS server role on a Windows Server 2012 or Windows Server 2012 R2 server. It does not require a fully configured WDS server, just the WDS service to be running. You can install the WDS role as part of the Network Unlock feature install or separately by using this:

```
Install-WindowsFeature WDS-Deployment
```

Confirm that the WDS service is running with this:

```
Get-Service WDSServer
```

Creating the Network Unlock certificate

On the WDS server, follow these steps to create the Network Unlock certificate if working in an environment with an existing certification authority (CA):

1. Open Certificate Manager on the WDS server using **certmgr.msc**.

2. Request a new personal certificate, as shown in Figure 2-31.

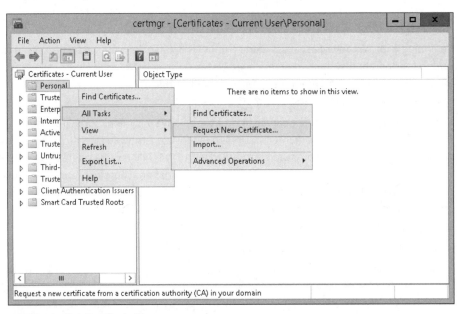

FIGURE 2-31 The Certificate Manager console

3. Click Next and select Active Directory Enrollment Policy; then click Next.

4. Choose the certificate template created for the Network Unlock on the domain controller and select Enroll.

5. Add a Subject Name value that clearly identifies the purpose of the certificate, such as **BitLocker Network Unlock Certificate for TreyResearch domain**.

6. Create the certificate and verify that the certificate appears in the Personal folder.

7. Export the public key certificate for Network Unlock using DER Encoded Binary X.509 format and do not export the private key. Export the key to a file with a .cer extension, such as BitLocker-NetworkUnlock.cer.

8. Export the public key with a private key for Network Unlock by selecting the previously created certificate and selecting All Tasks and then Export. Select Yes, Export The Private Key and save to a .pfx file.

In environments that do not have a fully functional CA, create a self-signed certificate by following these steps:

1. Create a new blank text file **BitLocker-NetworkUnlock.inf**.

2. Enter the following into the file using a plain text editor such as Notepad.exe:

```
[NewRequest]
Subject="CN=BitLocker Network Unlock certificate"
Exportable=true
RequestType=Cert
KeyLength=2048

[Extensions]
1.3.6.1.4.1.311.21.10 = "{text}"
_continue_ = "OID=1.3.6.1.4.1.311.67.1.1"

2.5.29.37 = "{text}"
_continue_= "1.3.6.1.4.1.311.67.1.1"
```

3. From an elevated prompt, create a new certificate with certreq.exe:

```
certreq -new BitLocker-NetworkUnlock.inf BitLocker-NetworkUnlock.cer
```

4. Verify that the certreq command created and imported the certificate by running certmgr.msc. The certificate should be in the Current User, Personal store.

5. Export the certificate to create a .pfx file.

Deploying a private key and certificate to a WDS server

To deploy the private key and certificate to the WDS server, follow these steps:

1. On the WDS server, from an elevated prompt, open a new Microsoft Management Console (MMC) with mmc.exe.

2. Add the Certificates snap-in. Select the Computer Account and Local Computer options.

3. Select BitLocker Drive Encryption Network Unlock in the console tree. Right-click and select Import from the All Tasks menu.

4. On the File To Import page, select the .pfx file you exported, as shown in Figure 2-32.

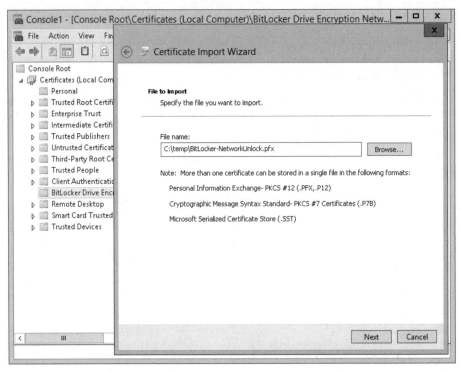

FIGURE 2-32 The Certificate Import Wizard

5.   Enter the password of the .pfx file you exported and complete the wizard.

Configuring Group Policy settings for Network Unlock

To configure the Group Policy settings for Network Unlock, you need to deploy the certificate to the clients that will use it. To do this, follow these steps:

1.   Copy the .cer file that was created earlier to a domain controller for the domain on which you're enabling Network Unlock.

2.   Open the Group Policy Management Console (GPMC).

3.   Create and edit a new GPO or modify an existing one to enable the Allow Network Unlock At Startup setting. This setting is in Computer Configuration\Policies\ Administrative Templates\Windows Components\BitLocker Drive Encryption\Operating System Drives.

4.   Select the Computer Configuration\Policies\Windows Settings\Security Settings\ Public Key Policies\BitLocker Drive Encryption Network Unlock Certificate folder in the console tree.

5.   Right-click and select Add Network Unlock Certificate to add the .cer file you copied from the WDS server.

Configuring BitLocker policies

Windows Server 2012 R2 has a full set of BitLocker policies. There are policies that affect all BitLocker drives; and different policies for fixed data drives, operating system drives, and removable data drives. The BitLocker policies are in the Computer Configuration\Policies\ Administrative Templates\Windows Components\BitLocker Drive Encryption folder. Table 2-2 lists the general BitLocker policies.

TABLE 2-2 General BitLocker policies

Setting	Default State
Stores BitLocker recovery information in AD DS (Windows Server 2008 and Windows Vista)	Not configured
Chooses default folder for recovery password	Not configured
Chooses how users can recover BitLocker-protected drives (Windows Server 2008 and Windows Vista)	Not configured
Chooses drive encryption method and cipher strength	Not configured
Chooses drive encryption method and cipher strength (Windows Vista, Windows Server 2008, Windows 7, Windows Server 2008 R2)	Not configured
Provides unique identifiers for your organization	Not configured
Prevents memory overwrite on restart	Not configured
Validates smart card certificate usage rule compliance	Not configured

The settings for fixed data drives are shown in Table 2-3.

TABLE 2-3 Fixed data drive BitLocker policies

Setting	Default State
Configures use of smart cards on fixed data drives	Not configured
Denies write access to fixed drives not protected by BitLocker	Not configured
Configures use of hardware-based encryption for fixed data drives	Not configured
Enforces drive encryption type on fixed data drives	Not configured
Allows access to BitLocker–protected fixed data drives from earlier versions of Windows	Not configured
Configure use of passwords for fixed data drives	Not configured
Choose how BitLocker–protected fixed drives can be recovered	Not configured

The settings for operating system drives are shown in Table 2-4.

TABLE 2-4 Operating system drive BitLocker policies

Setting	Default State
Allows Network Unlock at startup	Not configured
Allows Secure Boot for integrity validation	Not configured
Requires additional authentication at startup	Not configured
Requires additional authentication at startup (Windows Server 2008 and Windows Vista)	Not configured
Disallows standard users from changing the PIN or password	Not configured
Enables use of BitLocker authentication requiring preboot keyboard input on slates	Not configured
Allows enhanced PINs for startup	Not configured
Configures minimum PIN length for startup	Not configured
Configures use of hardware-based encryption for operating system drives	Not configured
Enforces drive encryption type on operating system drives	Not configured
Configures use of passwords for operating system drives	Not configured
Chooses how BitLocker–protected operating system drives can be recovered	Not configured
Configures TPM platform validation profile for BIOS-based firmware configurations	Not configured
Configures TPM platform validation profile (Windows Vista, Windows Server 2008, Windows 7, Windows Server 2008 R2)	Not configured
Configures TPM platform validation profile for native UEFI firmware configurations	Not configured
Resets platform validation data after BitLocker recovery	Not configured
Uses enhanced Boot Configuration Data (BCD) validation profile	Not configured

The settings for removable data drives are shown in Table 2-5.

TABLE 2-5 Removable data drive BitLocker policies

Setting	Default State
Controls use of BitLocker on removable drives	Not configured
Configures use of smart cards on removable data drives	Not configured
Denies write access to removable drives not protected by BitLocker	Not configured
Configures use of hardware-based encryption for removable data drives	Not configured
Enforces drive encryption type on removable data drives	Not configured
Allows access to BitLocker–protected removable data drives from earlier versions of Windows	Not configured
Configures use of passwords for removable data drives	Not configured
Chooses how BitLocker–protected removable drives can be recovered	Not configured

Configuring the EFS recovery agent

The EFS, which was introduced in Windows 2000, provides a method for users to encrypt and protect sensitive files and folders. To ensure that encrypted files can be recovered in the event of emergency, the Administrator account on the first domain controller in the domain is automatically designated the recovery agent for the domain, allowing this account to access and recover encrypted files.

In addition to the default data recovery agent for a domain, you can add additional recovery agents. To add a recovery agent, follow these steps:

1. Open the GPMC and select the GPO you want to configure. For an EFS recovery agent, it is usually the Default Domain Policy.

2. Right-click the policy and select Edit to open the Group Policy Management Editor. Select Computer Configuration\Policies\Windows Settings\Security Settings\Public Key Policies\Encrypting File System in the console tree, as shown in Figure 2-33.

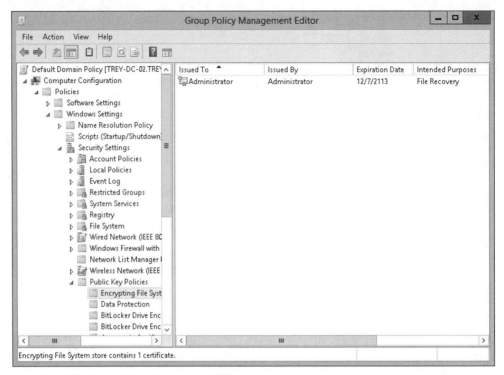

FIGURE 2-33 The Group Policy Management Editor

3. Right-click and select Add Data Recovery Agent. Click Next and then click Browse Folders. Select the certificate for the account that will be the data recovery agent.

The account used for data recovery should not be an account that is online and available under normal circumstances. You should export the private key for the account to a .pfx file, deleting the key during the export. Then move the key to removable media and store in a secure location.

> **NOTE CREATING A SELF-SIGNED FILE RECOVERY CERTIFICATE**
>
> If your domain does not include a CA, you can create a self-signed certificate for use as an EFS recovery agent. To create a self-signed certificate, use the cipher.exe command. From a command prompt, logged on as the account that will be the designated recovery agent, use this:
>
> ```
> Cipher /r:<filename>
> ```
>
> This command creates two files: a .cer file and a .pfx file. The .cer file is added to the GPO as a recovery agent, and the .pfx file should be copied to removable media and safely stored in a secure location and then deleted from the original location.

Managing EFS and BitLocker certificates, including backup and restore

It is important that you enable EFS and BitLocker recovery procedures for all encrypted data and volumes. Without a full backup of recovery information, vital information might be unavailable in an emergency. This recovery information is sensitive, however, and should be stored in secure locations and not be readily available except in an emergency. And in all cases, it should never be in the same location as the item it is protecting. (Printing out your BitLocker recovery key and then taping it to the back of your laptop is a really, really bad idea.)

Enabling AD DS storage of BitLocker recovery keys

You can enable the storage of BitLocker recovery keys in AD DS by enabling the GPO settings. There are three settings that control recovery key saving for Windows Server 2008 R2, Windows 7, Windows Server 2012, Windows 8, Windows Server 2012 R2, and Windows 8.1. These settings, which are in the Computer Configuration\Policies\Administrative Templates\ Windows Components\BitLocker Drive Encryption folder, are these:

- Choose How BitLocker-Protected Fixed Data Drives Can Be Recovered
- Choose How BitLocker-Protected Operating System Drives Can Be Recovered
- Choose How BitLocker-Protected Removable Drives Can Be Recovered

EXAM TIP

When you enable BitLocker policies, create them on the policy that applies to the computer on which you're enabling BitLocker. While you can use the Default Domain Policy for BitLocker policies, that doesn't allow you to save the recovery passwords for your BitLocker protected domain controllers.

When one of these policies is set to Enabled, you have additional options (see Figure 2-34), including the following:

- Allow Or Require 48-Digit Recovery Password
- Allow Or Require 256-Bit Recovery Password
- Save BitLocker Recovery Information To AD DS
- Backup Recovery Passwords And Key Packages

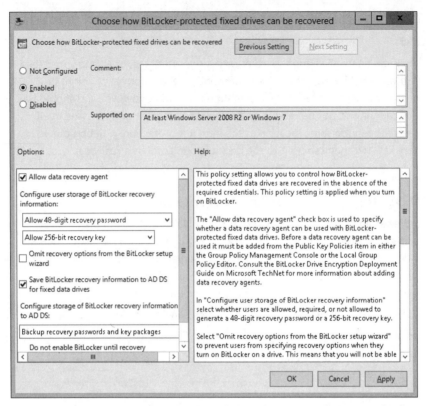

FIGURE 2-34 The Choose How BitLocker-Protected Fixed Drives Can Be Recovered policy setting page

After recovery password saving to AD DS is enabled, you can save the recovery password with the Backup-BitLockerKeyProtector cmdlet. Use the following commands to back up the Recovery Password for the operating system volume:

```
$blC = Get-BitLockerVolume -MountPoint C:
Backup-BitLockerKeyProtector `
        -MountPoint "C:" `
        -KeyProtectorId $blC.KeyProtector[1].KeyProtectorId
```

This will back up the second key protector for the drive mounted at C. The first key protector is the TPM whenever there is a TPM present. To recover the key, search the AD DS domain by following these steps:

1. Open Active Directory Users And Computers.

2. Right-click the domain in the console tree and select Find BitLocker Recovery Password from the Action menu.

3. Enter the first eight characters of the Password ID and click Search, as shown in Figure 2-35.

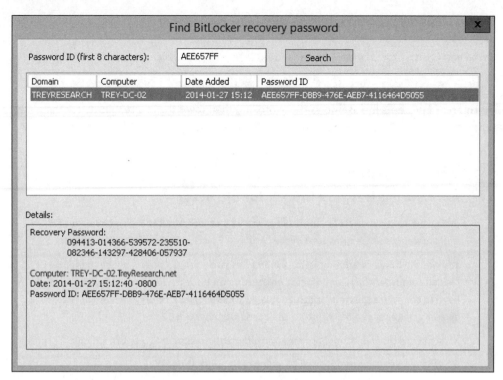

FIGURE 2-35 The Find BitLocker Recovery Password dialog box

Saving BitLocker recovery passwords

Although saving BitLocker recovery passwords to Active Directory is an excellent way to save them securely and where they can be easily recovered, you can also do the following:

- Print the recovery password
- Save it to a file
- Create a USB recovery key

Whatever methods you use, make sure that they are kept up to date, are secure, and are available when needed.

Saving EFS certificates

Although having an extra recovery agent for EFS is one form of backup, another important backup is to export the EFS certificates for users and back them up to secure storage. If this isn't done, and a user's computer needs to be rebuilt, the user could lose access to all EFS–protected files and folders on the computer. The simplest solution is to export the EFS certificate to a .pfx file, which can then be part of normal backup procedures.

You can automate the EFS certificate export with the following script:

```
$Cert=(Get-childitem -path cert:\CurrentUser\My | where {$_.Subject -match "OU=EFS" } )
Write-host "Enter the password for the .pfx file: " -nonewline
$pfxPW = read-host -assecurestring
Export-PfxCertificate -Cert $cert -password $pfxPW -filepath C:\MyEFScert.pfx
```

This script prompts the user for a password and then saves the EFS certificate for the current user in the file C:\MyEFScert.pfx, with the password typed in at the prompt.

Thought experiment

Configuring Network Unlock for BitLocker

In this thought experiment, apply what you've learned about this objective. You can find answers to these questions in the "Answers" section at the end of this chapter.

You are the network administrator for TreyResearch.net. Company policy mandates that all computers have multifactor encryption on boot devices and data drives. You have to configure the network to enable automatic unlock of boot drives for clients and servers that are hard-wired to the corporate network.

1. What are the minimum hardware requirements to support Network Unlock?

2. What server roles are needed to support Network Unlock?

3. What Group Policy settings need to be configured to support Network Unlock and require BitLocker encryption?

Objective summary

- Configure BitLocker policies to allow backup to Active Directory.
- Use Windows PowerShell to back up the BitLocker Recovery Password to Active Directory.
- Back up BitLocker recovery passwords to USB, files, and hard copy.
- Back up EFS certificates with Export-PfxCertificate.
- Enable the Network Unlock protector to allow automatic boot even with a TPM+PIN configuration.
- Create a BitLocker Network Unlock certificate and use Group Policy to distribute the public key. Use WDS to distribute the private key to allow Network Unlock.
- BitLocker Network Unlock certificates can be created with AD CS or by creating a self-signed certificate with certreq.exe.

Objective review

1. To which GPOs do you need to link to ensure that all BitLocker passwords can be backed up to Active Directory?

    A. Default Domain Policy

    B. Default Domain Controller Policy

    C. Both the A and B

    D. A new BitLocker GPO linked to the Domain Users folder

2. What features are required and installed for the BitLocker Drive Encryption feature? (Choose all that apply.)

    A. BitLocker Drive Encryption

    B. Remote Server Administration Tools - BitLocker Drive Encryption Administration Utilities

    C. Remote Server Administration Tools - AD DS Tools

    D. File Server VSS Agent Service

    E. Enhanced Storage

    F. BitLocker Network Unlock

3. Company policy requires that all servers be encrypted with BitLocker on all fixed internal drives and volumes. Several existing servers do not support a TPM. You created a special OU for these servers and linked a GPO to the OU. What policy do you need to configure to enable BitLocker encryption for the servers?

    A. Choose Drive Encryption Method And Cipher Strength

    B. Choose How BitLocker-Protected Fixed Drives Can Be Recovered

    C. Require Additional Authentication At Startup

    D. Use Enhanced Boot Configuration Data Validation Profile

    E. Allow Network Unlock At Startup

Objective 2.4: Configure advanced audit policies

Advanced audit policies extend the basic audit policies to provide granular auditing of events. Advanced audit policies were extended in Windows Server 2012 with Global Object Access Auditing and Dynamic Access Control (DAC) to allow for expression-based auditing, giving administrators more selective auditing of events. Also added in Windows Server 2012 is the ability to audit removable devices.

Implementing auditing using Group Policy and AuditPol.exe

You can implement advanced audit policies by configuring the Group Policy settings for the type of advanced auditing you want to enable. The advanced audit policies are grouped into 10 subcategories:

- Account Logon
- Account Management
- Detailed Tracking
- DS Access
- Logon/Logoff
- Object Access
- Policy Change
- Privilege Use
- System
- Global Object Access Auditing

Advanced auditing is located in Computer Configuration\Policies\Windows Settings\ Security Settings\Advanced Audit Policies. To configure advanced auditing, select a subcategory and then double-click the policy you want to configure and set the audit on success or failure. For example, to audit logon success, select the Logon/Logoff category and double-click Audit Logon to open the Audit Logon Properties dialog box shown in Figure 2-36. Select the Configure The Following Audit Events check box; select Success, Failure, or both; and click OK to apply.

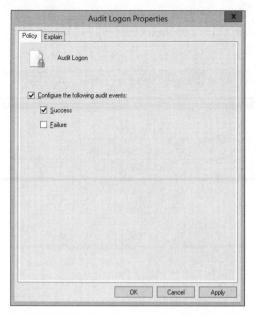

FIGURE 2-36 The Audit Logon Properties dialog box

The Logon/Logoff policy settings are straightforward success or failure settings. But other settings, such as those for Global Object Access Auditing, are more involved and are described in the following "Creating expression-based audit policies" section.

To ensure that advanced auditing isn't overridden by basic auditing policies, set the Force Audit Policy Subcategory Settings (Windows Vista Or Later) To Override Audit Policy Category Settings policy in the Computer Configuration\Policies\Windows Settings\Security Settings\Local Policies\Security Options folder to Enabled.

Creating expression-based audit policies

Windows Server 2012 enables expression-based audit policies that enable you to audit only the specific actions and users of interest. You can build expression-based audit policies for either the file system or the registry by using Global Object Access Auditing. To enable an expression-based audit of a file system folder, for example, follow these steps:

1. In the GPMC, select the GPO for which you want to enable an expression-based audit and select Edit from the context menu to open the Group Policy Management Editor.

2. Double-click File System under Global Object Access Auditing in the Advanced Audit Policy Configuration section of the Computer Configuration\Policies\Windows Settings\Security Settings folder.

3. Select Define This Policy Setting in the File System Properties dialog box and then click Configure to open the Advanced Security Settings for Global File SACL dialog box shown in Figure 2-37.

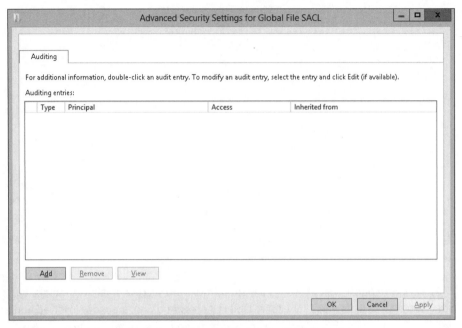

FIGURE 2-37 The Advanced Security Settings For Global File SACL dialog box

4. Click Add to open the Auditing Entry For Global SACL dialog box.

5. Click Select A Principal to open the familiar Select User, Computer, Service Account, Or Group dialog box. Add groups, computers, or users to audit and then click Next.

6. Select the Type of audit from the list.

7. Select the Permissions to audit.

8. Use the Add A Condition To Limit The Scope section to limit the scope of this audit, as shown in Figure 2-38, in which I'm building a condition that will tell me if any Domain Admins who are not also Enterprise Admins take ownership of a file.

9. Click OK to add the audit expression, as shown in Figure 2-39.

10. Click Apply to continue adding audit entries, or click OK to complete the audit entry and complete the configuration of the expression-based audit policy.

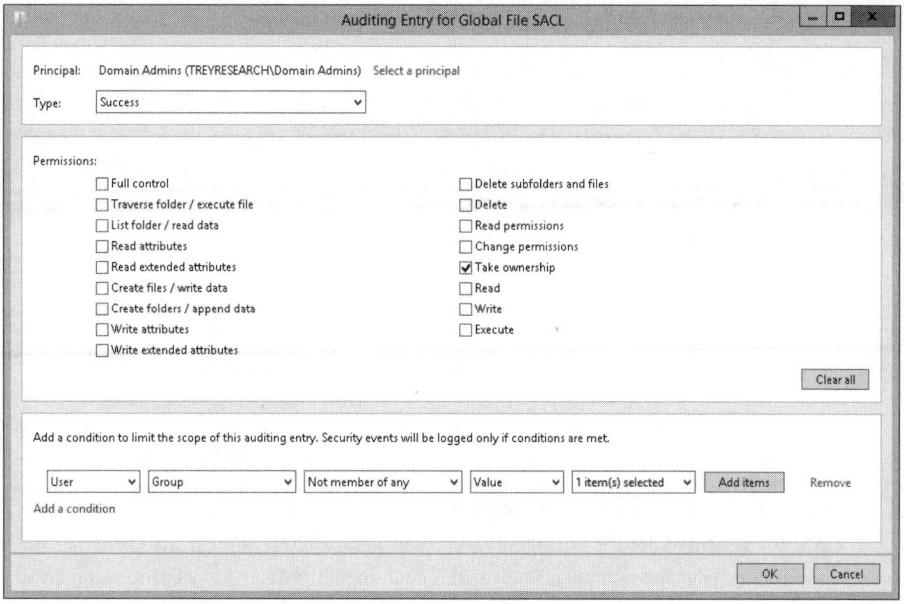

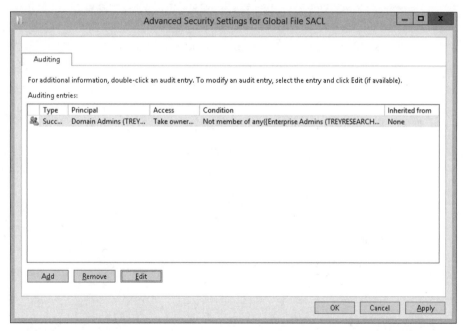

FIGURE 2-38 The Auditing Entry For Global File SACL dialog box

FIGURE 2-39 The Advanced Security Settings For Global File SACL dialog box with the auditing expression

Creating removable device audit policies

To audit the success or failure of access to removable devices, use the Audit Removable Storage setting in the Computer Configuration\Policies\Windows Settings\Security Settings\ Advanced Audit Policy Configuration\Audit Policies\Object Access folder. You can audit Success (event 4663), Failure (event 4656), or both. If you enable Failure tracking, you need to also enable the Audit Handle Manipulation For Failure events.

Thought experiment
Disabling and auditing removable USB drives

In this thought experiment, apply what you've learned about this objective. You can find answers to these questions in the "Answers" section at the end of this chapter.

You are the network administrator for TreyResearch.net. Because of past concerns and the sensitive nature of the research being conducted at Trey, the company has issued a policy that no one is to use USB flash drives on company computers. You have been asked to implement the policy. You have also been asked to audit any attempts to use USB drives, even though they are not allowed. Users will continue to be allowed to connect and use cell phones and media players, but all use of them is to be audited.

1. What settings do you need to enable to ensure that users can't use USB disks? All policies are in the \Computer Configuration\Policies\Administrative Templates\ System\Removable Storage Access folder. (Choose all that apply.)

   A. Enable All Removable Storage Classes: Deny All Access

   B. Disable All Removable Storage Classes: Deny All Access

   C. Enable Removable Disks: Deny Execute Access

   D. Enable Removable Disks: Deny Read Access

   E. Enable Removable Disks: Deny Write Access

   F. Disable Removable Disks: Deny Write Access

   G. Disable Removable Disks: Deny Read Access

   H. Disable Removable Disks: Deny Execute Access

2. What settings do you need to set to ensure that users can continue to connect their cell phones and media players? All policies are in the \Computer Configuration\Policies\Administrative Templates\System\Removable Storage Access folder. (Choose all that apply.)

A. Enable All Removable Storage Classes: Deny All Access

B. Disable All Removable Storage Classes: Deny All Access

C. Enable WPD Devices: Deny Read Access

D. Enable WPD Devices: Deny Write Access

E. Disable WPD Devices: Deny Read Access

F. Disable WPD Devices: Deny Write Access

3. What settings do you need to set to ensure that all attempts to use USB devices, including cell phones and media players, are audited for success and failure? All policies are in the Computer Configuration\Policies\Windows Settings\Security Settings\Advanced Audit Policy Configuration\Audit Policies folder. (Choose all that apply.)

A. Configure Audit Object Access Success

B. Configure Audit Object Access Failure

C. Configure Audit Handle Management Success

D. Configure Audit Handle Management Failure

E. Configure Audit File System Success

F. Configure Audit File System Failure

Finally, in thinking about the policy, what recommendations could you make to management to ensure that the policy accomplishes the goals described and what concerns do you have about the specific details of the policy? How will auditing help alleviate these concerns?

Objective summary

- Implement advanced audit policies in Group Policy to enable fine-grained control of auditing.
- Use the Force Audit Policy Subcategory Settings (Windows Vista Or Later) To Override Audit Policy Category Settings policy to enforce advanced audit policies.
- For even more specific auditing of file system and registry events, use expression-based audit policies based on DAC Global Object Access Auditing.
- Use GPOs to audit removable device access or attempts. You can audit the success or failure (or both) of attempts to use removable devices.
- Enabling Failure auditing of removable devices also requires enabling the Audit Handle Manipulation For Failure Events policy.

Objective review

1. You monitor changes to distribution groups and you don't want to get events from other account management events because it would tend to hide the specific events you're looking for in the high noise levels. What policy do you need to set and what setting should it have?

   A. Set the Computer Configuration\Policies\Security Settings\Local Policies\Audit Policy\Audit Account Management policy to Enabled, Audit Success.

   B. Set the Computer Configuration\Policies\Security Settings\Local Policies\Audit Policy\Audit Account Management policy to Enabled, Audit Failure.

   C. Set the Computer Configuration\Policies\Security Settings\Advanced Audit Policy Configuration\Audit Policies\Account Management\Audit Distribution Group Management policy to Enabled, Audit Success.

   D. Computer Configuration\Policies\Security Settings\Local Policies\Audit Policy\Audit Account Management policy to Enabled, Audit Failure.

2. What Group Policy setting do you need to enable in order to enable auditing of logoff events?

   A. Computer Configuration\Policies\Windows Settings\Security Settings\Advanced Audit Policies\Audit Logoff

   B. Computer Configuration\Policies\Windows Settings\Security Settings\Local Policies\Audit Logon Events

   C. User Configuration\Policies\Windows Settings\Security Settings\Advanced Audit Policies\Audit Logon

   D. User Configuration\Policies\Windows Settings\Security Settings\\Local Policies\Audit Logoff Events

3. What are the minimal Group Policy settings that you need to set in order to ensure that removable optical disks can be used to read data only? (Choose all that apply.)

A. Computer Configuration\Policies\Administrative Templates\System\Removable Storage Access\Removable Disks: Deny Execute Access

B. Computer Configuration\Policies\Administrative Templates\System\Removable Storage Access\ Removable Disks: Deny Write Access

C. Computer Configuration\Policies\Administrative Templates\System\Removable Storage Access\CD and DVD: Deny Execute Access.

D. Computer Configuration\Policies\Administrative Templates\System\Removable Storage Access\CD and DVD: Deny Write Access.

E. Computer Configuration\Policies\Administrative Templates\System\Removable Storage Access\All Removable Storage Classes: Deny All Access

Answers

This section contains the solutions to the thought experiments and answers to the lesson review questions in this chapter.

Objective 2.1: Thought experiment

1. **Correct answers:** C, D, E. You need to move the share to an NTFS volume before you can enable DFS for it. Creating a DFS-N with the shared folder then allows you to configure the replication in a hub/spoke configuration. A mesh configuration would work, but it would create more replication traffic, given that the description implies that the data is currently stored and created on the main corporate datacenter.

2. The change in content origination lends itself to a change in replication from hub/spoke to mesh to reduce the number of hops to fully replicate.

3. A combination of preseeding the changes to each of the branches and cloning the DFS database improves the initial DFS-R time.

Objective 2.1: Review

1. **Correct answer:** C

   A. **Incorrect**. This command adds a .cab or .msu package to a Windows image or, with the -online parameter, the currently running Windows.

   B. **Incorrect**. This command enables an optional feature on Windows, but can't be used to install a server role.

   C. **Correct**. This command installs the two DFS roles and the management tools.

   D. **Incorrect**. Although Add-WindowsFeature is an alias for Install-WindowsFeature, there isn't a feature named DFS; it is actually two features: FS-DFS-N and FS-DFS-R.

2. **Correct answers:** A, D

   A. **Correct**. Installs the RSAT DFS Management console along with the Windows PowerShell modules for DFS.

   B. **Incorrect**. Enables an optional feature on Windows, but there isn't a client feature named *DFS*.

   C. **Incorrect**. Only partially enables what needs enabling for remote management.

   D. **Correct**. Enables all the Windows PowerShell remoting features and also enables WinRM.

Objective 2.2: Thought experiment

1. Use the File By Owner report to identify the files owned by each user and how much space they take up. Use the Files By File Group report to tell what kinds of files are being stored on the server. Use the Large Files report to see whether there are very large files taking up excess space that might be a target for removal. The Large Files report is likely to be the least useful because substantial space is being used by the shared internal corporate resources and they are probably large files. However, you can include specific file name patterns to help narrow the scope of the report.

2. Yes. By enabling quotas with the Auto Apply Template And Create Quotas On Existing And New Subfolders option on the folder at the top of the Public share, you can enforce quotas on all users except administrators. You can then require an administrator to post any files that were to bypass the quotas, such as internal corporate resources. This is less than optimal, however, because it requires action by an administrator to add any new files to the share corporate resources if you want to avoid quota limits. A possible solution is to use soft quotas and use the Files By Owner report to identify problems.

3. By using the Files By File Group report, you can quickly identify where the problem file types are and then create a file screen to block any file types that shouldn't be there.

4. You can get around the limitations of the file screen by using a file screen exception on the specific path for corporate resources to allow the files blocked in the previous answer and then restricting the file saving to that path to specific users. Adding a different share name with share permissions that limit who can write to the exception path can also help. Ideally, the solution involves all four of these features of FSRM.

Objective 2.2: Review

1. **Correct answer:** D

   A. **Incorrect**. The (Get-Date).add(-3) portion of the command is a time only three seconds prior to the time the command is run.

   B. **Incorrect**. The (Get-Date).add(-3) portion of the command is a time only three seconds prior to the time the command is run.

   C. **Incorrect**. The .AddDays property is the correct property to use, and -3 is the correct number of days, but this command removes all the files newer than three days.

   D. **Correct**. Finds all files in the path that are three days or more old at the time the command is run and removes them.

2. **Correct answer:** A

    A. **Correct**. This is the least privilege that will allow the command to run.

    B. **Incorrect**. Domain Users isn't an option here; Furthermore, it would provide substantially more privilege than local service if it were available.

    C. **Incorrect**. Local System is full access and control. Way more than you need to use for this question.

    D. **Incorrect**. Protected Users is not an option and has no special limitations on privilege that would help even if it were an option.

3. **Correct answer:** B

    A. **Incorrect.** All Monitor templates are soft quotas and will warn but not actually limit.

    B. **Correct.** This template has a hard limit of 200 MB, with warnings, but automatically extends the limit to 250 MB.

    C. **Incorrect.** You can't create limits on shares; you can create limits only on file system folders or disks. Also, Monitor templates are soft quotas and will warn but not actually limit.

    D. **Incorrect.** You can't create limits on shares; you can create limits only on file system folders or disks.

Objective 2.3: Thought experiment

1. Wired network and a TPM. Further, the computers being unlocked must support DHCP in UEFI.

2. The WDS role must be enabled on the network on a Windows Server 2012 or Windows Server 2012 R2 server (you don't need to set up full WDS deployment.) AD DS and a working DHCP server must be present on the network (for Group Policy). Additionally, only computers running Windows 8 or Windows 8.1, or servers running Windows Server 2012 or Windows Server 2012 R2 can participate in Network Unlock, and the private and public keys for Network Unlock must be deployed.

3. To enable Network Unlock, use the Allow Network Unlock At Startup policy, and add the public key certificate from the WDS server to the BitLocker Drive Encryption Network Unlock Certificate folder. To require BitLocker encryption of data drives, use the Deny Write Access To Fixed Drives Not Protected By BitLocker policy; and to require BitLocker on the operating system drive, use the Require Additional Authentication At Startup policy for operating system drives. Set it to Allow TPM and Allow BitLocker Without A Compatible TPM.

Objective 2.3: Review

1. **Correct answer:** C

   A. **Incorrect**. This does not include the domain controllers

   B. **Incorrect**. This does not include computers that are not domain controllers

   C. **Correct**. Includes both domain controllers and nondomain controllers

   D. **Incorrect**. You can't link a GPO to the Domain Users folder.

2. **Correct answers:** A, B, C, E

   A. **Correct**. This is the correct name for the BitLocker feature.

   B. **Correct**. This is automatically installed by the GUI and should be included in the command line if you use Windows PowerShell to install BitLocker. It provides the tools to manage BitLocker.

   C. **Correct**. This is automatically installed by the GUI and is included if you use the -IncludeManagementTools parameter. It is required to configure AD DS storing of recovery passwords.

   D. **Incorrect**. This has nothing to do with BitLocker.

   E. **Correct**. This is automatically installed with BitLocker and is a required prerequisite.

   F. **Incorrect**. This is not required for BitLocker, though it is an optional feature for networks that choose to set it up.

3. **Correct answer:** C

   A. **Incorrect**. This sets the drive encryption method, but doesn't do anything to enable a non-TPM server to use BitLocker.

   B. **Incorrect**. This controls recovery methods.

   C. **Correct**. This policy includes an option for enabling BitLocker without a TPM.

   D. **Incorrect**. This sets enhanced BCD validation.

   E. **Incorrect**. This policy actually requires a TPM to work.

Objective 2.4: Thought experiment

1. **Correct answers:** C, D, E. Answers A and B affect *all* removable drives, including backup tapes and cell phones. Answers F, G, and H explicitly allow USB drive access.

2. **Correct answers:** E, F. Answers A and B affect *all* removable drives, including backup tapes and cell phones. Answers C and D explicitly prohibit the use of cell phones or media devices.

3. **Correct answers:** A, B, D. Both B and D are required to audit failures, C isn't required to audit USB drive access success, and E and F are not directly related to USB drives.

4. I have significant concerns about a policy that allows cell phones and media players because both can have significant file system access. By enabling auditing, you can mitigate this somewhat because you'll get an audit event if someone uses any USB device. A more restrictive policy that prohibits *all* removable devices, including Windows Portable Devices (WPDs), would be more effective in preventing data theft and malware insertion.

Objective 2.4: Review

1. **Correct answer:** C

   A. **Incorrect**. This would capture all successful account management changes and hide the events of interest in the overall noise level.

   B. **Incorrect**. This would capture all failures to change account management and would not capture successful changes. It would also be hidden in the overall noise level.

   C. **Correct**. This would capture only the successful changes to distribution groups.

   D. **Incorrect**. This would capture attempts to change distribution groups, but only if they failed.

2. **Correct answer:** A

   A. **Correct:** This uses the Advanced Auditing Policy setting to enable auditing of Logoff events.

   B. **Incorrect:** This is not an Advanced Auditing Policy setting and only audits success or failure of logon.

   C. **Incorrect.** All logon and logoff events are Computer Configuration policies, not user configuration policies.

   D. **Incorrect.** All logon and logoff events are Computer Configuration policies, not user configuration policies.

3. **Correct answers:** C, D

    A.   **Incorrect.** This would deny execute access to removable hard disks, but not affect optical disks.

    B.   **Incorrect.** This would deny write access to removable hard disks, but not affect optical disks.

    C.   **Correct.** This would deny execute access to optical disks, preventing them from being used to run programs.

    D.   **Correct.** This would deny write access to optical disks, preventing their use as removable writable media.

    E.   **Incorrect.** This would deny all access of any sort to removable media of all classes. This doesn't meet the minimal requirement of the question and furthermore doesn't allow the optical disks to be used to read data.

CHAPTER 3

Configure network services and access

This chapter covers essential network technologies that will play an important part in the exam: the Domain Name System (DNS); Virtual Private Networks (VPNs) and routing; and DirectAccess, which enables remote domain-joined computers to be managed by the same tools you use to manage locally connected computers, while optionally providing users who work remotely a seamless experience that allows them to work remotely as easily as in the office.

Objectives in this chapter:

- Objective 3.1: Configure DNS zones
- Objective 3.2: Configure DNS records
- Objective 3.3: Configure virtual private network (VPN) and routing
- Objective 3.4: Configure DirectAccess

Objective 3.1: Configure DNS zones

There are three basic types of DNS zones: primary, secondary, and stub. Primary zones can be Active Directory-integrated or can be conventional, stand-alone primary zones. A primary zone is a zone hosted on the DNS server that is both authoritative for the zone and the primary point of storage for the zone. The zone data can be hosted in Active Directory Domain Services (AD DS) or in a local file on the DNS server.

Secondary zones contain all the information that a primary zone contains, but get their information by transferring zone information from other DNS servers. Changes to DNS records can't originate in a secondary zone, and a secondary zone is never authoritative for the zone.

Stub zones are zones that contain only information about the servers that are authoritative for the zones. Stub zones are useful for distributing information about where the full information for a zone can be found, but don't have all the zone data.

Beginning with Windows Server 2012, there is full Windows PowerShell parity with the user interface and the legacy dnscmd.exe command-line tool. There are two Windows PowerShell modules that support DNS: DnsClient, and DnsServer.

Configuring primary and secondary zones

A primary DNS zone is required for DNS functionality and name resolution of any domain name. A primary DNS zone is both authoritative for the zone and the primary point of storage for the zone. Secondary zones are not required and not authoritative, but are useful to reduce network traffic and provide faster name resolution, especially when not using an Active Directory-integrated primary zone.

Configuring primary DNS zones

Primary DNS zones can be both forward lookup zones and reverse lookup zones. The most common use of a forward lookup zone is to translate a device name into the IP address that is represented by that name. A reverse lookup zone is used to obtain the device name when you only know the device's IP address.

The zone data can be hosted in AD DS or in a local file on the DNS server. If stored in a local file, it is in the %windir%\System32\Dns directory on the DNS server. The file name is *zonename*.dns where *zonename* is the name of the DNS zone.

A forward lookup zone, such as treyresearch.net, is composed of records of the names of devices in the treyresearch.net namespace and their corresponding IP addresses. If a client computer wants to connect to trey-dc-02.treyresearch.net, it requests the IP address for trey-dc-02 from the client's primary DNS server. If that server hosts the record, it replies immediately. If it doesn't, it either forwards that request to a server on its forwarders list, or looks up who the authoritative DNS server is for treyresearch.net and queries that server for the information and then returns the answer to the client that asked for the information in the first place.

A reverse lookup zone enables clients to look up the name of a device when all they know is the IP address for the device. So if I want to know the computer associated with

192.168.10.2, I would look it up on my local DNS server and it would reply immediately if it hosted the 10.168.192.in-addr.arpa zone. If my local DNS server didn't host the zone, it would forward the request to one of its forwarders.

To configure a new primary zone, use either the DNS Management console (dnsmgmt.msc) or Windows PowerShell. To create a new primary forward lookup zone for TailspinToys.com, follow these steps:

1. Open the DNS Manager console.

2. Expand the server you are adding the zone to and right-click Forward Lookup Zones.

3. Select New Zone from the menu to open the New Zone Wizard.

4. Click Next on the Welcome page and select Primary Zone.

5. If running the New Zone Wizard on a writeable domain controller, you can select the Store The Zone In Active Directory check box if you want to store the zone in Active Directory or clear the check box to use conventional files (see Figure 3-1).

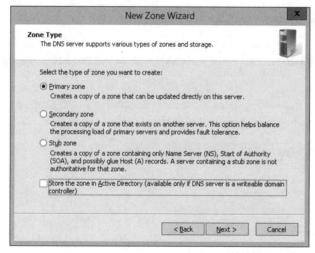

FIGURE 3-1 The New Zone Wizard

6. If storing the zone in Active Directory, click Next and specify which DNS servers to replicate the zone to, as shown in Figure 3-2. (Skip this if running zone files instead of AD DS-integrated zones.)

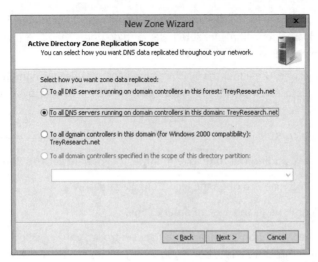

FIGURE 3-2 The Active Directory Zone Replication Scope page of the New Zone Wizard

7. Click Next and enter the Zone Name. Click Next again.

8. On the Zone File page of the New Zone Wizard, select Create A New File With This File Name and click Next. (Skip this step if this zone will be an Active Directory-integrated zone.)

9. Select whether to allow dynamic updates. If the zone is stored in Active Directory you have the option of using only secure dynamic updates, as shown in Figure 3-3.

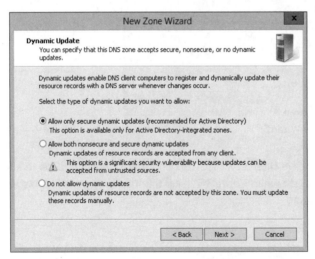

FIGURE 3-3 The Dynamic Update page of the New Zone Wizard

10. Click Next and then Finish to complete the wizard and create the primary DNS forward lookup zone.

To create a primary forward lookup zone by using Windows PowerShell, use the Add-DnsServerPrimaryZone cmdlet. To create an Active Directory-integrated primary zone for TailspinToys.com that allows only secure dynamic updates and is replicated to the entire Forest, use the following command:

```
Add-DnsServerPrimaryZone -Name 'TailspinToys.com' `
                         -ReplicationScope 'Forest' `
                         -DynamicUpdate 'Secure'
```

To create a reverse lookup zone, use the -NetworkID parameter. For example, use this command:

```
Add-DnsServerPrimaryZone -NetworkID 192.168.10.0/24 `
                         -ReplicationScope 'Forest' `
                         -DynamicUpdate 'Secure'
```

To create a file-based primary DNS zone for TailspinToys.com, use the following command:

```
Add-DnsServerPrimaryZone -Name 'TailspinToys.com' `
                         -ZoneFile 'TailspinToys.com.dns' `
                         -DynamicUpdate 'None'
```

EXAM TIP

The Windows PowerShell commands to create a DNS zone are fairly straightforward, but there are a couple of places that can easily create problems for the careless exam taker. For example, the -ReplicationScope parameter can't be used with the -ZoneFile parameter because zone files are used for storage only when the zone is not integrated into Active Directory and replication is possible only for an Active Directory-integrated zone. Another possible trip point is the -DynamicUpdate parameter. You can't have secure updates in a file-based DNS zone.

Configuring secondary zones

Secondary DNS zones can be both forward lookup zones and reverse lookup zones. The most common use of a forward lookup zone is to translate a device name into the IP address that is represented by that name. A reverse lookup zone is used to obtain the device name when you only know the device's IP address.

Secondary DNS zones depend on transferring the data for the zone from another DNS server. That other DNS server must have enabled zone transfers.

To create a secondary forward lookup zone, follow these steps:

1. Open the DNS Manager console.

2. Expand the server you are adding the zone to and right-click Forward Lookup Zones.

3. Select New Zone from the menu to open the New Zone Wizard.

4. Click Next on the Welcome page and select Secondary Zone.

5. On the Zone Name page, enter the name of the zone you want to create a secondary zone of, as shown in Figure 3-4, and then click Next.

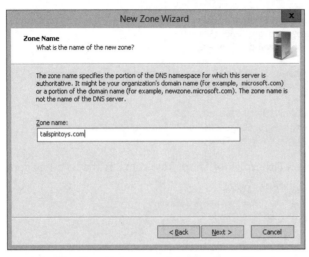

FIGURE 3-4 The Zone Name page of the New Zone Wizard

6. Enter the fully qualified domain name (FQDN) or IP address of the primary DNS server or other Master Server for the zone. You can enter an IPv4 or IPv6 address, or both.

EXAM TIP

The Master Server that you specify when creating a secondary DNS zone is usually the primary DNS server for the zone, especially when referencing an Active Directory-integrated zone, but that isn't a requirement. A secondary DNS server can act as a Master Server for other secondary servers.

7. If the IP address is correct, and the Master DNS server has enabled zone transfers to the secondary server, you'll see a green check mark, as shown in Figure 3-5. If not, you see a red X and you'll have to correct the issue before the zone transfer occurs.

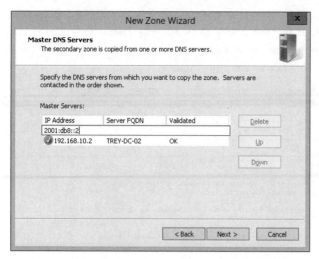

FIGURE 3-5 The Master DNS Servers page of the New Zone Wizard

8. Click Next and then Finish to create the secondary zone, as shown in Figure 3-6.

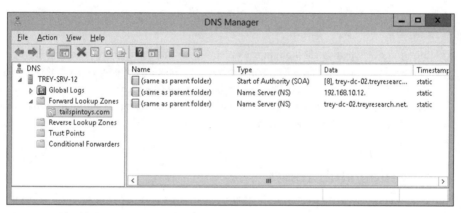

FIGURE 3-6 The DNS Manager console

To create a reverse lookup secondary zone, use the same procedure. There is no difference in the procedure regardless of whether the primary zone is Active Directory-integrated or file-based.

To create a new secondary zone at the command line by using Windows PowerShell, use the Add-DnsServerSecondaryZone cmdlet. For example:

```
Add-DnsServerSecondaryZone -Name 10.168.192.in-addr.arpa `
                    -ZoneFile "10.168.192.in-addr.arpa.dns" `
                    -MasterServers 192.168.10.2,2001:db8::2
```

If there is a problem with the zone transfer, the zone will still be created, and you can correct the issue and then reinitiate the transfer. (A failed zone transfer looks like Figure 3-7.) Correct the source of the problem and then reinitiate the transfer by right-clicking the failing zone and selecting Transfer From Master from the menu.

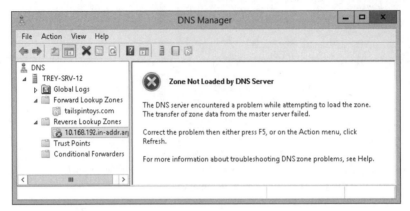

FIGURE 3-7 The DNS Manager console showing a failed initial zone transfer

EXAM TIP

Although not explicitly called out in the objective for this exam, there is one other way to create a primary or secondary DNS zone: convert an existing zone to a different type. So, for example, you can convert a file-based primary zone to a secondary zone as long as another primary zone exists. And you can convert a secondary zone to a primary zone as long as the creation doesn't result in more than one file-based primary zone.

Configuring stub zones

Stub DNS zones are zones that contain only data about a zone's name servers, without maintaining all the data for the entire zone. Stub zones are a useful way, for example, to keep track of the currently authoritative servers for a child zone without maintaining the full records of the child zone. Unlike secondary zones, stub zones contain only the records for the name servers of the zone. Also, unlike secondary zones, stub zones can be Active Directory-integrated. Stub zones can be created for both forward and reverse lookup zones.

Stub zones also alleviate a significant security concern about secondary zones. Because secondary zones contain a full copy of all DNS records in the zone, they provide a potential attacker with important information that could jeopardize network security. Stub zones expose only the IP addresses of the designated name servers. Because stub zones use standard DNS queries to obtain their information, they can be used even when the zone is marked "Do not transfer."

To create a stub zone, use essentially the same procedures as creating a primary or secondary server, as detailed in the following steps:

1. Open the DNS Manager console.

2. Expand the server you are adding the zone to and right-click Forward Lookup Zones.

3. Select New Zone from the menu to open the New Zone Wizard.

4. Click Next on the Welcome page and select Stub Zone on the Zone Type page.

5. Click Next and enter the Zone Name. Click Next.

6. Accept the default value in the Create A New File With This Name box and then click Next.

7. On the Master DNS Servers page, enter the IP address or FQDN of a Master Server in the zone for which you are creating a stub, click OK, and then click OK again.

To create a stub zone at the command line by using Windows PowerShell, use the Add-DnsServerStubZone cmdlet. For example:

```
Add-DnsServerStubZone -Name TailspinToys.com `
                      -MasterServers 192.168.10.4 `
                      -ReplicationScope "Tree"
```

Configuring conditional forwards

Conditional forwards allow you to specify a specific DNS server or servers to which you can forward DNS requests based on the DNS domain for which the request is made. This is useful when you have multiple internal namespaces (such as after a merger or acquisition). By creating conditional forwards, you allow DNS requests to stay internal without having to completely take over the DNS server role or create secondary zones. For example, if the DNS server at 192.168.10.2, which is a DNS server for the TreyResearch.net domain, receives a request for the address of tail-rdsh-105.tailspintoys.com, the DNS server would first look to see whether it hosted the domain or a stub for it. Failing that, it would check its cache to see whether it had already looked up the address. If it still didn't have the address, it would next forward a request to the Internet, either to a configured forwarding address or to the root DNS servers. But, if you have a conditional forwarder configured for TailspinToys.com at 192.168.10.102, it will instead send the request to the conditional forwarder.

Conditional forwarders can be maintained on an individual DNS server basis, or integrated into Active Directory and replicated. To configure a conditional forwarder, follow these steps:

1. Open the DNS Manager console.

2. Expand the server you are adding the forwarder to and right-click Conditional Forwarders.

3. Select New Conditional Forwarder from the menu to open the New Conditional Forwarder dialog box shown in Figure 3-8.

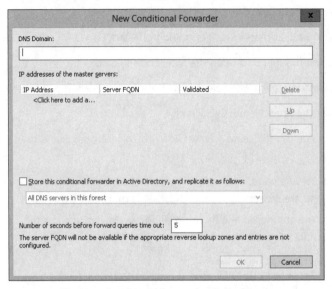

FIGURE 3-8 The New Conditional Forwarder dialog box

4. Enter the DNS domain to forward and the IP address of the target DNS server. (You can specify more than one target DNS server.)

5. Select Store This Conditional Forwarder In Active Directory, And Replicate It As Follows; then select the replication scope from the list.

6. Click OK, and the conditional forwarder is created.

You can also use the Add-DnsServerConditionalForwarderZone cmdlet. For example:

```
Add-DnsServerConditionalForwarderZone -Name treyresearch.net `
                              -MasterServers 192.168.10.2,2001:db8::2 `
                              -ForwarderTimeout 10 `
                              -ReplicationScope "Forest"
```

Configuring zone and conditional forward storage in Active Directory

When you create a zone, be it a primary zone or a stub zone, or you create a forwarder, you have the option of storing the data in Active Directory by choosing Active Directory-integrated. This option is *not* available for a secondary zone. A secondary zone can never be stored in Active Directory, which leads to an exam tip, of course.

EXAM TIP

Secondary zones are a seductive solution to many situations, but they have some limitations that exam question writers are likely to take advantage of. One is that they present a potential security consideration because the entire zone is available, so be leery of questions that include security as a called-out concern where a secondary zone appears to be the answer. The other limitation is that they can't be Active Directory-replicated because they can't be stored in Active Directory. Secondary zones are always file-based zones.

Zone and conditional forwarder storage is usually set at creation time, but you have the option to change it after the fact by using either the DNS Management console. To configure an existing conditional forwarder that is not stored in Active Directory to one that is, use the DNS Management console (the operation is not supported in Windows PowerShell). The same is true for converting a file-based DNS zone into an Active Directory-integrated one. Use the DNS Management console.

So to convert a DNS file-based stub zone into an Active Directory-integrated one, follow these steps:

1. Open the DNS Manager console.

2. Expand the server on which you are converting the stub zone.

3. Select the stub zone folder in the console tree and right-click.

4. Select Properties from the menu to open the Zone Properties dialog box shown in Figure 3-9.

FIGURE 3-9 The Zone Properties dialog box for tailspintoys.com

5. Click Change to open the Change Zone Type dialog box. Select the Store The Zone In Active Directory check box, as shown in Figure 3-10.

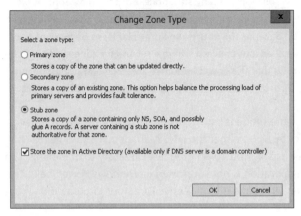

FIGURE 3-10 The Change Zone Type dialog box

6. Click OK and click Yes on the DNS prompt shown in Figure 3-11.

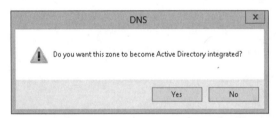

FIGURE 3-11 The DNS dialog box

7. Click OK, and the zone is converted.

EXAM TIP

With the nearly 100 percent coverage of the Windows PowerShell DNS cmdlets, you'd expect that you could convert a file-based zone to an Active Directory-integrated zone by using the appropriate Set-DnsServer* cmdlet. But that option fails with a "not supported" message. You should expect to see at least one question on the exam that revolves around that limitation.

Configuring zone delegation

Zone delegation allows you to delegate the administration of a portion of your DNS namespace, and to divide up a large zone into smaller subzones to distribute the load and improve performance.

To delegate a zone, follow these steps:

1. Open the DNS Manager console.

2. Expand the zone for which you are making the delegation.

3. Right-click the zone you want to delegate and select New Delegation from the menu.

4. On the Welcome screen, click Next. On the Delegated Domain Name page, enter the Delegated Domain, as shown in Figure 3-12, and click Next.

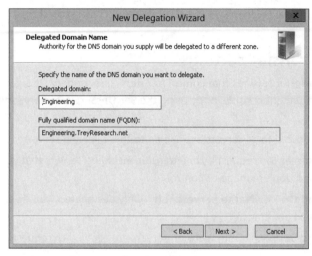

FIGURE 3-12 The New Delegation Wizard

5. On the Name Servers page, click Add and then enter the DNS name of the server that is authoritative for the zone to be delegated and click Resolve, as shown in Figure 3-13.

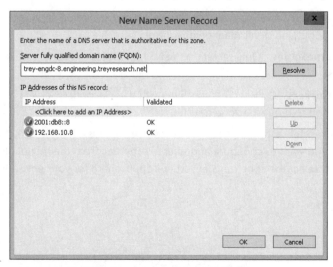

FIGURE 3-13 The New Name Server Record dialog box

6. Click OK to close the New Name Server Record dialog box and return to the Name Servers page of the New Delegation Wizard.

7. Click Next and then Finish to complete the delegation.

To create a zone delegation by using Windows PowerShell, use the Add-DnsServerZoneDelegation cmdlet. For example:

```
Add-DnsServerZoneDelegation -Name TreyResearch.net `
                            -ChildZoneName Engineering `
                            -IPAddress 192.168.10.8,2001:db8::8 `
                            -NameServer trey-engdc-8.engineering.treyresearch.net
```

Configuring zone transfer settings

You can configure the zone transfer settings that control transfers to secondary DNS zones either through the DNS Management console, or by using the Set-DnsServerPrimaryZone cmdlet.

Zone transfers can be disallowed to all servers or enabled to the following servers:

- **To Any Server**   Any server can request a zone transfer, including servers that you know nothing about and don't manage or control.

- **Only To Servers Listed On The Name Servers Tab**   Only designated Name Servers are allowed to request a zone transfer.

- **Only To The Following Servers**   Only specified servers are allowed to request a zone transfer.

The options for the Set-DnsServerPrimaryZone are worded slightly differently, but have the same effect. The choices for the -SecureSecondaries parameter are these:

- **NoTransfer**   No transfers are allowed for this zone from this server.

- **TransferAnyServer**   Any server can request a zone transfer, including servers that you know nothing about and don't manage or control.

- **TransferToZoneNameServer**   Only servers in the NS records for this zone are allowed to request transfers.

- **TransferToSecureServers**   Only servers specified with the -SecondaryServers parameter are allowed to request a zone transfer.

To configure the zone transfer settings in the DNS Management console, right-click the zone folder on the server you want to configure and select Properties from the menu. Click the Zone Transfers tab and select the zone transfer settings appropriate for your environment, as shown in Figure 3-14.

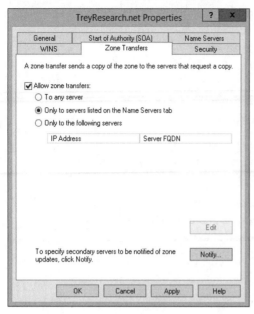

FIGURE 3-14 The Zone Transfers tab of the DNS Zone Properties dialog box

Configuring notify settings

You can configure which secondary servers are notified of changes to the zone by clicking the Notify button on the Zone Transfers tab of the DNS Manager console or by using the Set-DnsServerPrimaryZone cmdlet. The settings in the DNS Manager console are these:

- **Automatically Notify**   When disabled, no notifications are sent, and secondary servers need to manually request a zone transfer or update. When enabled, the primary DNS server will automatically notify the following:

  - **Servers Listed On The Name Servers Tab**   All servers for whom there are NS records in the zone are automatically notified whenever a change is made to the zone.

  - **The Following Servers**   Only the specifically listed servers are automatically notified of changes in the zone. Any other servers that are allowed to request zone transfers must request the transfer manually.

The equivalent Set-DnsServerPrimaryZone parameter is the -Notify parameter, which accepts the following strings:

- **NoNotify**   No notifications are sent, and secondary servers need to manually request a zone transfer or update.

- **Notify**   All servers for whom there are NS records in the zone are automatically notified whenever a change is made to the zone.

- **NotifyServers** Only servers specified by the -NotifyServers parameter are automatically notified of changes to the domain. Any other servers that are allowed to request zone transfers must request the transfer manually.

Thought experiment
Designing namespace and DNS zones

In this thought experiment, apply what you've learned about this objective. You can find answers to these questions in the "Answers" section at the end of this chapter.

You are the network administrator for Trey Research. Your Forest root zone is TreyResearch.net, with child domains of Engineering and Finance, and a tree domain of TailspinToys.com. Users are located in several branch locations, as well as a central main office, and all need access to resources in both trees.

You need to design your namespace and DNS zones to provide fast and efficient lookups while maintaining as secure an environment as possible, especially in branch office locations. Further, you need to minimize network traffic.

1. It has been suggested that you use secondary zones at the branch sites to provide a better resource lookup experience. The branch sites do not have domain controllers. What are the pluses and minuses of using secondary zones at the branch offices, and what other solutions might you consider?

2. There is a lot of computer name churn in the Engineering department as they continually build and rebuild clients and servers to support ever-changing project requirements. This name churn includes both static DNS names and DHCP names. What are your options to reduce the management overhead to the system administrators?

3. Consider the DNS churn and management overhead in the Engineering department DNS structure from a broader perspective. What other steps might you suggest?

Objective summary

- Windows DNS Server supports primary, secondary, and stub DNS zones.
- Primary and stub DNS zones can be Active Directory-integrated.
- Both forward and reverse lookup zones are supported.
- Starting with Windows Server 2012, full Windows PowerShell support for DNS servers is included.

- Use stub zones and conditional forwarders to replace the need for secondary zones.
- Conditional forwarders provide a means to manage to which DNS server a DNS query is forwarded for specific zones.
- You can change whether a zone or conditional forward is stored in Active Directory or in files, except for secondary zones, which are always file based.
- Use DNS zone delegation to delegate administration of a portion of your DNS namespace.
- Zone transfers are disallowed unless explicitly allowed.

Objective review

1. You need to create a new primary forward lookup zone for Engineering.TreyReseach. net. The zone should have its data stored in Active Directory and be available to all domain controllers in the domain. What Windows PowerShell commands would you use?

   A. Add-DnsServerPrimaryZone -Name 'Engineering.TreyResearch.net' -zone 'engineering.treyresearch.net.dns' -replication Domain

   B. Add-DnsServerPrimaryZone -Name 'Engineering.TreyResearch.net' -zone 'engineering.treyresearch.net.dns' -replication Forest

   C. Add-DnsServerPrimaryZone -Name 'Engineering.TreyResearch.net' -replication Domain

   D. Add-DnsServerPrimaryZone -Name 'Engineering.TreyResearch.net' -replication Forest

2. You need to create a new secondary reverse lookup zone for the TreyResearch.net, which uses 192.168.10.0 - 192.168.10.255 for network addresses. The Primary zone is hosted by trey-dc-02 at 192.168.10.2. What Windows PowerShell commands would you use?

   A. Add-DnsSecondaryZone -Name 'TreyResearch.net' -NetworkID "192.168.10.0/24" -Replication Domain -Master "trey-dc-02.treyresearch.net"

   B. Add-DnsSecondaryZone -NetworkID "192.168.10.0/24" -Master 192.168.10.2 -Zone "10.168.192.in-addr.arpa"

   C. Add-DnsSecondaryZone -NetworkID "192.168.10.0/24" -Master 192.168.10.2 -Zone "0.10.168.192.in-addr.arpa"

   D. Add-DnsSecondaryZone -NetworkID "192.168.10.0/24" -Master "trey-dc-02.treyresearch.net" -Zone "10.168.192.dns"

3. You are the enterprise administrator for Trey Research. Your domain name is TreyResearch.net, and your IPv4 address range is 192.168.10.0-192.168.10.255. Your IPv6 address range is 2001:db8:10::/64. The primary domain controller for TreyResearch.net is trey-dc-02 and it hosts the Active Directory-integrated DNS. The Engineering department is migrating to use a new child domain, Engineering. TreyResearch.net, with a domain controller of trey-engdc-8. What commands would you use to delegate this domain?

A. Add-DnsServerZoneDelegation -Name TreyResearch.net `
   -ChildZoneName Engineering `
   -IPAddress 192.168.10.8,2001:db8:10::8 `
   -NameServer trey-engdc-8.engineering.treyresearch.net

B. Add-DnsServerZoneDelegation -Name Engineering.TreyResearch.net `
   -ChildZoneName Engineering `
   -IPAddress 192.168.10.8,2001:db8:10::8 `
   -NameServer trey-dc-02.treyresearch.net

C. Add-DnsServerZoneDelegation -Name Engineering.TreyResearch.net `
   -ChildZoneName Engineering `
   -IPAddress 192.168.10.8,2001:db8:10::8 `
   -NameServer trey-engdc-02.engineering.treyresearch.net

D. Add-DnsServerZoneDelegation -Name TreyResearch.net `
   -ChildZoneName Engineering `
   -IPAddress 192.168.10.8,2001:db8:10::8 `
   -NameServer trey-dc-02.engineering.treyresearch.net

Objective 3.2: Configure DNS records

DNS servers support many different kinds of resource records. For the 70-411 exam, you should understand which resource record types are supported by the Windows Server 2012 and Windows Server 2012 R2 DNS server, and how to configure those records. You should also know how to configure zone and record options, as well as how to configure round robin load balancing.

This objective covers how to:

- Create and configure DNS resource records (RR) including A, AAAA, PTR, SOA, NS, SRV, CNAME, and MX records
- Configure zone scavenging
- Configure record options including Time To Live (TTL) and weight
- Configure round robin
- Configure secure dynamic updates

Creating and configuring DNS resource records

The DNS server in Windows Server supports a very wide variety of resource records, but the ones that most people have to deal with are the following:

- **A** An IPv4 host address record. The A record is a forward lookup record that translates a host name into an IPv4 address.

- **AAAA** An IPv6 host address record. The AAAA record is a forward lookup record that translates a host name into an IPv6 address.

- **CName** A canonical name record. The CName record allows the use of more than one resource record to refer to a single host.

- **MX** A Mail Exchanger record. The MX record identifies the email server for a domain. There can be multiple MX records for a domain, and they are used in order of precedence.

- **NS** A Name Server record. The NS record identifies a name server for the domain. There can be multiple NS records in a domain.

- **PTR** A pointer record. The PTR record is a reverse lookup record that translates an IP address into a host name. PTR records can be IPv4 or IPv6 addresses.

- **SOA** A Start of Authority record. The SOA record is a version number record identifying the version number of the DNS zone.

- **SRV** A Service record. The SRV record identifies the host name and port number of servers for the specified service.

All these resource records can be created or generated in the DNS Management console. They can also be created or generated by using Windows PowerShell, with the exception of the SOA record, which can't be directly manipulated by Windows PowerShell. You can use the general Add-DnsServerResourceRecord or Set-DnsServerResourceRecord for all the resource records listed except the SOA record, plus there are specific Add cmdlets for the A, AAAA, CName, MX, and PTR records.

There are a wide variety of other DNS record types, but they are rarely of concern on typical Windows networks and they are not called out in the description for this objective, so they are unlikely to be on the exam.

The procedure for setting these record types is essentially the same for all except the SOA and NS records.

Creating A resource records

The A resource record is a host address record that points to an IPv4 address. DNS clients query the DNS server with a name, and if it matches an A record, the DNS server returns an IPv4 address. You can create an A record with either the DNS Manager console or by using the Add-DnsServerResourceRecordA or Add-DnsServerResourceRecord cmdlet.

In most DHCP-managed networks, the A record is usually automatically generated when the IPv4 address is handed out to the DHCP client. This is the preferred method for DHCP clients whose address is subject to change, but you can create a static A record by manually creating it. The problem with static records is that they need to be manually maintained if there are changes in the network. However, if there are servers with static IP addresses (as opposed to DHCP reservations), you might need to manually create the records.

To create an A record with the DNS Manager console, follow these steps:

1. Open the DNS Manager console.

2. Expand the server on which you want to create the record and then expand Forward Lookup Zones.

3. Right-click the DNS domain name in which you want to create the record and select New Host (A Or AAAA).

4. Enter the host name in the Name box. (You don't need to enter the FQDN, just the host name.)

5. Enter the IPv4 address in the IP Address box, as shown in Figure 3-15, and select Create Associated Pointer (PTR) Record if you're using reverse lookup zones.

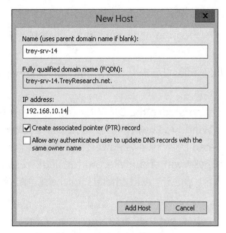

FIGURE 3-15 The New Host dialog box

6. Click Add Host to create the record.

To create the A record with Windows PowerShell, use the Add-DnsServerResourceRecordA cmdlet. For example:

```
Add-DnsServerResourceRecordA -ZoneName "TreyResearch.net" `
                             -Name trey-srv-14 `
                             -IPv4Address 192.168.10.14 `
                             -CreatePtr
```

You can also use the more general Add-DnsServerResourceRecord cmdlet to create the record. For example:

```
Add-DnsServerResourceRecord  -ZoneName "TreyResearch.net" `
                             -A `
                             -Name trey-srv-14 `
                             -IPv4Address 192.168.10.14 `
                             -CreatePtr
```

Both Windows PowerShell cmdlets create the exact same record and produce no output unless you include the -PassThru parameter. If you do include that, you see this:

```
HostName       RecordType Timestamp          TimeToLive   RecordData
--------       ---------- ---------          ----------   ----------
trey-srv-14    A          0                  01:00:00     192.168.10.14
```

Creating AAAA resource records

The AAAA resource record is a host address record that points to an IPv6 address. DNS clients query the DNS server with a name, and the DNS server returns an IPv6 address if it matches an AAAA record. You can create an AAAA record with either the DNS Manager console or by using the Add-DnsServerResourceRecordAAAA or Add-DnsServerResourceRecord cmdlet.

In most DHCP-managed networks, the AAAA record is usually automatically generated when the IPv6 address is handed out to the DHCP client. This is the preferred method for DHCP clients whose address is subject to change, but you can create a static AAAA record by manually creating it. The problem with static records is that they need to be manually maintained if there are changes in the network. However, if there are servers with static IP addresses (as opposed to DHCP reservations), you might need to manually create the records.

To create an AAAA record with the DNS Manager console, follow these steps:

1. Open the DNS Manager console.

2. Expand the server on which you want to create the record and then expand Forward Lookup Zones.

3. Right-click the DNS domain name in which you want to create the record and select New Host (A Or AAAA).

4. Enter the host name in the Name box. (You don't need to enter the FQDN, just the host name.)

5. Enter the IPv6 address in the IP Address box, as shown in Figure 3-16, and select Create Associated Pointer (PTR) Record if you're using reverse lookup zones.

FIGURE 3-16 New Host dialog box

6. Click Add Host to create the record.

7. Click OK to acknowledge the successful creation of the record and then click Done to exit out of the New Host dialog box.

To create the AAAA record with Windows PowerShell, use the Add-DnsServerResourceRecordAAAA cmdlet. For example:

```
Add-DnsServerResourceRecordAAAA -ZoneName "TreyResearch.net" `
                                -Name trey-srv-14 `
                                -IPv6Address 2001:db8::0e `
                                -CreatePtr
```

You can also use the more general Add-DnsServerResourceRecord cmdlet to create the record. For example:

```
Add-DnsServerResourceRecord  -ZoneName "TreyResearch.net" `
                             -AAAA `
                             -Name trey-srv-14 `
                             -IPv6Address 2001:db8::0e `
                             -CreatePtr
```

Both Windows PowerShell cmdlets create the exact same record and produce no output unless you include the -PassThru parameter. If you do include that, you see this:

```
HostName      RecordType Timestamp          TimeToLive    RecordData
--------      ---------- ---------          ----------    ----------
trey-srv-14   AAAA       0                  01:00:00      2001:db8::e
```

Creating CNAME resource records

The CNAME resource record is a canonical record that adds an additional host name for a server. It is also called an Alias. The CNAME record points to a host name record and provides an alternative name for that host name. DNS clients query the DNS server with a name, and if it matches an CNAME record, the DNS server looks up the IP address for the host name that the CNAME points to and returns an IPv4 address for that host name. You can create a CNAME record with the DNS Manager console or by using the Add-DnsServerResourceRecordCName or Add-DnsServerResourceRecord cmdlet.

CNAME records are typically used to provide an alternate host name during a transition phase or to point to specific services that run on the same server. So, for example, you might use a CNAME of ns1 to point to trey-dc-02 in the treyresearch.net zone and also use a CNAME of ns1 to point to tail-dc-102 in the tailspintoys.com zone, enabling you maintain a uniform naming convention across domains.

To create a CNAME record with the DNS Manager console, follow these steps:

1. Open the DNS Manager console.

2. Expand the server on which you want to create the record and then expand Forward Lookup Zones.

3. Right-click the DNS domain name in which you want to create the record and select New Alias (CNAME).

4. Enter the host name in the Name box. (You don't need to enter the FQDN, just the host name.)

5. Enter the FQDN of the target host, as shown in Figure 3-17.

FIGURE 3-17 The New Resource Record dialog box

6. Click OK to create the record.

To create the CNAME record with Windows PowerShell, use the Add-DnsServerResourceRecordCName cmdlet. For example:

```
Add-DnsServerResourceRecordCNAME -ZoneName "TreyResearch.net" `
                                 -Name dc1 `
                                 -HostNameAlias trey-dc-02.treyresearch.net
```

You can also use the more general Add-DnsServerResourceRecord cmdlet to create the record. For example:

```
Add-DnsServerResourceRecord -ZoneName "TreyResearch.net" `
                            -CName `
                            -Name dc1 `
                            -HostNameAlias trey-dc-02.treyresearch.net
```

Both Windows PowerShell cmdlets create the exact same record and produce no output unless you include the -PassThru parameter. If you do include that, you see this:

```
HostName RecordType Timestamp TimeToLive RecordData
-------- ---------- --------- ---------- ----------
dc1      CNAME      0         01:00:00   trey-dc-02.treyresearch.net.
```

Creating MX resource records

The MX resource record is a Mail Exchanger record that tells Simple Mail Transfer Protocol (SMTP) servers which host or hosts handle email for the domain. The MX record points to a host name record and includes a Mail Server Priority box that allows you to have backup mail servers with the email always being delivered to the mail server with the lowest value available. DNS clients query the DNS server for the MX record. If there is one or more, the DNS server returns the host names that the MX records point to, along with the priority for each server. You can create an MX record with the DNS Manager console or by using the Add-DnsServerResourceRecordMX or Add-DnsServerResourceRecord cmdlet.

To create an MX record with the DNS Manager console, follow these steps:

1. Open the DNS Manager console.

2. Expand the server on which you want to create the record and then expand Forward Lookup Zones.

3. Right-click the DNS domain name in which you want to create the record and select New Mail Exchanger (MX).

4. Enter a Host Or Child Domain if appropriate. (In most environments, you can leave this box blank.)

5. Enter the FQDN of the mail server in the Fully Qualified Domain Name (FQDN) Of Mail Server box.

6. Enter the Mail Server Priority, as shown in Figure 3-18.

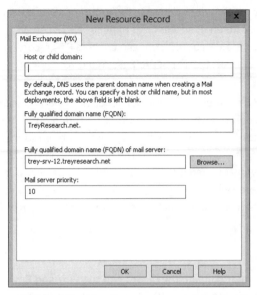

FIGURE 3-18 The New Resource Record dialog box for an MX Record

7. Click OK to create the record.

To create the MX record with Windows PowerShell, use the Add-DnsServerResourceRecordMX cmdlet. For example:

```
Add-DnsServerResourceRecordMX -ZoneName "TreyResearch.net" `
                              -Name "." `
                              -MailExchange trey-srv-12.treyresearch.net `
                              -Preference 10
```

You can also use the more general Add-DnsServerResourceRecord cmdlet to create the record. For example:

```
Add-DnsServerResourceRecord -ZoneName "TreyResearch.net" `
                            -Name "." `
                            -MX
                            -MailExchange trey-srv-12.treyresearch.net `
                            -Preference 10
```

Both Windows PowerShell cmdlets create the exact same record and produce no output unless you include the -PassThru parameter. If you do include that, you see this:

```
HostName RecordType Timestamp TimeToLive RecordData
-------- ---------- --------- ---------- ----------
@        MX         0         01:00:00   [10][trey-srv-12.treyresearch.net.]
```

Creating PTR resource records

The PTR resource record is a pointer record that does a reverse lookup to point to a host name. DNS clients query the DNS server with an IP address. If it matches a PTR record, the DNS server returns the host name for that IP address. You can create a PTR record with the DNS Manager console or by using the Add-DnsServerResourceRecordPTR or Add-DnsServerResourceRecord cmdlet.

Reverse lookup zones are not required for most Windows networks, but when they are used, the PTR record is automatically generated when the IP address is handed out to the DHCP client or when the A or AAAA record is manually created. This is the preferred method, but you can create a static PTR record by manually creating it. The problem with static records is that they need to be manually maintained if there are changes in the network. However, if you don't initially create a reverse lookup zone and then decide that you need one, you might well have servers with static addresses that need manually created records.

To create PTR record with the DNS Manager console, follow these steps:

1. Open the DNS Manager console.

2. Expand the server on which you want to create the record and then expand Reverse Lookup Zones. For an IPv4 address in the 192.168.10/24 network, this is the 10.168.192. in-addr.arpa zone; for an IPv6 address in the 2001:db8::/64 network, the zone is the 0.0.0.0.0.0.0.0.8.b.d.0.1.0.0.2.ip6.arpa zone.

3. Right-click the zone in which you want to create the record and select New Pointer (PTR).

4. Enter the IP address in the Host IP Address box. (You don't need to enter the FQDN, just the IP address.)

5. Enter the FQDN in the Host Name box, as shown in Figure 3-19.

6. Click OK to create the record.

To create the PTR record with Windows PowerShell, use the Add-DnsServerResourceRecordPtr cmdlet. For example:

```
Add-DnsServerResourceRecordPtr -ZoneName 10.168.192.in-addr.arpa `
                               -Name "14" `
                               -PtrDomainName "trey-srv-14.treyresearch.net"
```

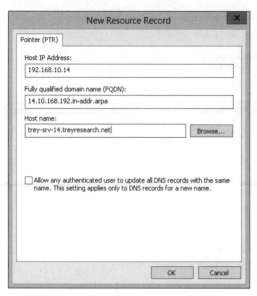

FIGURE 3-19 The New Resource Record dialog box for creating a PTR record

You can also use the more general Add-DnsServerResourceRecord cmdlet to create the record. For example:

```
Add-DnsServerResourceRecordPtr -ZoneName 10.168.192.in-addr.arpa `
                               -PTR
                               -Name "14" `
                               -PtrDomainName "trey-srv-14.treyresearch.net"
```

Both Windows PowerShell cmdlets create the exact same record, and produce no output unless you include the -PassThru parameter. If you do include that, you see the following:

```
HostName RecordType Timestamp TimeToLive RecordData
-------- ---------- --------- ---------- ----------
14       PTR        0         01:00:00   trey-srv-14.treyresearch.net.
```

Creating SRV resource records

The SRV resource record is a service location record that points to the location of key network resources. SRV records are required for AD DS domain controllers, but can also be required for other services. The necessary SRV records for domain controllers are created as part of the process of promoting a server to be a domain controller. Typically, _ldap and _kerberos SRV records are created in the _msdcs.<domainname> zone. The _kerberos record has a protocol of _tcp and a port number of 88, as shown in Figure 3-20.

FIGURE 3-20 The Properties dialog box for the _kerberos SRV record

The _ldap record is similar to the _kerberos record, except that it uses a port of 389. You usually should not modify these records, but it might be necessary to re-create them in the case of recovery from an unplanned event. Alternately, you might want to adjust the weight and priority of individual servers providing the service to manage load.

Other services that can use SRV records typically create their own records in DNS as part of their installation process, but you might have to manually create them as well. One other Microsoft service that uses SRV records is Microsoft Exchange, which uses SRV records to allow Outlook and other clients to autodiscover the Exchange server.

You can create an SRV record with the DNS Manager console or by using the Add-DnsServerResourceRecord cmdlet. To create an SRV record with the DNS Manager console, follow these steps:

1. Open the DNS Manager console.

2. Expand the server you on which you want to create the record and then expand Forward Lookup Zones.

3. Right-click the DNS domain name in which you want to create the record and select Other New Records.

4. Select Service Locator (SRV) from the list on the Resource Record Type dialog box, as shown in Figure 3-21, and click Create Record.

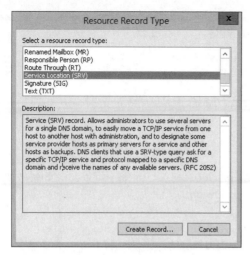

FIGURE 3-21 The Resource Record Type dialog box

5. Fill in the Service, Protocol, Priority, Weight, Port Number, and Host Offering This Service boxes on the New Resources Record dialog box, as shown in Figure 3-22.

FIGURE 3-22 The New Resource Record dialog box for a new SRV record

6. Click OK to create the record.

To create the SRV record with Windows PowerShell, use the Add-DnsServerResourceRecord cmdlet with the -SRV parameter set. For example:

```
Add-DnsServerResourceRecord -ZoneName "TreyResearch.net" `
                            -Name _nntp._tcp `
                            -SRV `
                            -DomainName "trey-edge-1.treyresearch.net" `
                            -Port 119 `
                            -Priority 0 `
                            -Weight 0 `
                            -PassThru
```

The Windows PowerShell cmdlet doesn't produce output unless you include the -PassThru parameter. If you do include it, you see the following:

```
HostName  RecordType  Timestamp  TimeToLive  RecordData
--------  ----------  ---------  ----------  ----------
_nntp     SRV         0          01:00:00    [0][0][113][trey-edge-1.treyresearch.net.]
```

Creating NS resource records

The NS resource record is a name server record that identifies a name server for the domain. You can create an NS record with the DNS Manager console or by using the Add-DnsServerResourceRecord cmdlet.

NS records are usually created automatically when servers are promoted to a domain controller, but you might have to manually create the NS record.

To create an NS record with the DNS Manager console, follow these steps:

1. Open the DNS Manager console.

2. Expand the server on which you want to create the record and then expand Forward Lookup Zones.

3. Right-click the Zone Name for the zone for which you want to create an NS record and select Properties from the menu.

4. Select the Name Servers tab and click Add to open the New Name Server Record dialog box shown in Figure 3-23.

5. Enter FQDN of the new name server in the Server Fully Qualified Domain Name (FQDN) box and click the Resolve button.

6. Click OK and then OK again to create the record.

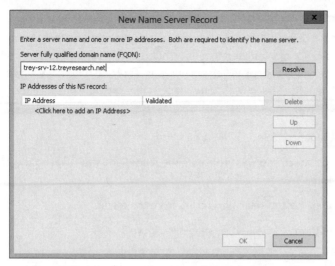

FIGURE 3-23 The New Name Server Record dialog box

To create the NS record with Windows PowerShell, use the Add-DnsServerResourceRecord cmdlet. For example:

```
Add-DnsServerResourceRecord   -ZoneName "TreyResearch.net" `
                              -NS `
                              -Name "." `
                              -NameServer trey-srv-12.treyresearch.net `
                              -PassThru
```

The Windows PowerShell cmdlet produces no output unless you include the -PassThru parameter. If you do include it, you see this:

```
HostName   RecordType Timestamp   TimeToLive RecordData
--------   ---------- ---------   ---------- ----------
@          NS         0           01:00:00   trey-srv-12.treyresearch.net.
```

EXAM TIP

The NS record is a bit different from other resource records, and it's easy to get the fields wrong with the Windows PowerShell cmdlet. The Name field needs to be "(same as parent folder)" (without the quotes), and the way to enter it is with a value of "." for the -Name parameter. There are several compelling alternatives that the exam writers might offer as distractors, but don't be seduced by them.

Configuring SOA resource records

The SOA resource record is a Start of Authority record that sets the version number of a DNS zone. Typically, this record is not manipulated manually, but is automatically incremented whenever there is a change to the zone. The version number is used to determine which zone record is authoritative if there have been DNS zone changes in more than one location.

To update a SOA record with the DNS Manager console, follow these steps:

1. Open the DNS Manager console.

2. Expand the server on which you want to create the record and then expand the Zone you want to configure.

3. Right-click the zone name and select Properties from the menu.

4. Click the Start Of Authority (SOA) tab, as shown in Figure 3-24.

FIGURE 3-24 The Start Of Authority (SOA) tab of the zone Properties dialog box

5. Enter the host name in the Primary Server box.

6. Click Increment to increment the Serial Number for the record.

7. Set Refresh Interval, Retry Interval, Expires After, Minimum TTL, and TTL For This Record and then Click OK to update the zone.

Configuring zone scavenging

You can enable DNS scavenging and aging on a per-zone basis or for all zones on an Active Directory-integrated DNS server. To enable and configure scavenging for all zones on the server, follow these steps:

1. Open the DNS Manager console.

2. Right-click the server name and select Set Aging/Scavenging For All Zones.

3. On the Server Aging/Scavenging Properties dialog box, shown in Figure 3-25, select Scavenge Stale Resource Records.

FIGURE 3-25 The Server Aging/Scavenging Properties dialog box

4. Adjust the no-refresh and refresh intervals if necessary and then click OK.

5. On the Server Aging/Scavenging Confirmation dialog box, shown in Figure 3-26, select Apply These Settings To The Existing Active Directory-Integrated Zones and then click OK.

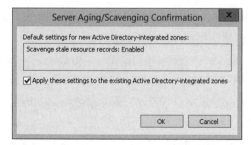

FIGURE 3-26 The Server Aging/Scavenging Confirmation dialog box

Next, enable scavenging on at least one DNS server hosting Active Directory-integrated primary DNS zones:

6. Right-click the name of the DNS server in the console tree of the DNS Manager console and select Properties from the menu.

7. Click the Advanced tab, shown in Figure 3-27, and select Enable Automatic Scavenging Of Stale Records.

FIGURE 3-27 The Advanced tab of the DNS Server Properties dialog box

8. Set the Scavenging Period as appropriate for your environment (the default is 7 days.)

9. Click OK to close the Properties dialog box and enable automatic scavenging.

You can control which zones are subject to scavenging on a zone-by-zone basis. To enable or disable scavenging for an individual zone, follow these steps:

1. Open the DNS Manager console and expand the server name that hosts the primary zone for which you want to enable or disable scavenging.

2. Right-click the zone you want to configure and select Properties. You can set aging and scavenging on both forward lookup zones and reverse lookup zones.

3. On the General tab, click Aging to open the Zone Aging/Scavenging Properties, shown in Figure 3-28.

4. Select or clear the Scavenging Stale Resource Records check box to enable or disable scavenging for the zone.

5. If enabled, you can also set the No-Refresh Interval and Refresh Interval.

FIGURE 3-28 The Zone Aging/Scavenging Properties dialog box

6. Click OK and then OK again to close the Zone Properties dialog box.

Alternately, you can use Windows PowerShell to set the scavenging settings, by using the Set-DnsServerScavenging cmdlet. For example, to configure the settings for all zones, set a scavenging interval of three days, and enable scavenging on new zones by default, use the following command:

```
Set-DnsServerScavenging -ScavengingState:$True `
                        -ScavengingInterval 3:00:00:00 `
                        -ApplyOnAllZones `
                        -PassThru
```

This command returns the following (because the -PassThru parameter is set):

```
NoRefreshInterval   : 7.00:00:00
RefreshInterval     : 7.00:00:00
ScavengingInterval  : 3.00:00:00
ScavengingState     : True
LastScavengeTime    :
```

To set the aging and scavenging for an individual zone, use Set-DnsServerZoneAging to enable aging and scavenging for a zone, and use Set-DnsServerResourceRecordAging to set a timestamp on the records in a zone and begin the aging. For example:

```
Set-DnsServerZoneAging -Name TreyResearch.net `
                       -Aging:$True `
                       -RefreshInterval 3:00:00:00 `
                       -NoRefreshInterval 3:00:00:00 `
                       -ScavengeServers 192.168.10.2 `
                       -PassThru
```

This command returns the following (because the -PassThru parameter is set):

```
ZoneName              : TreyResearch.net
AgingEnabled          : True
AvailForScavengeTime  : 4/7/2014 10:00:00 AM
RefreshInterval       : 3.00:00:00
NoRefreshInterval     : 3.00:00:00
ScavengeServers       : 192.168.10.2
```

Next, begin the aging process on the zone with the following:

```
Set-DnsServerResourceRecordAging -ZoneName TreyResearch.net
```

Configuring record options including Time To Live (TTL) and weight

You can configure resource record options for record types that support individual configuration of options, such as SRV resource records. The combination of weight and priority control the server that will deliver specific services. So, for example, if you have multiple Network News Transfer Protocol (NNTP) servers that use SRV records, you can set both a Priority value and a Weight value. For example, assume that you have two SRV records for the service, each with a priority of 1 and each pointing to a different service provider. If one has a weight of 2, and the other a weight of 8, a query for the service will return the SRV record with the weight of 8 four times for every one time it returns the SRV record with a weight of 2.

MX resource records support a Preference setting. This is equivalent to the Priority setting on an SRV record. The record returned includes the Preference or Priority value, and the lowest Preference (MX) or Priority (SRV) value is used if the server it points to is available.

To set the weight on an SRV record, follow these steps:

1. Open the DNS Manager console and navigate to the zone that hosts the SRV record.

2. Right-click the SRV record and select Properties from the menu.

3. Enter the weight and priority in the appropriate boxes and click OK to update the record and close the Property dialog box.

To set the weight at the command line, use the DnsServerResourceRecord cmdlets. For example, to set the weight of the _nntp SRV record to 10, use the following commands:

```
$NewRRObj = $OrigRRObj = Get-DnsServerResourceRecord -Name _nntp `
    -ZoneName TreyResearch.net `
    -RRType SRV
$NewRRObj.RecordData.Weight = 20
Set-DnsServerResourceRecord -NewInputObject $NewRRObj `
    -OldInputObject $OrigRRObj `
    -ZoneName treyresearch.net
```

You can also use this same technique to set the TTL for an individual resource record. For example, to change the A record for server trey-wds-11 to have a TTL of two hours, use the following:

```
$NewRRObj = $OrigRRObj = Get-DnsServerResourceRecord -Name trey-wds-11 `
    -ZoneName TreyResearch.net `
    -RRType A
$NewRRObj.TimeToLive = [System.TimeSpan]::FromHours(2)
Set-DnsServerResourceRecord -NewInputObject $NewRRObj `
    -OldInputObject $OrigRRObj `
    -ZoneName treyresearch.net `
    -PassThru
```

HostName	RecordType	Timestamp	TimeToLive	RecordData
trey-wds-11	A	0	02:00:00	192.168.10.11

Configuring round robin

Round robin load balancing is an easy and unsophisticated way to distribute load across a group of servers that provide the same service. The basic process is to create A or AAAA records with the same name pointing to each of the servers in the round robin. By default, round robin is enabled on Windows Server 2012 R2 DNS servers. If the service uses an SRV record, the SRV record should use that A or AAAA record name in the Host Offering This Service box.

Each time a new client requests the service or server, the DNS server returns one of the IP addresses that matches the host name queried. After clients have cached the DNS information locally, they usually won't need to request it again until the record they've cached ages out. But different clients get a different IP address in the round robin group.

Windows Server also uses netmask ordering to attempt to connect to the service or server that is closest. This proximity awareness is used to return the A or AAAA record whose IPv4 address is in the same subnet, or whose IPv6 address has the longest prefix match. When both netmask ordering and DNS round robin are enabled, round robin load balancing might not always return a load balanced address.

Configuring secure dynamic updates

Another option you can configure for resource records is what type of update is permitted. By default, Active Directory-integrated zones are set to allow only secure dynamic updates. When DNS records are created or updated by a Windows DHCP server, the update automatically updates the A or AAAA record and the PTR record. It can be further configured on the DHCP server to enable DHCP Name Protection. If DHCP Name Protection is enabled, the DHCP server attempts to register the A or AAAA and PTR records for the client, but if a different client already has the name registered on the DNS server, the new registration will fail.

Enabling Name Protection is possible only with Secure Dynamic Updates enabled. Enabling Name Protection will set the following DHCP server settings:

- DHCP Server honors requests for registration from Windows DHCP clients.
- DHCP Server dynamically updates A (or AAAA) and PTR records for non-Windows DHCP clients.
- DHCP Server discards the A (or AAAA) and PTR records when the client lease is deleted.

The Secure Updates option is set in the DNS Manager console and is set at the zone level. To change the setting, open the DNS Manager, right-click the zone you want to change, and select properties from the menu. On the General tab, select one of three options:

- **Secure Only**   Only devices that are in the same DNS domain are permitted to register their DNS records.
- **Nonsecure And Secure**   Any device can update a dynamic DNS record.
- **None**   No dynamic updates are accepted. All DNS records must be manually maintained.

Thought experiment
Configuring round robin

In this thought experiment, apply what you've learned about this objective. You can find answers to these questions in the "Answers" section at the end of this chapter.

You are the network administrator for TreyResearch.net. Engineering users run specialized applications on a trio of dedicated Remote Desktop Session Host (RDSH) servers to reduce the need to install them on each workstation locally. Especially because there is a large amount of computer churn in the department as compute resources get scavenged for other uses. These computers are all on the same subnet, and each has a single IP address.

1. Currently, users connect to one or another RDSH server, depending on how their client is configured. If their primary RDSH is down, they connect to one of the alternate ones manually, which doesn't provide a good user experience. How can you use DNS round robin to distribute the load across the RDSH servers and improve the user experience?

2. How would you configure the round robin records? (Assume that the three RDSH servers are rdsh1, rdsh2, and rdsh3.)

Objective summary

- The DnsServer Windows PowerShell module includes cmdlets to create and manage DNS resource records.
- The Windows DNS server supports a wide variety of resource records, including A, AAAA, PTR, SOA, NS, SRV, CNAME, and MX records.
- You can use the DNS Manager console or Windows PowerShell to manage DNS record options such as TTL.
- DNS resource records can be used to do basic round robin load balancing.
- Use DHCP Name Protection with DNS secure dynamic updates to ensure that you don't end up with conflicting DNS records.
- Use DNS zone scavenging and aging to remove stale records from your DNS servers.

Objective review

1. Which records do you need to create to support a new application server that uses both IPv4 and IPv6? (Choose all that apply.)

   A. MX

   B. SRV

   C. A

   D. AAAA

   E. PTR

   F. CNAME

2. What command should you use to create a new name server record for ns13.treyresearch.net at 192.168.10.13?

   A. Add-DnsServerResourceRecord -ZoneName "treyresearch.net" -NS -Name "." -NameServer "ns13.treyresearch.net"

   B. Add-DnsServerResourceRecord -ZoneName "treyresearch.net" -NS -Name "ns13" -NameServer "ns13.treyresearch.net"

   C. Add-DnsServerResourceRecord -Name "treyresearch.net" -NS -NameServer "ns13.treyresearch.net"

   D. Add-DnsServerResourceRecord -ZoneName "treyresearch.net" -NS -Name "ns13.treyresearch.net" -NameServer "."

3. How do you update the SOA resource record?

   A. Use the Set-DnsServerResourceRecordSOA cmdlet

   B. Use the Add-DnsServerResourceRecordSOA cmdlet

   C. Use the DNS Manager console Properties of the zone

   D. Use the DNS Manager console Properties of the server

Objective 3.3: Configure virtual private network (VPN) and routing

The traditional methods of providing remote access include dial-in modems and virtual private network (VPN) connections. Dial-in modems use standard telephone lines and hardware or software modems that enable a direct connection from a remote client to the internal network without using the Internet at all. They have the advantage that they require only an available telephone line; no Internet connection is necessary. Their disadvantages, however, include their speed—they are limited to the speed of the modem and they are hardware-intensive, requiring a dedicated bank of phone lines and modems.

By contrast, VPNs require no additional hardware beyond that required for Internet connectivity; they use the public Internet as the transmission medium. VPN remote access creates a dedicated encrypted tunnel between a client computer and a VPN endpoint computer on the internal network. VPNs, however, have some limitations of their own. The biggest is that VPNs limit the ability of the connected client to be managed.

Routing and Network Address Translation (NAT) are two technologies used by internal computers accessing the Internet. Routing controls which path a packet takes to get to its destination; NAT maps internal private IP addresses to external public addresses, enabling a single public IP address to serve for many internal devices.

Finally, Web Application Proxy is a Remote Access role service in Windows Server 2012 R2 that provides a reverse proxy that allows remote users to access web applications on the internal network from anywhere.

This objective covers how to:

- Install and configure the Remote Access role
- Implement Network Address Translation (NAT)
- Configure VPN settings
- Configure remote dial-in settings for users
- Configure routing
- Configure Web Application proxy in passthrough mode

Installing and configuring the Remote Access role

The first step of implementing VPNs and routing is installing the Remote Access role and doing the basic initial configuration.

Installing the Remote Access role

Installing the Remote Access role is the same basic process as installing any other role in Windows Server. You can install the role from Server Manager by using the Add Roles And Features Wizard or you can use the Install-WindowsFeature cmdlet. To install by using Server Manager, follow these steps:

1. Open Server Manager either locally on the edge server that will host the Remote Access role or on a computer that has Server Manager configured to connect to the edge server.

2. Select Add Roles And Features from the Manage menu. Click Next on the Before You Begin page if it is displayed.

3. Select Role-Based Or Feature-Based Installation and click Next.

4. Choose Select A Server From The Server Pool and then select the server that will host the role. Click Next.

5. On the Select Server Roles page, shown in Figure 3-29, select Remote Access. Click Next and then click Next again.

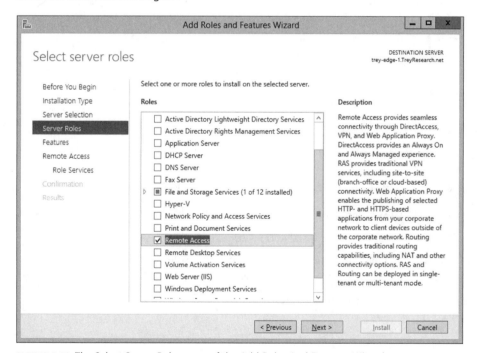

FIGURE 3-29 The Select Server Roles page of the Add Roles And Features Wizard

6. Read the Remote Access page and then click Next.

7. On the Select Role Services page, shown in Figure 3-30, select which role services you want to enable on this server. The choices are these:

- DirectAccess and VPN (RAS)
- Routing
- Web Application Proxy

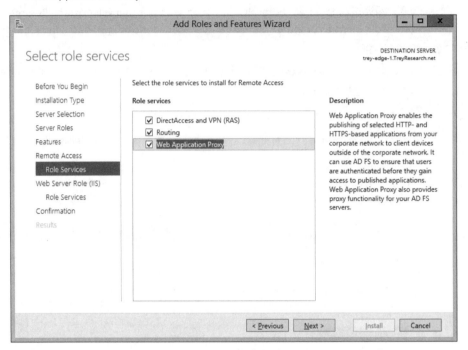

FIGURE 3-30 The Select Role Services page of the Add Roles And Features Wizard

8. Click Add Features if prompted by selecting a Role Service.

9. Click Next as required until the Confirm Installation Selections page is displayed.

10. Click Install; when the installation is complete, click Close.

To install the Remote Access role, including all the Role Services, you can use the Install-WindowsFeature cmdlet. For example:

```
Install-WindowsFeature -Name RemoteAccess `
                -IncludeAllSubFeatures `
                -IncludeManagementTools
```

Initial configuration

The initial configuration of the Remote Access role can be done by using the Getting Started Wizard, or the Remote Access Setup Wizard from the Remote Access Management console, as shown in Figure 3-31. The Getting Started Wizard is a quick way to get a VPN and

DirectAccess configured and set up. It makes all the initial settings and configuration decisions based on default recommended settings, and it is a huge improvement over the early days of setting up DirectAccess, especially. However, because it hides most of the choices, it's not particularly appealing to write exam questions about.

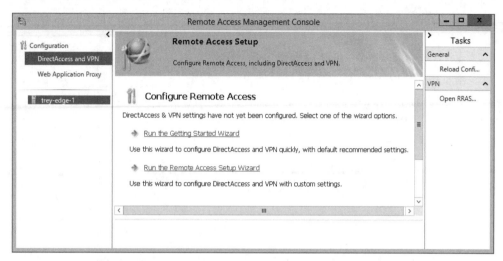

FIGURE 3-31 The Configure Remote Access screen of the Remote Access Management console

Regardless of whether you choose the Configure Remote Access Wizard or the Getting Started Wizard, the first page of each wizard is essentially the same—you need to choose what kind of Remote Access you want to deploy. The choices are these:

- **Deploy Both DirectAccess And VPN**   Configures the server as a VPN endpoint and also configures DirectAccess (DirectAccess is covered in Objective 3.4).

- **Deploy DirectAccess Only**   Configures the server as a DirectAccess server and enables DirectAccess client computers.

- **Deploy VPN Only**   Configures the servers as a VPN endpoint by using the Routing And Remote Access console. VPNs can be remote client VPNs or site-to-site VPNs.

For the sections in this objective, configure the Remote Access server by using the Deploy VPN Only option. (The Web Access Proxy is configured separately and is not dependent on which option you choose for this initial configuration.)

To do the initial configuration of the Remote Access server, follow these steps:

1. Open the Remote Access Management Console by selecting Remote Access Management from the Tools menu in Server Manager.

2. Click DirectAccess And VPN under the Configuration option in the left pane, as shown in Figure 3-31.

3. Select Run The Remote Access Setup Wizard in the Remote Access Setup pane to open the Configure Remote Access page shown in Figure 3-32.

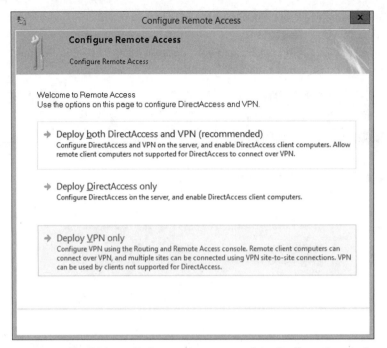

FIGURE 3-32 The Welcome To Remote Access page of the Configure Remote Access Wizard

4. Select Deploy VPN Only to open the Routing And Remote Access console, as shown in Figure 3-33.

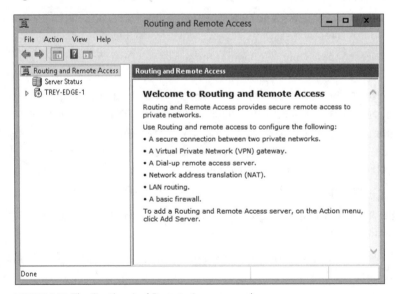

FIGURE 3-33 The Routing And Remote Access console

5. Select the server you are configuring and then select Configure And Enable Routing And Remote Access from the Action menu.

6. Click Next on the Welcome page of the Routing And Remote Access Server Setup Wizard.

7. Select Virtual Private Network (VPN) Access And NAT on the Configuration page and click Next.

8. On the VPN Connection page, select the network interface that connects the server to the Internet, as shown in Figure 3-34.

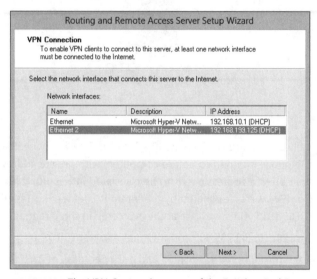

FIGURE 3-34 The VPN Connection page of the Routing And Remote Access Server Setup Wizard

9. If you're using DHCP on your network, select Automatically on the IP Address Assignment page or select From A Specified Range Of Addresses to have the Remote Access server assign the IP addresses of incoming VPN connections. Click Next.

10. On the Managing Multiple Remote Access Servers page, select No, Use Routing And Remote Access To Authenticate Connection Requests.

11. Click Next and then click Finish to return to the Remote Access Management console.

Implementing Network Address Translation (NAT)

NAT allows computers with private IP addresses to share a single public IP address. NAT can be implemented on Windows Server by using the Remote Access role or can be implemented on a network edge device such as a router or firewall. When you configure Windows Server as a NAT device, the server requires at least two network adapters: one connected to the private network and the second to the public network, as shown in Figure 3-35.

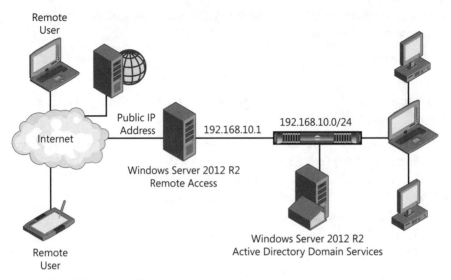

FIGURE 3-35 NAT network design

Internal networks are typically configured with private IP addresses. These private IP addresses cannot be routed to the public Internet, so before computers with private addresses can connect to the Internet, their private address needs to be translated into a public IP address. Private address ranges for IPv4 were designated by the Internet Engineering Task Force (IETF) Request for Comment (RFC) 1918. Those private addresses come in three ranges:

- **10.0.0.0/8**   10.0.0.0 through 10.255.255.255 and a subnet mask of 255.0.0.0

- **172.16.0.0/12**   172.16.0.0 through 172.32.255.255 and a subnet mask of 255.255.0.0

- **192.168.0.0/16**   192.168.0.0 through 192.168.255.255 and a subnet mask of 255.255.0.0

When you run the Routing And Remote Access Server Setup Wizard, it enables NAT on the IPv4 address of the public facing network adapter. The second adapter is connected to the private, internal local area network (LAN). Packets to the public Internet are translated to show that they came from the public IP address of the public facing network adapter. When a reply comes back from the Internet, the Remote Access server reads the packet and routes it onto the private internal LAN to the originating device.

When you configure NAT using the Routing And Remote Access console, you specify which network adapter is connected to your private network and which adapter is connected to the public network. The Routing And Remote Access Server Setup Wizard creates two additional network interfaces, as shown in Figure 3-36: an internal interface, and a loopback interface.

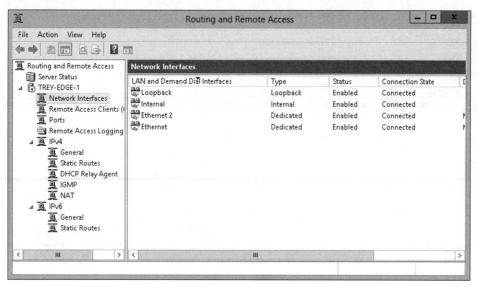

FIGURE 3-36 The Network Interfaces in the Routing And Remote Access console

You can specify specific services that are available on your internal network and map ports and protocols to the servers providing that service across the NAT boundary. For example, if you have a mail server at 192.168.10.5, you can configure port mapping on the public fac-ing network interface to forward all SMTP packets (port 25) to the server at 192.168.10.5, as shown in Figure 3-37. However, this port mapping capability should *not* be substituted for a firewall.

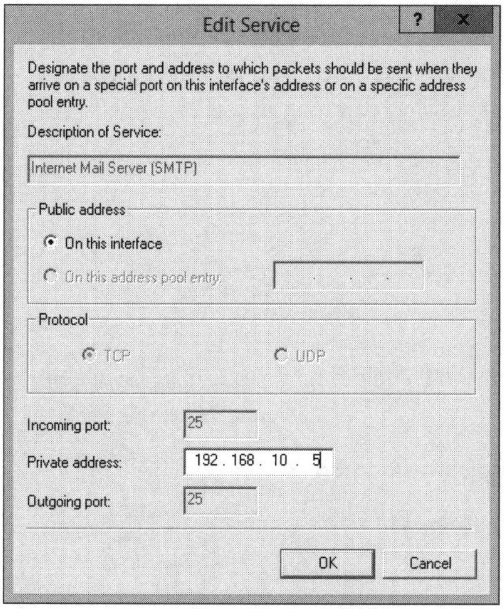

FIGURE 3-37 The Edit Service dialog box

Configuring VPN settings

Windows Server 2012 R2 supports four different VPN protocols, Point to Point Tunneling Protocol (PPTP), Layer 2 Tunneling Protocol (L2TP), Internet Key Exchange version 2 (IKEv2), and Secure Socket Tunneling Protocol (SSTP). These protocols are compared in Table 3-1. By default, when you use the Routing And Remote Access Server Setup Wizard to configure VPN, it creates VPN ports for all four protocols with a maximum of 128 ports each.

TABLE 3-1 VPN Protocols

Protocol	IP Protocol and Ports	Security	Comments
PPTP	TCP 1723; GRE 47	Low	Widely available across virtually all platforms.
L2TP	UDP 500, UDP 4500, UDP 1701; ESP 50	High	Uses IPSec, IKEv1. Difficult to configure, but suitable for site-to-site VPNs and client VPNs. Supported by Windows 2000, Windows XP, Windows Server 2003, Windows Vista, and Windows Server 2008.
SSTP	TCP 443 (SSL)	High	Easily used from almost any location. High overhead Supported on Windows Vista SP1 and later, and on Windows Server 2008. Used for Client VPN only, not site-to-site VPN. Not cross-platform.
IKEv2	UDP 500, UDP 4500, UDP 1701; ESP 50	High	Supports VPN Reconnect. Supports NAT Transversal. Supported by Windows Server 2008 R2, Windows 7, Windows Server 2012, Windows Server 2012 R2 and Windows 8.x.

Windows Server 2012 added support for many VPN management operations. The two modules that include VPN-related cmdlets are the RemoteAccess module and the VpnClient module. The related cmdlets in the RemoteAccess module are for VPN server operations, and the cmdlets in the VpnClient module are client operations. You can get a complete list of VPN-related cmdlets by using the following command:

```
Get-Command -Module RemoteAccess,VpnClient `
    | Sort-Object module,noun,verb `
    | where {$_.Noun -match "Vpn" } `
    | ft -auto verb,noun,Module
```

Configuring available VPN protocols

You can configure which protocols are available for VPN. The default is to use any available protocol; follow these steps to remove a protocol:

1. Open the Routing And Remote Access console (rrasmgmt.msc).

2. Select and expand the VPN server you want to manage.

3. Right-click Ports and select Properties.

4. Select the Device for which you want to remove support and click Configure.

5. Clear the check box for Remote Access Connections (Inbound Only).

6. Clear the check box for Demand-dial Routing Connections (Inbound And Outbound) if it is selected.

7. Change Maximum Ports to 0, as shown in Figure 3-38.

FIGURE 3-38 The Configure Device - WAN Miniport dialog box

8. Click OK and click Yes to acknowledge that you're reducing the number of ports for the connection. Any users using the ports you're eliminating will be disconnected.

9. Click OK to return to the Routing And Remote Access console.

You can add support for the removed protocol by reversing the preceding process.

Configuring DHCP and security settings for VPN connections

If you took the default settings when you configured VPN by using the Routing And Remote Access Server Setup Wizard, VPN clients will get their IP address from your existing DHCP server if one was detected. You can change this by configuring Routing And Remote access service (RRAS) to issue an IP address from a set block of addresses rather than requesting an address from the DHCP server. You can also change which network interface RRAS uses to request a DHCP address for the client. Follow these steps to configure DHCP on the server:

1. Open the Routing And Remote Access console (rrasmgmt.msc).

> **NOTE DIFFERENT IF DIRECTACCESS IS ENABLED**
>
> If you have both DirectAccess and VPN enabled, you must configure DHCP and authentication settings from the Remote Access Management console, not RRAS. The settings are the same, but the location is different.

2. Select the VPN server you want to manage and right-click.

3. Select Properties from the menu and then click the IPv4 tab shown in Figure 3-39.

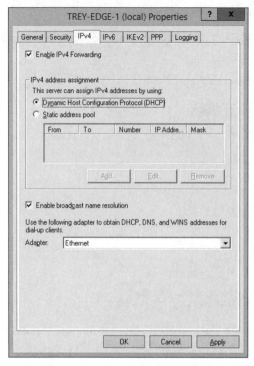

FIGURE 3-39 The IPv4 tab of the RRAS Server Properties dialog box

4. Select Dynamic Host Configuration Protocol (DHCP) to use network DHCP servers or Static Address Pool to issue IP addresses from the VPN server.

5. If using a static address pool, click Add to add a range of IP addresses to use for VPN clients, as shown in Figure 3-40.

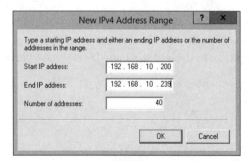

FIGURE 3-40 The New IPv4 Address Range dialog box

> **IMPORTANT** **DHCP EXCLUSION**
>
> If you choose to use a static IP address range for VPN clients, make sure to exclude that range from DHCP servers on the network to avoid an IP address conflict.

6. Select Enable Broadcast Name Resolution to specify the adapter to use for DHCP, DNS, and WINS.

7. Select the IPv6 tab to configure IPv6 properties, as shown in Figure 3-41.

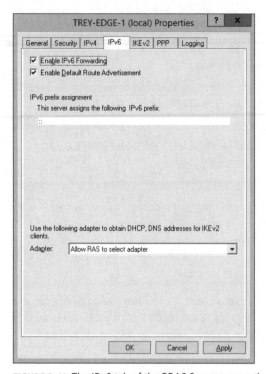

FIGURE 3-41 The IPv6 tab of the RRAS Server properties dialog box

8. Select the Security tab to configure security settings for remote access clients. The settings are these:

- **Authentication Provider** Choose Windows Authentication or RADIUS Authentication. Click the Authentication Methods button to select the authentication methods that are allowed. Choices include EAP, MS-CHAPv2, CHAP, PAP, unauthenticated, and machine certificates for IKEv2.

- **Accounting Provider** Choose Windows Accounting or RADIUS Accounting.

- **Allow Custom IPsec Policy For L2TP/IKEv2 Connection** When selected, you can enter a Pre-shared Key.

- **Use HTTP** When selected, SSL Certificate Binding can use HTTP. When deselected, specify the certificate that SSTP should use.

EXAM TIP

Support for the MS-CHAP, SPAP, and EAP-MD5 protocols ended with Windows Server 2008, and these protocols are no longer supported beginning with Windows Server 2008 R2.

9. Select the General tab to enable or disable portions of RRAS. In the Enable This Computer As A section, the options are these:

    ■ **IPv4 Router**   Enabled by default. When enabled, can be set to Local Area Network (LAN) routing only, or LAN And Demand-Dial Routing (default).

    ■ **IPv6 Router**   Disabled by default. When Enabled, can be set to Local Area Network (LAN) routing only or to LAN And Demand-Dial Routing.

    ■ **IPv4 Remote Access Server**   Enabled by default.

    ■ **IPv6 Remote Access Server**   Disabled by default.

Use the Set-VpnIPAddressAssignment cmdlet to set IP address assignment to DHCP or Static, and if static, to set a range of addresses to use. For example:

```
Set-VpnIPAddressAssignment `
    -IPAssignmentMethod StaticPool `
    -IPAddressRange "192.168.10.200","192.168.10.239"
```

Use the Set-VPNAuthProtocol cmdlet to set acceptable authentication protocols, and the Set-VPNAuthType cmdlet to set to "Windows" or "ExternalRadius"; if set to ExternalRadius, set the RadiusServer, SharedSecret, RadiusScore, RadiusTimeout, and RadiusPort parameters.

Configuring remote dial-in settings for users

The Routing And Remote Access console is also the interface for configuring remote dial-in settings. To enable dial-up remote access, open the Routing And Remote Access console and follow these steps:

1. Select the server you want to configure in the Tree pane and select Configure And Enable Routing And Remote Access from the Action menu.

2. Click Next on the Welcome page and then select Remote Access (Dial-Up Or VPN) on the Configuration page shown in Figure 3-42.

3. Click Next and select Dial-Up on the Remote Access page shown in Figure 3-43. You can also select VPN. If you do, you'll get a slightly different page progression through these steps.

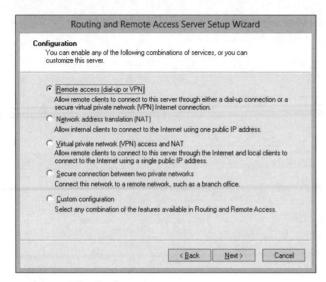

FIGURE 3-42 The Configuration page

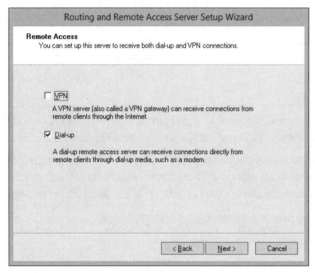

FIGURE 3-43 The Remote Access page

4. Click Next and select the network that dial-up clients will be connected to.

5. Click Next and specify whether to assign IP addresses Automatically or From A Specified Range Of Addresses. Automatically depends on an available DHCP server.

6. Click Next and specify whether to use Routing And Remote Access to authenticate connection requests or to use an RADIUS server. Click Next.

7. If you selected RADIUS, specify the details of the RADIUS server on the RADIUS Server Selection page shown in Figure 3-44. Click Next.

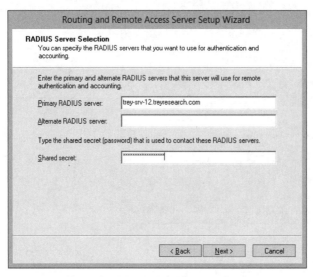

FIGURE 3-44 The RADIUS Server Selection page

8. Click Finish; the server is configured for dial-up remote access.

Configuring routing

You can configure the Remote Access server to also do routing between the LAN and the Internet, with or without NAT. When you install NAT, routing is also configured and enabled.

You can see the routing table for a default installation in Figure 3-45 by right-clicking the Static Routes node under IPv4 in the Routing And Remote Access console. The public facing IP address is 192.168.199.125, and the private LAN IP address is 192.168.10.1 for this figure.

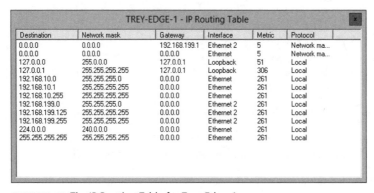

FIGURE 3-45 The IP Routing Table for Trey-Edge-1

Adding a new routing protocol

You can add the Routing Information Protocol (RIP) version 2 routing protocol to the Routing And Remote Access server by following these steps:

1. Open the Routing And Remote Access console (rrasmgmt.msc).

2. Expand the server to which you want to add the protocol in the console tree.

3. Right-click the General node of the IPv4 folder and select New Routing Protocol, as shown in Figure 3-46.

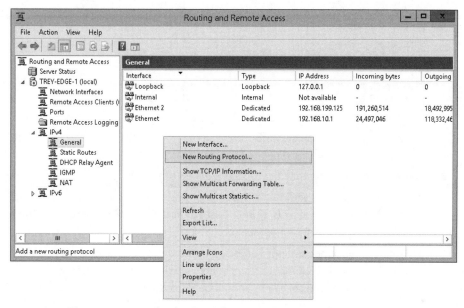

FIGURE 3-46 The context menu for the General IPv4 node

4. On the New Routing Protocol dialog box, select RIP Version 2 For Internet Protocol and click OK. A New RIP node is added to the IPv4 folder of the server. (There is no RIP or equivalent protocol for IPv6.)

5. Right-click the new RIP node and select New Interface from the menu.

6. Select the interface on which you want to enable RIP, usually the Internet facing interface, and click OK.

7. On the RIP Properties page, shown in Figure 3-47, set the options for RIP.

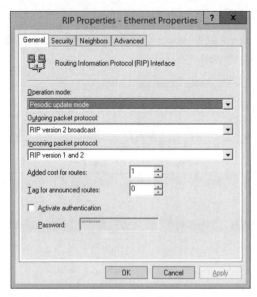

FIGURE 3-47 The RIP Properties dialog box

8. There are four tabs on the RIP Properties dialog box:

■ **General**   Includes settings for Operation Mode, Outgoing Packet Protocols, Incoming Packet Protocols, Added Cost For Routes, Tag For Announced Routes, and an option to Activate Authentication.

■ **Security**   Includes settings For Incoming Routes and For Outgoing Routes. You can choose to Accept All Routes or specify the incoming route ranges to accept or ignore, and you can specify to announce all routes, announce only specified routes, or not announce specified routes.

■ **Neighbors**   Includes settings for how the router interacts with neighboring RIP routers. You can use Broadcast Or Multicast Only, Use Neighbors In Addition To Broadcast Or Multicast, or Use Neighbors Instead Of Broadcast Or Multicast. You can specify the IP Address of neighbors.

■ **Advanced**   Includes timing settings and processing options, as shown in Figure 3-48.

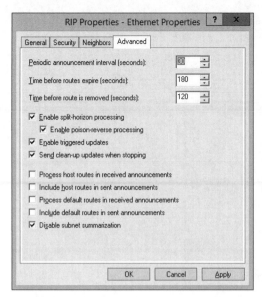

FIGURE 3-48 The Advanced tab of the RIP Properties dialog box

9. After you make any choices appropriate for your environment on the RIP Properties dialog box, click OK; the interface is added to the RIP node.

You can add the DHCPv6 Relay Agent routing protocol to the Routing And Remote Access server by following these steps:

1. Open the Routing And Remote Access console (rrasmgmt.msc).

2. Expand the server to which you want to add the protocol in the console tree.

3. Right-click the General node of the IPv6 folder and select New Routing Protocol from the menu.

4. In the New Routing Protocol dialog box, select DHCPv6 Relay Agent and click OK. A new DHCPv6 Relay Agent node is added to the IPv6 folder.

5. Right-click the new DHCPv6 Relay Agent node and select New Interface from the menu.

6. Select the interface on which you want to relay DHCPv6 packets and click OK to open the DHCP Relay Properties dialog box for that interface, as shown in Figure 3-49.

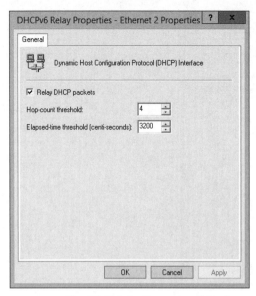

FIGURE 3-49 The DHCP Relay Properties dialog box

7. Click OK to enable the DHCPv6 Relay Agent.

Adding static routes

In addition to adding routing protocols, you can manually configure the RRAS server to use specific static routes. To add a static route, follow these steps:

1. Open the Routing And Remote Access console (rrasmgmt.msc).

2. Select and expand the server to which you want to add a route in the console tree.

3. Select IPv4 to add an IPv4 static route or IPv6 to add an IPv6 static route.

4. Right-click in the details pane and select New Static Route from the menu.

5. On theIPv4 Static Route dialog box (or the IPv6 Static Route dialog box), select the Interface and enter a Destination, Network Mask, Gateway, and Metric for the route, as shown in Figure 3-50.

6. Click OK to create the static route.

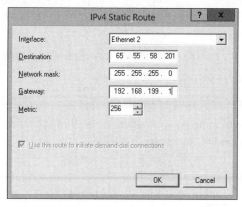

FIGURE 3-50 The IPv4 Static Route dialog box

Configuring Web Application Proxy in passthrough mode

Web Application Proxy can be configured to do passthrough preauthentication without requiring Active Directory Federation Services (AD FS) to publish applications. When Web Application Proxy is used in pass-through mode, domain users who have authenticated to the domain as part of their sign in on their computer can then access the application by passing through their AD DS credentials. When configured this way, the applications can't take advantage of Workplace Join, Multi-Factor Authentication (MFA), or Multi-factor Access Control. These features require AD FS. The flow for Web Application Proxy in passthrough mode is as follows:

1. A client attempts to connect to a public resource URL for an application. This URL is a public address that the Web Application Proxy listens on for HTTPS requests.

2. The Web Application Proxy passes the HTTPS request to the backend server hosting the application via HTTP or HTTPS.

3. Optionally, the user authenticates directly to the backend server or application.

4. If the user successfully authenticates (or if no authentication is required), the client now has access to the published application.

To publish an application using passthrough mode, follow these steps:

1. Open the Remote Access Management Console and click Web Application Proxy.

2. Right-click Web Application Proxy and select Publish.

3. Click Next. On the Preauthentication page of the Publish New Application Wizard, click Pass-Through and then Next.

4. On the Publish Settings page, do the following:

- Enter a friendly name in the Name box.

- In the Enter URL box, enter the fully qualified resource URL for the application.

- Select a certificate from the External Certificate list. Click Next.

5. Click Publish and then Close when the application publish completes.

The Windows PowerShell method for publishing an application in passthrough mode, uses the Add-WebApplicationProxyApplication cmdlet. For example:

```
Add-WebApplicationProxyApplication `
    -BackendServerURL "https://app.treyresearch.net/" `
    -ExternalCertificateThumbprint '1a2b3c4d5e6f1a2b3c4d5e6f1a2b3c4d5e6f1a2b' `
    -ExternalURL "https://app.treyresearch.net/" `
    -Name "Trey App" `
    -ExternalPreAuthentication PassThrough
```

Thought experiment
Configuring VPN protocols

In this thought experiment, apply what you've learned about this objective. You can find answers to these questions in the "Answers" section at the end of this chapter.

You are the network administrator for TreyResearch.net. You need to deploy VPN to support legacy remote users and non-domain-joined remote clients, including includes both Windows and non-Windows devices. You also have users running Windows 8 and Windows 8.1 who need to use VPN as a fallback for their DirectAccess connection.

1. What protocols provide the widest range of support for different operating systems and devices? Do you really need or want all four available protocols?

2. You currently use DirectAccess with Windows Authentication, but you want to move to two-factor authentication for DirectAccess and VPN. What are your options?

Objective summary

- Windows Server 2012 introduced the new combined Remote Access role that combines Routing, VPN, DirectAccess, and Web Application Proxy.

- A single Remote Access server can provide both VPN and DirectAccess.

- Network Address Translation (NAT) allows multiple computers to share a single public IP address.

- The RemoteAccess Windows PowerShell module provides support for some VPN Server management functions, and the VpnClient module is used for VPN client functions.

- The Routing And Remote Access console is used to configure routing, NAT, and dial-up remote access and VPN remote access.

- Windows Server 2012 supports four VPN protocols: PPTP, L2TP, IKEv2, and SSTP.

- Windows Server optionally supports the RIPv2 routing protocol.

- Windows Server 2012 R2 adds Web Application Proxy as a reverse proxy to make applications available for external access. Web Application Proxy can publish applications in passthrough mode.

Objective review

1. What command do you use to install *only* VPN and NAT and their management tools?

    A. Enable-WindowsOptionalFeature -FeatureName RRAS -online

    B. Add-WindowsFeature -Name RemoteAccess -IncludeManagementTools

    C. Add-WindowsFeature -Name DirectAccess-VPN,Routing `
        -IncludeManagementTools

    D. Add-WindowsFeature -Name RRAS -IncludeManagementTools

2. You need to configure VPN to only support clients using the SSTP protocol. What changes do you need to make to the default VPN configuration in Windows Server 2012 R2?

    A. Add the WAN Miniport for SSTP and set the maximum number of ports. Restart the RemoteAccess service.

    B. Remove the PPTP WAN Miniport and set the maximum number of ports for PPTP to zero.

    C. Clear Remote Access Connections for the WAN Miniport (PPTP), WAN Miniport (IKEv2), and WAN Miniport (L2TP).

    D. Enable demand-dial for the WAN Miniport (PPPOE).

3. You use DirectAccess for all Windows 8 and later remote clients, but you use VPN to support Windows 7 clients. You need to configure VPN to use IP addresses controlled by the Remote Access server. What settings do you need to make? (Choose all that apply.)

   A. In the Routing And Remote Access console, select Assign Addresses Automatically.

   B. In the Routing And Remote Access console, select Assign Addresses From A Static Pool.

   C. In the DHCP Management console, create DHCP reservations for the IP addresses assigned to VPN clients.

   D. In the DHCP Management console, create a DHCP exclusion for the IP addresses assigned to VPN clients.

   E. In the Remote Access Management console, select Assign Addresses Automatically.

   F. In the Remote Access Management console, select Assign Addresses From A Static Address Pool.

Objective 3.4: Configure DirectAccess

Originally introduced in Windows Server 2008 R2 and Windows 7, DirectAccess is an always-on technology that allows remote management of domain-joined computers and optionally a transparent, always available, remote connection to the domain network that provides users remote access without having to initiate a VPN connection.

A DirectAccess remote connection has the following benefits as compared with VPNs:

- **Always-on** With a VPN, a user needs to initiate a connection before the computer is connected. With DirectAccess, the computer is connected to the domain network as soon as it has an Internet connection.

- **Seamless** A DirectAccess connected computer is transparently connected to the domain network. The computer seems to users as if they are directly connected to the domain network, with the exception of the connection speed, which is dependent on the Internet connection speed.

- **Security** A VPN connection is an unmanaged connection with Group Policy not enforced. A DirectAccess connection is a fully managed connection with all Group Policy Objects enforced; and management tools, such as Microsoft System Center Configuration Manager, can manage the client computer just as they do when it is connected locally. DirectAccess uses IPSec to authenticate the user and computer, and to encrypt communication.

Installing DirectAccess

There are two different scenarios for DirectAccess: remote management only or remote management plus remote access. In either scenario, the DirectAccess server can be directly connected to the Internet as the edge device or connected behind an edge device. When connected directly to the Internet, the DirectAccess server needs at least two network adapters. When connected behind an edge device, the DirectAccess server can have a single network adapter if the edge device is doing NAT.

Follow the steps in the section titled "Installing the Remote Access role" in Objective 3.3 to install the Remote Access role on the DirectAccess server. The Getting Started Wizard or the Remote Access Setup Wizard from the Remote Access Management console can be used to initially configure the Remote Access role (refer to Figure 3-31). Each enables you to install both DirectAccess and VPN on the same server. The Getting Started Wizard is a very useful tool for configuring DirectAccess with only a very few mouse clicks, but that process is not terribly interesting from an exam viewpoint. It also hides a lot of the decisions by making default choices. For this objective, focus on using the Remote Access Setup Wizard and installing the DirectAccess role only.

When you install DirectAccess, there are four stages of the installation:

- **Configure DirectAccess Client** DirectAccess clients can be configured for both remote access and remote management, or remote management only. You also need to configure which security groups to enable for DirectAccess. Only client computers that are explicitly allowed can connect via DirectAccess. You can also enable DirectAccess for mobile computers only. This is the default for the Getting Started Wizard.

- **Configure DirectAccess Server** The DirectAccess server configuration varies, depending on the physical topology of the network. You configure where the server is located on your network and what network configuration to use.

- **Configure Infrastructure Servers** The DirectAccess Infrastructure Server Setup Wizard is used to configure settings for the network location server, the DNS server, and management servers used by DirectAccess clients.

- **Configure Internal Application Servers** The DirectAccess Application Server Setup page enables you to configure IPsec authentication for end-to-end authentication and encryption to specified servers, if desired. Traffic between the DirectAccess client and the DirectAccess server is always authenticated and encrypted with IPsec.

Implementing client configuration

The first step of installing and configuring DirectAccess is to set the client configuration. These steps are performed at the server or by using the Remote Server Administrative Tools (RSAT). To install DirectAccess after the Remote Access role is installed, follow these steps:

1. Open the Remote Access Management console and select DirectAccess And VPN in the left pane (refer to Figure 3-31).

2. Click Run The Remote Access Setup Wizard to open the Welcome To Remote Access page of the Configure Remote Access Wizard, as shown in Figure 3-51.

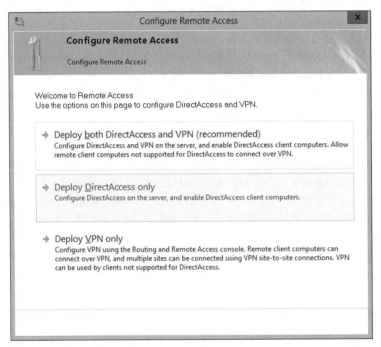

FIGURE 3-51 The Welcome To Remote Access page of the Configure Remote Access Wizard

The choices are as follows:

- **Deploy Both DirectAccess And VPN**   Configures the server as a VPN endpoint and also configures DirectAccess.

- **Deploy DirectAccess Only**   Configures the server as a DirectAccess server and enables DirectAccess client computers.

- **Deploy VPN Only**   Configures the servers as a VPN endpoint by using the Routing And Remote Access console. VPNs can be remote client VPNs or site-to-site VPNs. (VPNs are covered in Objective 3.3.)

For the sections in this objective, configure the Remote Access server by using the Deploy DirectAccess Only option.

3. Select Deploy DirectAccess Only to open the Configure Remote Access, Including The DirectAccess And VPN page, as shown in Figure 3-52.

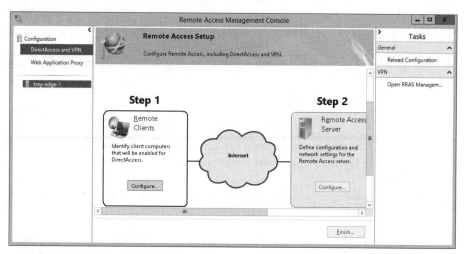

FIGURE 3-52 The Configure Remote Access, Including DirectAccess And VPN page

4. Click Configure in the Step 1 Remote Clients box to open the DirectAccess Client Setup Wizard shown in Figure 3-53. Choose whether DirectAccess clients will have remote access and remote management, or only remote management.

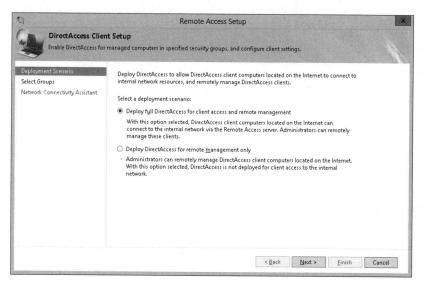

FIGURE 3-53 The Deployment Scenario page of the DirectAccess Client Setup Wizard

5. Click Next to open the Select Groups page of the DirectAccess Client Setup Wizard, as shown in Figure 3-54. The options are the following:

- Click Add to open the standard Select Groups dialog box to add security groups that will have DirectAccess enabled.

- Select Enable DirectAccess For Mobile Computers Only if you want DirectAccess to be enabled only on laptop and tablet computers.

EXAM TIP

The default for the Quick Start Wizard is to limit DirectAccess to mobile computers only. This sets up a scenario for which it is particularly easy to write an exam question. Why can laptops connect to the corporate network but not desktop computers?

- Select Use Force Tunneling to force DirectAccess clients to send all Internet traffic through the corporate network.

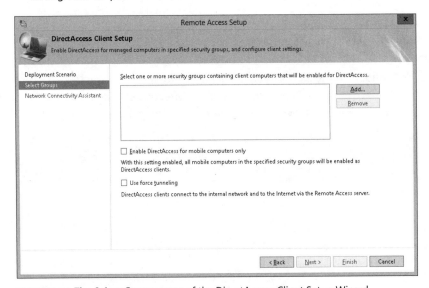

FIGURE 3-54 The Select Groups page of the DirectAccess Client Setup Wizard

6. Click Next to open the Network Connectivity Assistant page of the Direct Access Client Setup Wizard, as shown in Figure 3-55.

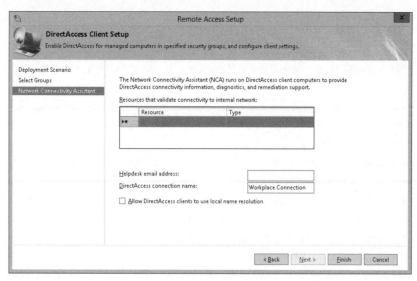

FIGURE 3-55 The Network Connectivity Assistant page of the DirectAccess Client Setup Wizard

7. Double-click in the first line in the Resources That Validate Connectivity To Internal Network box to open the Configure Corporate Resources For NCA dialog box shown in Figure 3-56. You can enter an HTTP address or a PING address that the Network Connectivity Assistant (NCA) can use to verify connectivity. You can add multiple resources if desired.

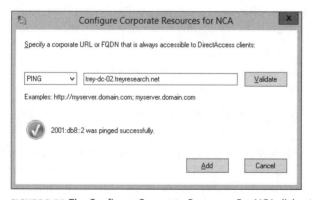

FIGURE 3-56 The Configure Corporate Resources For NCA dialog box

8. Select PING or HTTP for the resource type and enter the URL or FQDN of the resource. Click Validate to ensure that the resource is reachable.

9. Click Add to add the resource and return to the NCA page. On this page, you can also configure the following:

   - **Helpdesk Email Address** An email address dedicated to resolving DirectAccess client problems for remote users.

   - **DirectAccess Connection Name** A connection name that users will see on DirectAccess connected clients for the DirectAccess connection.

   - **Allow DirectAccess Clients To Use Local Name Resolution** When enabled, clients can use the broadcast protocols of NetBIOS over TCP/IP and Link-Local Multicast Name Resolution (LLMNR) to resolve single-level names when they can't resolve them through DNS. Local name resolution also needs to be configured on the Infrastructure Server Setup Wizard for this to work.

10. Click Finish; the DirectAccess Client Setup Wizard closes, and you're back at the main Configure Remote Access page. Step 1 now shows Edit instead of Configure.

Implementing server requirements

After you complete the client configuration section of Step 1 in the Configure Remote Access Wizard, the Configure button is enabled on Step 2. You can configure the DirectAccess server by following these steps:

1. Click the Configure button in Step 2 of the Remote Access Setup pane of the Remote Access Management console.

2. On the Network Topology page of the Remote Access Server Setup Wizard, select the topology that best describes your network. The choices are these:

   - **Edge** The DirectAccess server is at the edge of the internal network. The server has two network adapters, one of which is configured with a public IP address and is connected to the Internet. The second adapter is connected to the internal private network and has a private IP address.

   - **Behind An Edge Device (With Two Network Adapters)** The DirectAccess server is deployed behind an edge firewall or device. The server has two network adapters, one of which is connected to the perimeter network, and the other is connected to the internal private network. If the edge device uses NAT, only IP over HTTPS (IP-HTTPS) is deployed.

   - **Behind An Edge Device (With One Network Adapter)** The DirectAccess server is deployed with a single network adapter that is connected to the internal network. The edge device does NAT.

3. Enter the public DNS name or IPv4 address that remote clients use to connect to the remote access server, as shown in Figure 3-57.

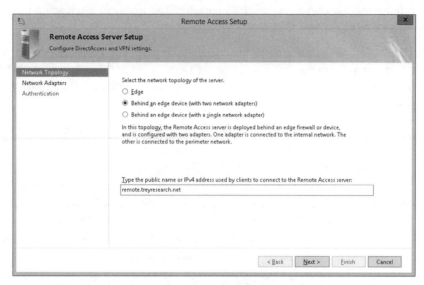

FIGURE 3-57 The Network Topology page of the Remote Access Server Setup Wizard

4. Click Next to open the Network Adapters page. The Remote Access Server Setup Wizard will attempt to determine your network adapter settings and configure them, as shown in Figure 3-58.

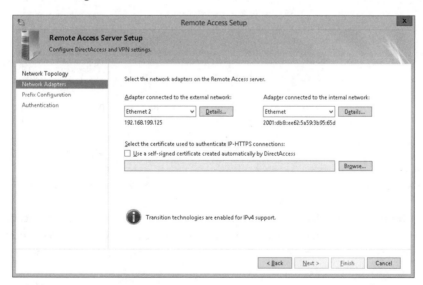

FIGURE 3-58 The Network Adapters page of the Remote Access Server Setup Wizard

5. Specify the certificate to use for IP-HTTPS connections. It can be a self-signed certificate that is automatically created by DirectAccess, or you can use a public certificate that matches the public DNS name or IP address you specified on the Network Topology page. Click Next.

6. On the Prefix Configuration page, the IPv6 prefix settings that have been detected are displayed, along with the IPv6 prefix that will be assigned to DirectAccess clients. You can edit these settings if they don't look right, but the wizard is usually correct. Click Next.

7. On the Authentication page, shown in Figure 3-59, specify the authentication used. The choices on the page are these:

   - **User Authentication**   Active Directory credentials is the default choice. You can, however, specify Two-Factor Authentication, which uses a smart card or one-time password (OTP). Beginning with Windows Server 2012, the client computer's Trusted Platform Module (TPM) can be used as a virtual smart card. OTP requires configuring RADIUS and other configuration steps that are beyond the scope of this portion of the exam, although you should know that it is an option.

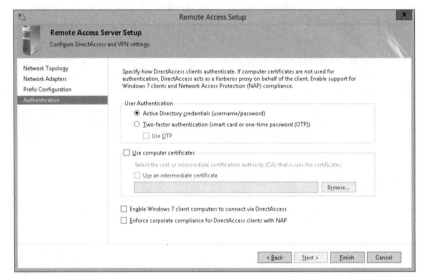

FIGURE 3-59 The Authentication page of the Remote Access Server Setup Wizard

   - **Computer Certificates**   The default is to use Kerberos for client authentication, which doesn't require a certificate. However, certificate authentication is required for two-factor authentication, for a multisite deployment, and for Windows 7 DirectAccess clients.

   - **Windows 7 Clients**   Windows 7 clients can't connect to a Windows Server 2012 DirectAccess deployment unless you configure computer certificates. If you select this box, it automatically selects the Use Computer Certificates box.

- **Network Access Protection** NAP is not supported for new DirectAccess deployments beginning with Windows Server 2012 R2.

8. Click Finish to close the Remote Access Server Setup Wizard and return to the Configure Remote Access Wizard. Step 2 now has an Edit button; and Step 3, Infrastructure Servers, has the Configure button enabled.

The settings on the Authentication page can also be configured with the Set-DAServer cmdlet.

Configuring DNS for DirectAccess

This item in the objective domain for the exam actually aligns with Step 3, the Infrastructure Server configuration, although Step 3 includes other name and location services. To run the Infrastructure Server Setup Wizard, follow these steps:

1. Click the Configure button in Step 3 of the Remote Access Setup pane of the Remote Access Management console.

2. On the Network Location Server page, enter the URL of the Network Location server if the server is on a remote web server and then click Validate. This is the preferred solution, but you can also host the network location server on the DirectAccess server. However, if you do, you need to provide a certificate or use a self-signed certificate, as shown in Figure 3-60.

3. On the DNS page of the Infrastructure Server Setup Wizard, shown in Figure 3-61, double-click the DNS Server Address to open the DNS Server Addresses dialog box.

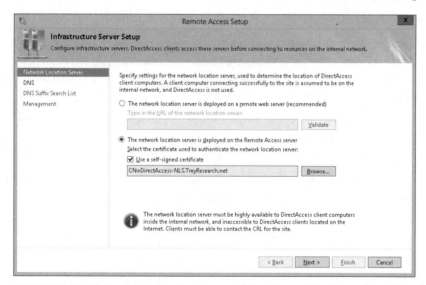

FIGURE 3-60 The Network Location Server page of the Infrastructure Server Setup Wizard

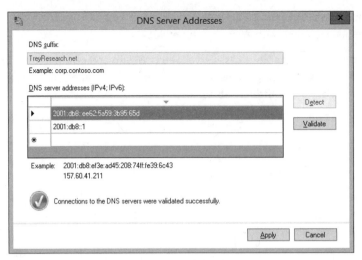

FIGURE 3-61 The DNS Server Addresses dialog box

4. Click the Validate button to validate the DNS Server address and DNS Suffix, and then click Apply to return to the DNS page. Select from the three Local Name Resolution options:

   - Use Local Name Resolution If The Name Does Not Exist In DNS. (Most restrictive)

   - Use Local Name Resolution If The Name Does Not Exist In DNS, Or DNS Servers Are Unreachable When The Client Computer Is On A Private Network. (Default, recommended)

   - Use Local Name Resolution For Any Kind Of DNS Resolution Error. (Least restrictive)

5. Click Next. On the DNS Suffix Search List page, shown in Figure 3-62, configure the Domain Suffixes to use for DNS search. The default values should include all detected internal domain DNS names. To add a suffix, use the New Suffix box plus the Add button. Use the up and down arrow buttons to reorder the list.

6. Click Next and enter any Management Servers on the Management page of the Infrastructure Server Setup Wizard. Any automatically discovered System Center Configuration Manager servers are added to the list after the wizard completes.

7. Click Finish to complete Step 3, Infrastructure Servers. Step 3 is changed to an Edit button, and Step 4 is now active with an enabled Configure button.

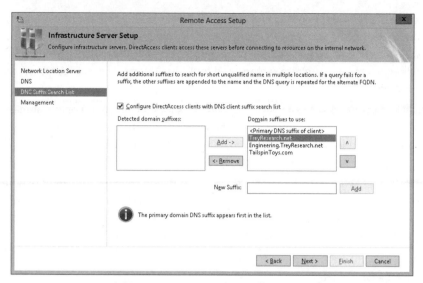

FIGURE 3-62 The DNS Suffix Search List page of the Infrastructure Server Setup Wizard

Step 4 of the Configure Remote Access Wizard is the DirectAccess Application Server Setup page. This page enables you to configure end-to-end authentication and encryption between the DirectAccess client and selected internal application servers. This is a single page with the option to Extend Authentication To Selected Application Servers, as shown in Figure 3-63.

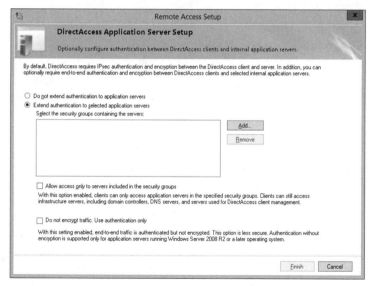

FIGURE 3-63 The DirectAccess Application Server Setup page

Add servers to the list for end-to-end authentication by adding the security group containing the servers to the list. You can restrict access to application servers to *only* the servers in the list by selecting Allow Access Only To Servers Included In The Security Groups. It does not restrict access to infrastructure servers used for DirectAccess, such as DNS servers and domain controllers.

You can also specify that the end-to-end scenario is for authentication only, but that encryption stops at the DirectAccess server. This less-secure option is available only for application servers running Windows Server 2008 R2 or later operating systems.

When you configure the Application Server settings, click Finish and then Finish again on the Remote Access Setup page to complete the configuration changes. The Remote Access Review page shown in Figure 3-64 opens. This page lists the GPO settings, Remote Clients settings, Remote Access Server settings, Infrastructure Server settings, and Application Server settings. You can save all these settings to a file by clicking the Save To A File link.

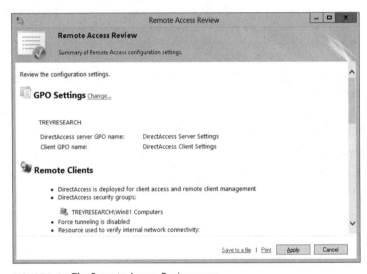

FIGURE 3-64 The Remote Access Review page

When you click Apply, the wizard will attempt to make the changes shown in the Remote Access Review page. If the wizard experiences a problem, it will identify it and then either roll back or issue a warning, as shown in Figure 3-65.

FIGURE 3-65 The Applying Remote Access Setup Wizard Settings dialog box

You can correct any errors and restart the applying step of the wizard from the main Remote Access Management console.

Configuring certificates for DirectAccess

Beginning with Windows Server 2012 and Windows 8, DirectAccess clients are configured to use Kerberos authentication by default. This means that Windows 8 and later clients do not need a certificate to connect. If you enable connecting with Windows 7 clients to a Windows Server 2012 or Windows Server 2012 R2 DirectAccess server, you need to enable computer certificate authentication. You also need to enable computer certificate authentication for two-factor authentication or for a multisite deployment of DirectAccess.

To enable computer certificate authentication, follow these steps:

1. Open the Remote Access Management console and select DirectAccess And VPN in the Configuration section of the left pane.

2. Click Edit in Step 2 Remote Access Server in the Remote Access Setup pane.

3. Click Authentication in the left pane and select Use Computer Certificates.

4. Select Use An Intermediate Certificate if you want to use an intermediate certificate authority certificate, such as the DirectAccess RADIUS certificate.

5. Click Browse to open a list of available certificates, as shown in Figure 3-66.

6. Select the certificate you want to use and click OK.

FIGURE 3-66 The Remote Access Setup Select A Certificate dialog box

Thought experiment

Configuring two-factor authentication

In this thought experiment, apply what you've learned about this objective. You can find answers to these questions in the "Answers" section at the end of this chapter.

You are the network administrator for TreyResearch.net. You're migrating from purely VPN remote access to primarily DirectAccess for remote access, with VPN for fallback only.

The sensitive nature of much of the research data that users work with is a compelling driver in the move to DirectAccess. You want to be sure that you can remotely manage the computers that are connecting to your network and that those computers are meeting all company policies.

1. You want to include two-factor authentication in your rollout of DirectAccess. What are the choices available, and what are the factors favoring each? What hardware or software considerations does your choice of two-factor authentication entail?

2. Because you intend to keep VPN available as a fallback option, what changes can you make to ensure that VPN also works with two-factor authentication? What other suggestions do you have for improving the security of the VPN fallback?

Objective summary

- DirectAccess can be installed for remote access and remote management, or for remote management only.
- Windows 8 and later clients do not require certificates for DirectAccess.
- To support Windows 7, DirectAccess must be configured with computer certificates.
- DirectAccess can be installed with one or two network adapters, and can be installed directly connected to the Internet, in a perimeter network, or behind a NAT device.
- Client computers must be explicitly allowed to connect via DirectAccess.
- DirectAccess is configured in four steps: Client, Server, Infrastructure Servers, and Application Servers.
- You can limit DirectAccess to mobile computers only.
- All DirectAccess computers must be domain joined.
- DirectAccess can be co-installed with VPN.

Objective review

1. You are the network administrator for TreyResearch.net. You have deployed DirectAccess, and initial acceptance has been good, but now some users report that they cannot connect to the corporate network since the rollout, but have used VPN as a fallback. Other users report that they can connect via DirectAccess without problems. Upon investigation, all users reporting that they cannot connect are on desktop computers. What are the possible causes? (Choose all that apply.)

   A. During initial setup, you configured DirectAccess with the Quick Start Wizard.

   B. During initial setup, you configured DirectAccess with the Remote Access Setup Wizard and cleared both the Use Force Tunneling and Enable DirectAccess for Mobile Computers Only check boxes in the DirectAccess Client Setup Wizard.

   C. During initial setup, you configured DirectAccess with the Remote Access Setup Wizard, and added the Mobile Computers Security Group and the Home Computers Security Group to the Enabled For DirectAccess field.

   D. All of the above.

   E. None of the above.

2. You are the network administrator for TreyResearch.net. Your current network topology has a single-edge device that performs firewall and NAT functions. All client computers run Windows 8.1 and use VPN for remote access. Your ISP has provided you with a single, static public IP address. You have been asked to deploy DirectAccess for remote access, and a server has been identified for the project. The server has a single network adapter. What are the minimum steps you need to do before you can enable DirectAccess? (Choose all that are required.)

   A. Purchase and install an additional network adapter for the identified server.

   B. Install Windows Server 2012 R2 on the identified server.

   C. Install the Remote Access role as a role on the server.

   D. Purchase an additional static IP address from your ISP.

   E. Decommission your existing edge device.

   F. All of the above.

   G. None of the above.

3. You are the network administrator for TreyResearch.net. After an initial test deployment of DirectAccess, which reported no issues, you have now deployed DirectAccess across all remote users. Users are reporting a significant slowing of Internet access. What are the possible causes? (Choose all that apply.)

   A. During initial setup, you configured DirectAccess with the Quick Start Wizard.

   B. During initial setup, you configured DirectAccess with the Remote Access Setup Wizard and selected Use Force Tunneling.

   C. During initial setup, you configured DirectAccess with the Remote Access Setup Wizard and selected Enable DirectAccess for Mobile Computers Only.

   D. None of the above.

Answers

This section contains the solutions to the thought experiments and answers to the lesson review questions in this chapter.

Objective 3.1: Thought experiment

1. Secondary zones provide fast and efficient lookups because they need updating only when there are actual changes. They are local to the users who use them, reducing network traffic. But they are a security concern because they have the full list of all servers and clients in the zone, and they are located in what is often a less-secure environment of the branch office. Other solutions that could be considered are stub zones or conditional forwarders. Both would have a higher initial network traffic, but local caching would quickly overcome that. Another possible solution is to consider putting a Read-Only Domain Controller (RODC) at the branch offices. Doing so would provide faster resource lookups with the Active Directory-integrated zones loaded as read-only DNS records and also enable faster logons because logons wouldn't have to authenticate to the main office.

2. This is a classic scenario for zone delegation. Create the zone delegations and give limited admin privilege to someone in the Engineering group who can take control of the process.

3. Looking beyond just DNS zones, you might consider setting up an aggressive DNS record aging and scavenging schedule to keep the zones from building up lots of dead records. Also consider creating DHCP reservations for most or all the computers in use. As the computers get repurposed and renamed, they continue to get the same IP address and settings, which will simplify keeping track of machines. Also, if there's a lot of full rebuild going on, this is a perfect fit for enabling Windows Deployment Services (WDS) in the department.

Objective 3.1: Review

1. **Correct answer:** C
    A. **Incorrect**. You can't have both a zone file and a replication parameter.
    B. **Incorrect**. You can't have both a zone file and a replication parameter, and the replication is to the Forest, not the domain.
    C. **Correct**. Creates a primary zone, replicated to the domain.
    D. **Incorrect**. Creates a primary zone, but with Forest-wide delegation.

2. **Correct answer:** B

   A. **Incorrect**. Secondary zones can't be Active Directory-integrated, so they can't have a Replication parameter.

   B. **Correct**. The NetworkID, zone master, and zone file name are all correctly identified.

   C. **Incorrect**. The zone file name is incorrect. It should be "10.168.192.in-addr.arpa".

   D. **Incorrect**. The zone file name is not in the required .in-addr.arpa format.

3. **Correct answer:** A

   A. **Correct**. Creates a delegation of the child zone named Engineering to the domain controller trey-engdc-8.engineering.treyresearch.net.

   B. **Incorrect**. The Name parameter should point to the parent domain, and the NameServer parameter should point to the name server of the child domain.

   C. **Incorrect**. The Name parameter should point to the parent domain.

   D. **Incorrect**. The NameServer parameter should point to the DNS server of the child domain.

Objective 3.2: Thought experiment

1. Because all three servers are on the same subnet, netmask ordering will treat them as equivalent. Therefore, by using round robin load balancing, users connect to "rdsh". The first user gets connected to rdsh1, the second to rdsh2, and the third to rdsh3. The fourth gets connected to rdsh1, and so on. If the Remote Desktop Gateway (RD Gateway) is configured correctly, when one of the servers is unavailable, it is dropped from the rotation.

2. If you have three RDSH servers—rdsh1, rdsh2, and rdsh3—start by making three new A records: rdsh pointing to the IP address of rdsh1, a second rdsh pointing to the IP address of rdsh2, and a third rdsh A record pointing to the IP address of rdsh3. You then create an RD Gateway–managed computer group and add rdsh plus rdsh1, rdsh2, and rdsh3 to the group; and create an RDSH farm with appropriate resource authorization policy (RAP) and connection authorization policy (CAP) policies for it.

Objective 3.2: Review

1. **Correct answers:** C, D, E

   A. **Incorrect**. MX records are required only for mail servers.

   B. **Incorrect**. Depending on the specific application and the service it is providing, you might need to create one or more SRV records. In a real exam question, this would be very clearly called out.

   C. **Correct**. The basic Address record is required.

   D. **Correct**. The basic IPv6 Address record is required.

   E. **Correct**. If the network is using reverse lookup zones, one or two PTR records should be created (one for IPv4, and possibly one for IPv6 if the network uses reverse lookup records for IPv6). As with answer B, a real exam question would call out clearly whether reverse lookup was being used.

   F. **Incorrect**. CNAME records are usually needed for very specialized circumstances. Although it's possible that a particular application server might require one, especially during a transition period from an earlier version, normally CNAME records are not used.

2. **Correct answer:** A

   A. **Correct**. Creates a new name server record with the name "(same as parent folder)".

   B. **Incorrect**. Creates a separate folder with the name ns13 instead of creating the NS record in the parent folder with (same as parent folder).

   C. **Incorrect**. Misses the ZoneName parameter; instead, it has the zone name as the Name parameter.

   D. **Incorrect**. Has the NameServer and Name parameters reversed.

3. **Correct answer:** C

   A. **Incorrect**. You can't create or update the SOA record explicitly from Windows PowerShell.

   B. **Incorrect**. You can't create or update the SOA record explicitly from Windows PowerShell.

   C. **Correct**. The zone properties allow you to increment the version of the zone, which updates the SOA record.

   D. **Incorrect**. You don't modify the SOA record at the server level, but at the zone level.

Objective 3.3: Thought experiment

1. Unfortunately, the VPN protocol with the widest range of support is the one you probably don't want to use: PPTP. There are a number of security vulnerabilities related to PPTP, so it is no longer recommended. Many older clients using PPTP supported only MS-CHAP, which is now gone from the PPTP list of authentication providers. L2TP is also reasonably well supported by a wide range of clients.

2. Beginning with Windows Vista, Windows clients all support SSTP, which has the distinct advantage of being able to work behind virtually any firewall. However, it is not well supported natively by other operating systems, although there are third-party products that provide support.

3. Beginning with Windows 7, Windows clients support IKEv2, also known as VPN Reconnect. IKEv2 supports user or machine authentication and has the capability to seamlessly reconnect the VPN when the network adapter changes.

4. Both smart cards and OTPs can be used with VPN and DirectAccess. With smart cards, Windows 8 and later mobile users who have a TPM chip on their computer can use virtual smart cards to simplify the user experience.

5. Regardless of whether you choose smart cards or OTPs, you have to implement a Public Key Infrastructure (PKI) to support computer certificates. If you choose OTP, you also have to implement RADIUS.

Objective 3.3: Review

1. **Correct answer:** C

    A. **Incorrect**. This is a client-only cmdlet from the DISM module.

    B. **Incorrect**. Installs the Remote Access role, but not the VPN or Routing role features.

    C. **Correct**. Installs the Remote Access role and the DirectAccess-VPN and Routing role features. The DirectAccess-VPN role feature meets the VPN requirement in the question, and the Routing role feature meets the NAT requirement. The -IncludeManagementTools parameter ensures that all management tools are also installed.

    D. **Incorrect**. Not an available Windows role. The RRAS role has been replaced by the Remote Access role, and VPNs have been combined with DirectAccess in a unified remote access role.

2. **Correct answer:** C

   A. **Incorrect**. All WAN miniport devices are installed by default.

   B. **Incorrect**. Removes one of the WAN miniports, but leaves L2TP and IKEv2 still available.

   C. **Correct**. Disables remote access for these protocols.

   D. **Incorrect**. This is an outgoing protocol, not an incoming one.

3. **Correct answers:** D, F

   A. **Incorrect**. Because DirectAccess is enabled, you make VPN changes on the Remote Access Management console.

   B. **Incorrect**. Because DirectAccess is enabled, you make VPN changes on the Remote Access Management console.

   C. **Incorrect**. You don't make DHCP reservations; instead, make a DHCP exclusion.

   D. **Correct**. You have to make a DHCP exclusion to ensure that the Remote Access server doesn't give a remote client the same IP address as an internal one.

   E. **Incorrect**. This would use DHCP, and the address assigned to the remote client would not be controlled by the Remote Access server.

   F. **Correct**. Enables the Remote Access server to control the assignment of IP addresses for remote VPN clients.

Objective 3.4: Thought experiment

1. Three choices are available: physical smart cards, virtual smart cards, and OTPs.

2. Physical smart cards are expensive and complicated to deploy, but can be easily integrated into the VPN strategy. You have to ensure that all users have a smart card reader, and provide a solution to reset the smart cards, and so on.

3. Virtual smart cards require only a TPM, and it is already company policy to require a TPM and BitLocker on all company mobile devices because they routinely work with sensitive data. With a TPM already assured, using virtual smart cards is a compelling solution. It does not, however, solve the issue of remote users who are on non-TPM desktop computers, and those users need to be addressed. However, the new corporate desktop specification includes at least two desktop options that have a TPM, so rolling that out to remote users should be a priority.

4. OTPs are simple and easy to use, require only a smartphone app for users to generate their password, and need no extra hardware for desktop users. However, they require deploying RADIUS servers, and do nothing to address desktop remote users who do not have a TPM and BitLocker, so you'd likely want to consider upgrading them even though you didn't plan to use virtual smart cards.

5. You should require two-factor authentication of VPN as well as DirectAccess, and deploy the same solution across both. Also consider removing PPTP and L2TP as VPN protocols.

Objective 3.4: Review

1. **Correct answer:** A

    A. **Correct**. The Quick Start Wizard defaults to selecting the Enable DirectAccess for Mobile Computers Only option.

    B. **Incorrect**. By clearing the Enable DirectAccess for Mobile Computers Only check box, DirectAccess is allowed for both mobile and non-mobile devices.

    C. **Incorrect**. By adding the Home Computers and Mobile Computers security groups, both home users' and mobile users' computers are enabled for DirectAccess.

    D. **Incorrect**. Only answer A is a possible cause of only mobile computers being able to connect via DirectAccess.

    E. **Incorrect**. Only answer A is a possible cause of only mobile computers being able to connect via DirectAccess.

2. **Correct answers:** B, C

    A. **Incorrect**. DirectAccess can be installed with a single network adapter.

    B. **Correct**. Windows Server must be installed on the server.

    C. **Correct**. The Remote Access role must be installed on the server.

    D. **Incorrect**. Only a single public IP address is required.

    E. **Incorrect**. With a single network adapter, DirectAccess can be installed behind a NAT device. If the edge device were decommissioned, you'd also need to add an additional network adapter, but you would have additional options for DirectAccess protocols.

    F. **Incorrect**. Incorrect because A, D, and E are incorrect.

    G. **Incorrect**. Incorrect because B and C are correct.

3. **Correct answer:** B

   A. **Incorrect.** Using the Quick Start Wizard would not have created a configuration that was affected by the number of actual users on the system.

   B. **Correct.** By selecting Use Force Tunneling, you have forced all remote traffic through the company's network connection. This actually causes a double load on the Internet connection, since remote users have to first connect inbound, and then outbound through the company's Internet connection. The extra load wasn't particularly noticeable for a few test users, but with many remote users you are now saturating the Internet connection, causing a general slowdown.

   C. **Incorrect.** This would have no effect on Internet connection speed for users.

   D. **Incorrect.** Since answer B is a possible answer, this can't be correct.

CHAPTER 4

Configure a Network Policy Server infrastructure

The Network Policy Server (NPS) is used to create and enforce network access policies for client health and the authentication and authorization of connection requests. NPS can be configured as a Remote Authentication Dial-In User Service (RADIUS) server or RADIUS proxy to forward connection requests to other NPS or RADIUS servers. Windows Server 2012 includes a new NPS module for Windows PowerShell.

Objectives in this chapter:

- Objective 4.1: Configure Network Policy Server (NPS)
- Objective 4.2: Configure NPS policies
- Objective 4.3: Configure Network Access Protection (NAP)

Objective 4.1: Configure Network Policy Server (NPS)

NPS can be configured as a RADIUS server, as a RADIUS proxy, and as a Network Access Protection (NAP) server. NPS can be configured as any combination of these three servers. This objective covers how to configure RADIUS and RADIUS proxy, leaving the NAP configuration for Objective 4.3.

> **This objective covers how to:**
> - Configure a RADIUS server, including RADIUS proxy
> - Configure multiple RADIUS server infrastructures
> - Configure RADIUS clients
> - Manage RADIUS templates
> - Configure RADIUS accounting
> - Configure certificates
> - Configure NPS templates

Configuring a RADIUS server, including RADIUS proxy

You can install the Network Policy and Access Services (NPAS) role to enable Windows Server to act as a RADIUS server. To do that, follow these steps on Windows Server 2012 R2:

1. In Server Manager, select Add Roles And Features from the Manage menu.

2. If you see the Before You Begin page, click Next.

3. Select Role-based Or Feature-based Installation and click Next.

4. Select the server on which you want to install NPS and click Next.

5. On the Select Server Roles page, select Network Policy And Access Services.

6. On the Add Features That Are Required For Network Policy And Access Services page, click Add Features to return to the Select Server Roles page.

7. Click Next twice, read the Network Policy And Access Services page, and click Next again.

8. On the Select Role Services page, shown in Figure 4-1, select Network Policy Server. You don't need either of the other two roles right now.

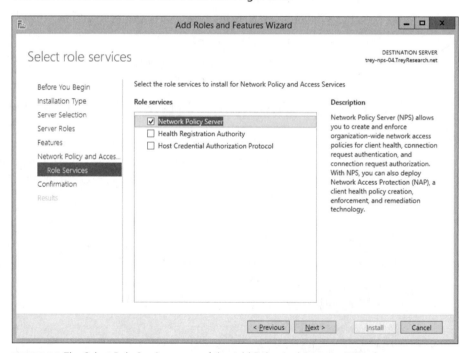

FIGURE 4-1 The Select Role Services page of the Add Roles And Features Wizard

9. Click Next and then click Install. When the installation is complete, click Close to close the Add Roles And Features Wizard.

To install the NPAS role, including only the NPS role service, by using Windows PowerShell, use the following command:

```
Install-WindowsFeature -Name NPAS,NPAS-Policy-Server -IncludeManagementTools
```

EXAM TIP

NPS can't be installed on a failover cluster, nor can it be installed on a Windows Server Core installation. These are the kinds of details that exam writers like.

Configuring RADIUS server for VPN

After NPS is installed, you have to do basic configuration: set a friendly name, the IP address, and a shared secret with the virtual private network (VPN) client.

To configure NPS as a RADIUS server for VPN, follow these steps:

1. Open the Network Policy Server console, shown in Figure 4-2, from Server Manager or by typing **nps.msc** at an elevated command prompt.

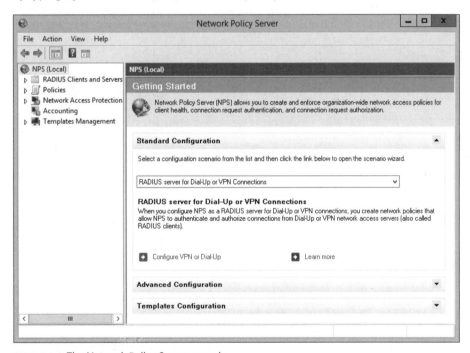

FIGURE 4-2 The Network Policy Server console

2. In the Standard Configuration pane, select RADIUS Server For Dial-up Or VPN Connections from the list.

3. Click Configure VPN Or Dial-up. Select Virtual Private Network (VPN) Connections and click Next to accept the default text for the connection.

4. On the Specify Dial-up Or VPN Server page, click Add to add a RADIUS client.

NOTE **RADIUS CLIENTS**

RADIUS clients are not Windows client computers; they are VPN servers such as Windows Server 2012 R2 running the Remote Access role. The VPN server is a client of the authorization and authentication service of the RADIUS server. The NPS or RADIUS server services authentication requests from RADIUS clients (VPN servers).

5. On the New RADIUS Client page, shown in Figure 4-3, enter a name in the Friendly Name box.

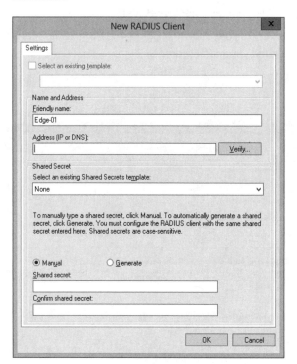

FIGURE 4-3 The New RADIUS Client dialog box

6. Enter the IP address or DNS name of the VPN server (RADIUS Client). Click Verify.

7. In the Verify Address dialog box, shown in Figure 4-4, click Resolve to verify that the name or IP address can be resolved.

FIGURE 4-4 The Verify Address dialog box

8. Click OK to return to the New RADIUS Client dialog box.

9. In the Shared Secret section of the New Radius Client dialog box, select Manual to type in a manual shared secret. Or select Generate and then click Generate to generate a very long, random shared secret.

> **NOTE** **LONG SHARED SECRETS**
>
> The shared secret generated by the wizard is longer than some RADIUS clients can support. You can shorten it by deleting a portion and still retain the preferred randomness of the shared secret. However, if your RADIUS client is Windows Server 2012 R2 with the Remote Access role installed, the full length of the generated secret can be used.

10. Copy the shared secret and paste into the RADIUS client, as shown in Figure 4-5. (This is a Windows Server 2012 R2 server with the Remote Access role installed, configured for VPN, but there is an equivalent for any brand or type of RADIUS client.)

11. Click OK to add the RADIUS client. Click Add to add additional clients, Edit to change the settings for a client, or Remove to remove a client from the list of supported RADIUS clients.

12. Click Next to open the Configure Authentication Methods page shown in Figure 4-6. The authentication methods supported are as follows:

   - **Extensible Authentication Protocol** Use this protocol to support smart cards, Protected Extensible Authentication Protocol (PEAP), and EAP-MSCHAPv2.

   - **Microsoft Encrypted Authentication Version 2 (MS-CHAPv2)** The default; it allows users to specify a password for authentication.

   - **Microsoft Encrypted Authentication (MS-CHAP)** Use only if you need to support operating systems that don't support MS-CHAPv2.

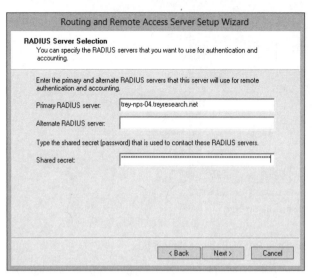

FIGURE 4-5 The Routing And Remote Access Server Setup Wizard

FIGURE 4-6 The Configure Authentication Methods page of the Configure VPN Or Dial-Up Wizard

13. Click Next; on the Specify User Groups page, add the security groups that should be allowed to connect via VPN. Click Next.

14. On the Specify IP Filters page, shown in Figure 4-7, you can specify input and output filters for IPv4, IPv6, or both. You can choose from a filter template or specify directly. IP filters allow you to specify source or destination network ranges, along with the protocols that are allowed or disallowed.

FIGURE 4-7 The Specify IP Filters page of the Configure VPN Or Dial-Up Wizard

15. Click Next to specify the level of encryption that will be supported:

- Basic Encryption (MPPE 40-bit)
- Strong Encryption (MPPE 56-bit)
- Strongest Encryption (MPPE 128-bit)

16. Deselect any encryption levels you don't need to support and click Next.

17. In Specify A Realm Name, you can specify a realm name that an ISP can use to specify which connections should be routed to this server.

18. Click Next, confirm the settings, and then click Finish to complete the wizard.

Configuring RADIUS server for dial-up

The steps for configuring the RADIUS server for dial-up connections are identical to those for VPN connections. The only difference is in the first page. The Type Of Connections, as shown in Figure 4-8, sets the portion of the name related to the type.

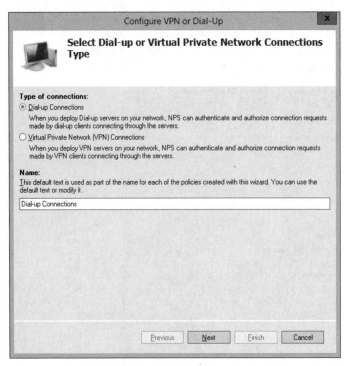

FIGURE 4-8 The Select Dial-Up Or Virtual Private Network Connections Type page

Even if the wizard makes no other distinction during the process of creating the policies for VPN and dial-up clients, the resulting policies are different. The policy for a VPN connection is to use a NAS port type of Virtual (VPN). For dial-up, it is Async (Modem) OR ISDN Sync OR ISDN AsyncV.120 OR ISDN Async V.110.

You can also configure a different set of users, authentication methods, realm, and encryption strength for dial-up and VPN clients, even when using the same server to support both methods of remote access.

Configuring a RADIUS proxy

You can configure a RADIUS server to act as a proxy that forwards requests for RADIUS authentication to other RADIUS servers, depending on the client making the request and the connection request policies configured on the RADIUS server. A RADIUS proxy can also act as a proxy for RADIUS Accounting, described later in this objective.

A RADIUS proxy acts as a traffic coordinator between RADIUS clients and other RADIUS servers or other RADIUS proxies. An NPS server acting as a RADIUS proxy can connect to other Microsoft NPS servers or third-party RADIUS servers, or any combination thereof. Figure 4-9 shows a Microsoft NPS server acting as a RADIUS proxy.

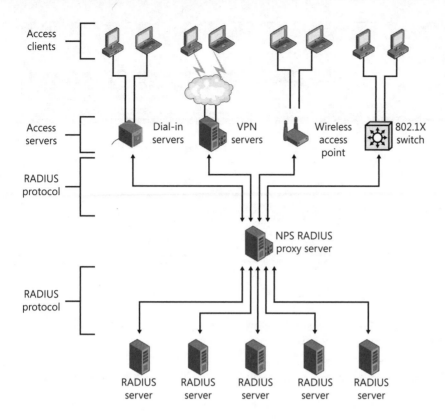

FIGURE 4-9 A RADIUS architecture with an NPS RADIUS proxy

To enable an NPS server to act as a RADIUS proxy, follow these steps:

1. Open the Network Policy Server console.

2. Select NPS (Local) at the top of the console tree.

3. In the Getting Started details pane, expand the Advanced Configuration section.

4. Scroll down to the Configure RADIUS Proxy section near the bottom of the Getting Started section, as shown in Figure 4-10.

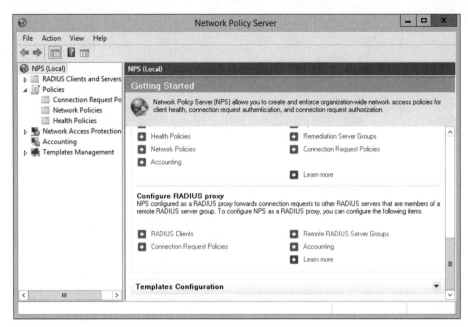

FIGURE 4-10 The Network Policy Server console

5. Click RADIUS Clients to specify which RADIUS clients will connect through this proxy.

FIGURE 4-11 The New RADIUS Client dialog box

6. Right-click in the RADIUS Clients details pane and select New from the menu to open the New RADIUS Client dialog box shown in Figure 4-11.

7. Specify the friendly name, IP address and shared secret to connect with the client.

8. Click Advanced to specify a specific RADIUS vendor and specify additional options, as shown in Figure 4-12.

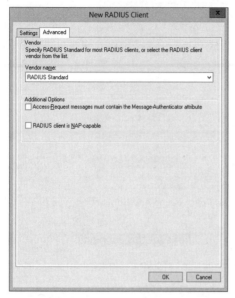

FIGURE 4-12 The Advanced tab of the New RADIUS Client dialog box

9. Click OK to return to the Network Policy Server console.

10. Right-click Connection Request Policy in the Policies folder of the console tree and select New from the menu to open the New Connection Request Policy Wizard.

11. Enter a Policy Name and specify a Type Of Network Access Server, as shown in Figure 4-13.

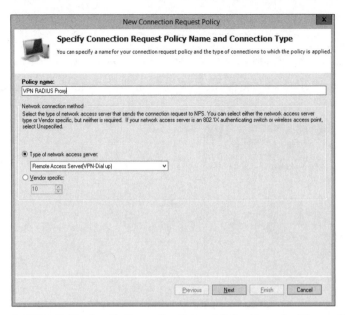

FIGURE 4-13 The Specify Connection Request Policy Name And Connection Type page

12. Click Next and then Add to specify the conditions for this connection request policy.

13. Select a condition from the Select Condition list shown in Figure 4-14 and click Add.

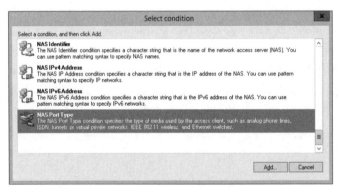

FIGURE 4-14 The Select Condition page

14. In the condition dialog box for the specified condition, select the appropriate conditions. For the shown NAS Port Type, you would specify Virtual (VPN) to build a policy for VPNs.

15. Click OK to return to the Select Condition page. If you want to add additional conditions, click Add again and repeat steps 13 and 14 as desired. Click Next to select the Specify Connection Request Forwarding page shown in Figure 4-15.

FIGURE 4-15 The Specify Connection Request Forwarding page

16. Select the server group to which this RADIUS server should forward authentication requests. You can create a new group of servers by clicking New and defining a new RADIUS server group.

17. Select Accounting in the Settings pane to specify forwarding of RADIUS Accounting to a RADIUS server group.

18. Click Next to open the Configure Settings page shown in Figure 4-16.

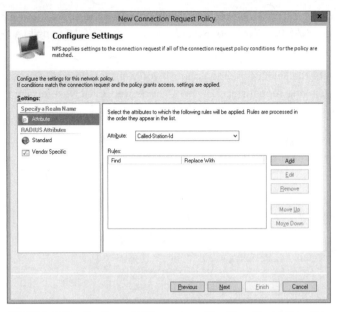

FIGURE 4-16 The Configure Settings page of the New Connection Request Policy Wizard

19. Specify any additional settings, such as the Realm Name Attribute, click Next, and then click Finish to complete the policy creation.

20. You can also configure Remote RADIUS Server Groups And Accounting from the Getting Started details pane if you need to add a new group of servers.

Configuring multiple RADIUS server infrastructures

You can use NPS as a RADIUS proxy to build a multiple RADIUS server infrastructure. Acting as a RADIUS proxy, NPS can forward requests to different RADIUS servers based on the RADIUS client criteria, type of authentication or port used, or the originating or targeted IP address of the request. Remote RADIUS servers do not need to be in a trusted domain, allowing you to use NPS to service authentication requests against a RADIUS server that is not part of the Windows domain.

Use RADIUS server groups to configure a named group that has one or more RADIUS servers. Each member of a RADIUS server group must have a unique IP address or DNS name that resolves to a unique IP address. You can forward authentication requests, accounting requests, or both to each member of a remote RADIUS server group.

Using priority and weight settings for the group members in a remote RADIUS server group enables you to do load balancing for the group. Within a group, the primary server has a priority of 1. All members of the group with the same priority are sent RADIUS messages in weighted order. Consider server group RADIUS1, with three members (server1, server2, and server3) in the group. All servers have a priority of 1, and the servers have the following weights:

- Server1, weight 10
- Server2, weight 15
- Server3, weight 25

If the RADIUS proxy has 100 RADIUS messages for the group to process, server1 will be sent 20 to process, server2 will get 30 messages, and server3 will process 50 messages.

EXAM TIP

Exam writers like to use features like priority and weight to build questions that test not only your understanding of basic math, but also your understanding of precedence. Be alert for combinations that go against expectations, such as a low priority number and a low weight combined with a higher priority number and higher weight.

You can create a remote RADIUS server group while configuring a connection policy with the New Connection Request Policy Wizard, or by following these steps:

1. Open the Network Policy Server console.

2. Expand NPS (Local) at the top of the console tree.

3. Right-click Remote RADIUS Server Groups in the RADIUS Clients And Servers folder. Select New from the menu.

4. In the New Remote RADIUS Server Group dialog box shown in Figure 4-17, enter a Group Name and then click Add to add a server to the group.

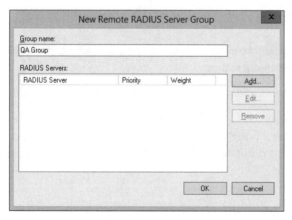

FIGURE 4-17 The New Remote RADIUS Server Group dialog box

5. On the Address tab of the Add RADIUS Server dialog box, specify the IP address or DNS name for the server. Click the Authentication/Accounting tab.

6. On the Authentication/Accounting tab shown in Figure 4-18, you can specify the details for the server, including Authentication Port, Shared Secret, Accounting Port, and a separate shared secret for the accounting function if needed.

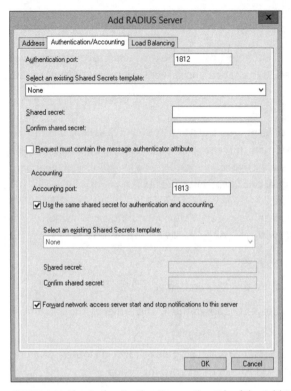

FIGURE 4-18 The Authentication/Accounting tab of the Add RADIUS Server dialog box

7. Click the Load Balancing tab shown in Figure 4-19, to specify Priority and Weight for the new server, along with timeout settings.

8. Click OK to close the dialog box and add the RADIUS server to the server group.

9. Click Add to add additional servers to the Remote RADIUS Server Group, Edit to change an existing server's settings, Remove to delete a server from the group, or OK to finish adding servers to the group and return to the Network Policy Server console.

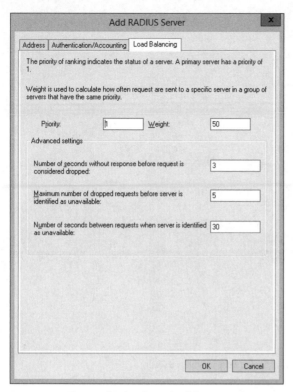

FIGURE 4-19 The Load Balancing tab of the New RADIUS Server dialog box

Configuring RADIUS clients

You need to configure RADIUS clients to connect to the RADIUS server. To configure an existing RADIUS client, right-click the client in the RADIUS Clients node of the RADIUS Clients And Servers folder of the Network Policy Server console and select Properties from the menu. To configure a new RADIUS client, follow these steps:

1. Open the Network Policy Server console (nps.msc) and expand NPS (Local) in the console tree.

2. In the RADIUS Clients and Servers folder, right-click RADIUS Clients and select New from the menu.

3. On the Settings page of the New RADIUS Client dialog box shown in Figure 4-20, enter a Friendly Name to identify the RADIUS client, and then enter the DNS name or IP address of the RADIUS client.

FIGURE 4-20 The New RADIUS Client dialog box

4. Click Verify to open the Verify Address dialog box shown in Figure 4-21. Click Resolve to resolve the address. If more than one IP address is identified for the client, select the preferred IP address and click OK.

FIGURE 4-21 The Verify Address dialog box

5. Enter and Confirm a shared secret, or select Generate and click the Generate button to generate a very long, random shared secret. This shared secret is case-sensitive and must be entered into the shared secret box on the RADIUS client exactly.

6. Click the Advanced tab to configure the RADIUS Vendor and additional options. Choose RADIUS Standard for the Vendor Name unless your RADIUS client specifically requires a vendor-specific setting.

7. If your RADIUS client supports the Message-Authenticator attribute, select Access-Request Messages Must Contain The Message-Authentication Attribute to improve security when using MS-CHAPv2.

8. Click OK to create the new RADIUS client.

You can create a new RADIUS client with the New-NpsRadiusClient cmdlet, as shown here:

```
New-NpsRadiusClient `
        -Name trey-edge-01 `
        -Address 192.168.10.1 `
        -SharedSecret "qboTFf^&JK#kHq17ffHXwIK2WcVLzNcABv"
```

Managing RADIUS templates

You can create templates that simplify setting and configuring NPS across multiple servers and clients, as follows:

- Shared secrets
- RADIUS clients
- Remote RADIUS servers
- IP filters
- Health policies
- Remediation server groups

Each template contains the settings for that type of configuration, and can be saved and used to simplify configuring additional items. In addition, the templates can be exported and used on other NPS RADIUS servers.

To create a new shared secrets template, follow these steps:

1. In the Network Policy Server console, expand the Templates Management node.

2. Right-click Shared Secrets and select New.

3. In the New RADIUS Shared Secret Template dialog box, enter a name for the template.

4. Select Manual to manually enter a shared secret or Generate to generate a very long random secret, as shown in Figure 4-22.

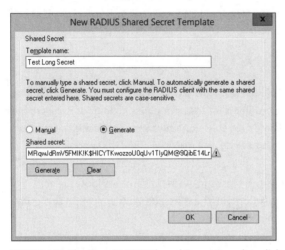

FIGURE 4-22 The New RADIUS Shared Secret Template dialog box

5. Click Generate to generate the shared secret and then click OK to save the template.

To create a template for RADIUS clients, right-click RADIUS Clients in Templates Management and select New from the menu. Follow the steps described earlier in the "Configuring RADIUS clients" section to configure the template; the settings will be saved as a template when you finish and click OK. You can use a similar process to create templates for Remote RADIUS Servers, IP filters, health policies, and Remediation Server Groups.

Configuring RADIUS accounting

In addition to authenticating and authorizing access, NPS supports RADIUS Accounting to log user authentication and accounting requests to either a local file or a SQL Server XML-compliant database. You can configure accounting to four different modes:

- **SQL logging only** Configures NPS to connect log accounting data to a SQL Server database.

- **Test logging only** Configures NPS to log accounting data to a local text file.

- **Parallel logging** Configures NPS to log to both a local text file and a SQL Server database.

- **SQL logging with backup**   Configures NPS to log to a SQL Server database, and configures text logging to be used if the SQL Server logging fails.

To configure RADIUS accounting to a local file, follow these steps:

1. In the Network Policy Server console, select the Accounting node in the console tree and click Configure Accounting in the details pane.

2. On the Introduction page, click Next. On the Select Accounting Options page, select Log To A Text File On The Local Computer and click Next.

3. On the Configure Local File Logging page shown in Figure 4-23, select which events to log and specify a new location to store the logs.

FIGURE 4-23 The Configure Local File Logging page of the Accounting Configuration Wizard

4. The default log file location is C:\Windows\system32\LogFiles. This location should be changed, ideally to a separate partition, because an active RADIUS server can generate large amounts of log data. Click Browse to select a new location to use for accounting logs.

5. If you want users to be able to connect even if there is a problem with accounting, clear the If Logging Fails, Discard Connection Requests check box.

6. Click Next and then Next again on the Summary page. The accounting configuration is complete. Click Close to exit the wizard.

The NPS server can be configured to use SQL Server for logging. When you configure SQL Server Logging, the Accounting Configuration Wizard configures the data connection to the SQL Server and either configures an existing database or creates a new one. The choices of what to log and whether to fail connection requests if the logging is unavailable are the same as for file logging. The Data Link Properties dialog box is shown in Figure 4-24.

FIGURE 4-24 The Data Link Properties dialog box

Configuring certificates

The NPS server can be configured to do certificate-based authentication PEAP and Extensible Authentication Protocol (EAP) authentication, which requires a Workstation Authentication certificate for the client computer and a Server Authentication certificate for the NPS server. Full coverage of how to configure Active Directory Certificate Services (AD CS) is in Exam 70-412, but what you need to know for this exam is the type of certificate template to use and how to configure for autoenrollment.

Configuring autoenrollment

If you're using AD CS, configure Group Policy to autoenroll certificates to both servers and clients by configuring the Default Domain Policy. To enable autoenrollment, follow these steps:

1. Open the Group Policy Management Console (gpmc.msc); in the console tree, expand the domain you want to configure.

2. Expand Group Policy Objects and right-click Default Domain Policy. Select Edit from the menu.

3. In the Group Policy Management Editor, navigate to Computer Configuration/Policies/ Windows Settings/Security Settings/Public Key Policies.

4. In the Object Type pane, double-click Certificate Services Client - Auto-Enrollment.

5. On the Enrollment Policy Configuration tab shown in Figure 4-25, select Enabled from the Configuration Model list.

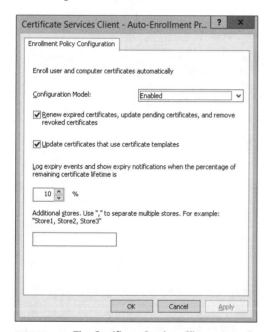

FIGURE 4-25 The Certificate Services Client - Auto-Enrollment Properties dialog box

6. Select the Renew Expired Certificates, Update Pending Certificates, And Remove Revoked Certificates check box, and then select Update Certificates That Use Certificate Templates.

7. Click OK, and then exit out of the Group Policy Management Editor and the Group Policy Management Console.

Configuring computer certificates for client and server authentication

You need to configure the *purpose* of the certificate you will use to support client and server authentication. To do this, start with the Workstation Authentication certificate template.

EXAM TIP

Some certificates are created with a purpose named All. This kind of certificate is intended to work for all purposes, but does not work for NPS client authentication or server authentication. Sounds like an exam question to me!

To configure a certificate for use by NPS, follow these steps on the AD CS computer:

1. Open the Certificate Authority and expand the domain for which you're creating the certificate.

2. Right-click Certificate Templates and select Manage from the menu.

3. In the Certificate Templates Console shown in Figure 4-26, right-click Workstation Authentication and select Duplicate Template from the menu.

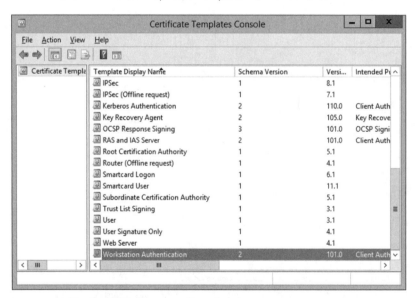

FIGURE 4-26 The Certificate Templates Console

4. On the General tab, type a new Template Display Name that describes the use of the certificate, such as **NPS Client-Server Authentication**, and select Publish Certificate In Active Directory.

5. Click the Extensions tab shown in Figure 4-27 and then click Edit.

FIGURE 4-27 The Extensions tab of the Properties of New Template dialog box

6. In the Edit Application Policies Extension, click Add and then select Server Authentication from the list of Application Policies, as shown in Figure 4-28.

FIGURE 4-28 The Add Application Policy dialog box

7. Click OK and then OK again to return to the Properties dialog box.

8. Click the Security tab and select Domain Computers.

9. Select the Allow box for Autoenroll. Click OK to close the Properties dialog box.

10. Close the Certificate Templates Console.

11. In the Certification Authority console, right-click Certificate Templates and select New and then Certificate Template To Issue.

12. In the Enable Certificate Templates dialog box shown in Figure 4-29, select the certificate template you just configured and click OK.

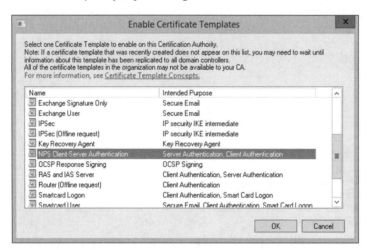

FIGURE 4-29 The Enable Certificate Templates dialog box

13. Close the Certificate Authority console.

Configuring NPS templates

The configuration of several RADIUS–related NPS templates were shown earlier in the "Managing RADIUS templates" section, but there are a couple of additional template types you should know about: the health policies and remediation server groups templates.

The health policies templates cover the system health validator (SHV) checks. To create a new health policy template, follow these steps:

1. Expand the Templates Management node of the Network Policy Server console and right-click Health Policies.

2. In the Create New Health Policy dialog box shown in Figure 4-30, enter a Policy Name and specify the client reporting of the SHVs.

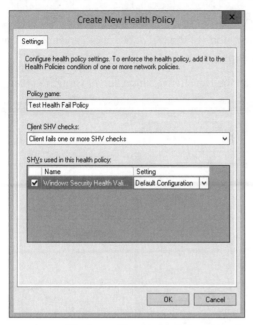

FIGURE 4-30 The Create New Health Policy dialog box

3. The options for Client SHV Checks are these:

   ■ Client Passes All SHV Checks

   ■ Client Fails All SHV Checks

   ■ Client Passes One Or More SHV Checks

   ■ Client Fails One Or More SHV Checks

   ■ Client Reported As Transitional By One Or More SHVs

   ■ Client Reported As Infected By One Or More SHVs

   ■ Client Reported As Unknown By One Or More SHVs

4. Under SHVs Used In This Health Policy, select Windows Security Health Validator with the Default Configuration, as shown in Figure 4-30.

5. Click OK to create the template.

> **NOTE NAP**
>
> The details for creating, configuring, and using SHVs are covered in Objective 4.3. This objective deals only with how to create a template that uses an SHV.

You can create a remediation server group template by following these steps:

1. Expand the Templates Management node of the Network Policy Server console and right-click Remediation Server Groups.

2. Select New from the menu to open the New Remediation Server Group template shown in Figure 4-31.

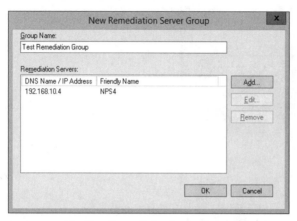

FIGURE 4-31 The New Remediation Server Group dialog box

3. Type a Group Name for the template group.

4. Click Add to add servers to the group.

5. Enter a Friendly Name for the server and then enter the IP Address Or DNS Name of the server. Click Resolve to resolve an IP address for a DNS name.

6. Click OK to add the server to the group.

7. You can add additional servers to the group by repeating steps 4–6.

8. Click OK after you finish adding servers to the group, and the template is created.

Thought experiment
Configuring different servers for different users

In this thought experiment, apply what you've learned about this objective. You can find answers to these questions in the "Answers" section at the end of this chapter.

You are the network administrator for TreyResearch.net and are designing a Remote Access policy to support connection for different groups of users. Network administrators will have access to dial-up modems, and the HR department has special requirements to ensure additional security.

1. How do you need to configure the dial-up access? Will you need to have a separate NPS server?

2. How can you configure extra security for HR without requiring it for everyone?

3. Can you use a single server to implement these requirements? What are the considerations?

Objective summary

- NPS can be configured as a RADIUS server or a RADIUS proxy.
- RADIUS can be used for both VPN and dial-up authentication and authorization.
- As a RADIUS proxy, NPS can connect to other Microsoft NPS servers or to third-party RADIUS servers.
- Use priority and weighting to load balance groups of RADIUS servers in RADIUS server groups.
- RADIUS clients can be network access servers or other RADIUS servers.
- NPS and RADIUS settings can be configured in templates to simplify deployment.
- RADIUS Accounting logs user authentication and accounting requests, and can use a local file or a SQL Server database.
- Use certificates for client authentication and server authentication.

Objective review

1. When installing NPS as a RADIUS proxy, which NPS role services are required in Windows Server 2012 R2? (Choose all that apply.)

   A. NPS

   B. Health Registration Authority

   C. Host Credential Authorization Protocol

   D. Routing and Remote access service (RRAS)

2. Certificates with which purposes can be used for mutual authentication of NPS and client computers? (Choose all that apply.)

   A. All Purpose certificates

   B. Server authentication certificates

   C. Root certificates

   D. Client authentication certificates

3. When you configure NPS as a RADIUS proxy, it means the following:

   A. It acts as a RADIUS client, authenticating all connection requests locally and notifying the RADIUS server group that the request should have access.

   B. It acts as a member of a RADIUS server group that accepts requests from RADIUS clients and authenticates them.

   C. It acts as a member of a RADIUS server group that accepts authenticated requests from RADIUS clients and assigns remote computers to a network.

   D. It acts as a RADIUS client, forwarding connection requests to a RADIUS server group for authentication and authorization.

Objective 4.2: Configure NPS policies

NPS supports three different kinds of policies: connection request policies, network policies, and health policies. I'll leave health policies for Objective 4.3, but focus here on the first two policies.

Together, the client request policy and the network policy control which clients are allowed to connect to the network. The connection request policy handles the initial request by a client to connect to the network, and (depending on what port it came in on and other factors) it passes the connection to the appropriate network policy. The network policy determines how a client is authenticated, and whether a client is authorized to connect to the network.

> **This objective covers how to:**
> - Configure connection request policies
> - Configure network policies for VPN clients
> - Manage NPS templates
> - Import and export NPS configuration

Configuring connection request policies

NPS creates a dial-up or VPN connection policy when you initially configure the RADIUS
server. You can modify that policy or create a new one from scratch. Each policy is evaluated
as part of the network policies to determine whether access is granted or denied.

Creating a new connection request policy

To create a new connection request policy, follow these steps:

1. In the Network Policy Server console, expand Policies and right-click Connection
    Request Policies.

2. Select New from the menu to open the New Connection Request Policy Wizard.

3. Enter a name in the Policy Name box and select the type of policy from the Type Of
    Network Access Server list, as shown in Figure 4-32.

FIGURE 4-32 The Specify Connection Request Policy Name And Connection Type page

4. Click Next to open the Specify Conditions page. Click Add to open the Select Condition dialog box shown in Figure 4-33. For a full list of conditions, see Table 4-1.

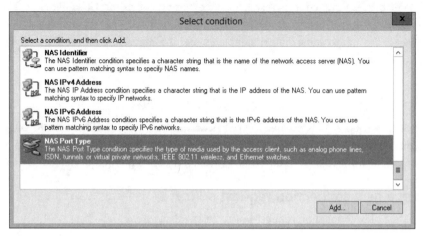

FIGURE 4-33 The Select Condition dialog box

5. Select the condition type and click Add. Fill in additional details appropriate to the condition type and click OK.

6. Add additional conditions as appropriate. The conditions are additive, meaning that all separate conditions must be met before a connection request is accepted. Within conditions, the conditions are OR'd.

7. Click Next to open the Specify Connection Request Forwarding page shown in Figure 4-34. On this page, specify whether requests are authenticated locally, or forwarded to a RADIUS server group (RADIUS proxy). Only users who meet the conditions specified can be accepted without validating credentials.

8. Click Next to open the Specify Authentication Methods page. On this page, you can choose to override the network policy authentication settings to require specific authentication for this connection policy.

9. Click Next to open the Configure Settings page. On this page, you can specify a realm name, RADIUS standard attribute, or a vendor-specific attribute.

10. Click Next and then Finish to create the policy.

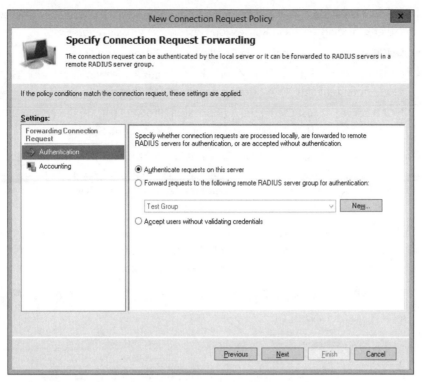

FIGURE 4-34 The Specify Connection Request Forwarding page

Configuring an existing connection request policy

After the New Connection Request Policy Wizard completes, you can fine-tune the settings for a connection. You can configure both a connection request policy and a network policy for each connection.

To configure additional settings for the connection request policy, follow these steps:

1. Open the Network Policy Server console and expand Policies in the console tree.

2. Select the connection request policy in the console tree and right-click the policy for which you want to configure additional settings in the Connection Request Policies detail pane and select Properties from the menu.

3. On the Overview tab, you can specify the Policy Name, Type Of Network Access Server, and whether the policy is enabled or disabled. The type of access servers supported are the following:

    ■ **Remote Access Server (VPN-Dial up) server** A Microsoft or other VPN or dial-up remote access server acting as a RADIUS client.

- **Remote Desktop Gateway server**   A Remote Desktop Gateway (RD Gateway) server providing access to RD Session Hosts or RD Virtualization Hosts.
- **DHCP server**   A Dynamic Host Configuration Protocol server.
- **Health Registration Authority server**   A Health Registration Authority (HRA) server obtains health certificates on behalf of NAP clients.
- **HCAP server** A Host Credential Authorization Protocol (HCAP) server is used to integrate Microsoft NAP with Cisco Network Access Control Server.

4. On the Conditions tab, you can specify the details for the type of connection you are configuring. These conditions can include User Names, IP addresses, Framing Protocol type, Service Type, Tunnel Type, date and time restrictions, and NAS type. For a full list of conditions, see Table 4-1.

5. On the Settings tab, shown in Figure 4-35, you can configure authentication methods, allowing you to override the network policy for the authentication method, and configure whether authentication occurs locally or on another RADIUS server (proxy).

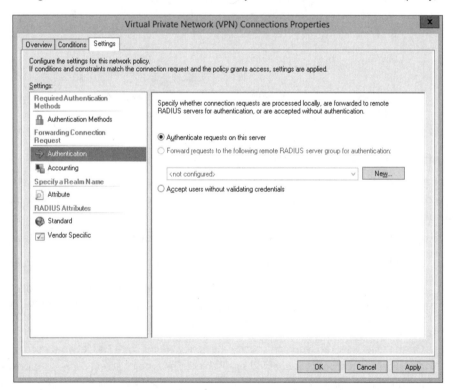

FIGURE 4-35 The Settings tab of the Virtual Private Network (VPN) Connections Properties Wizard

6. Select Accounting in the left pane to configure where accounting requests are forwarded to.

7. Configure a Realm Name, and any RADIUS Standard or Vendor-specific attributes, and then click OK to close the dialog box and implement the changes.

TABLE 4-1 Connection request policy conditions

Condition	Description
Location Groups	The HCAP Location Groups specifies the HCAP that matches the policy.
User Name	A character string typically combined with the realm name by the access client. (Pattern matching supported.)
Access Client IPv4 Address	Limits the policy to Access Clients with an IPv4 address matching the policy. (Pattern matching supported.)
Access Client IPv6 Address	Limits the policy to Access Clients with an IPv6 address matching the policy. (Pattern matching supported.)
Framed Protocol	Limits the policy to clients using specific framing protocol for incoming packets. Typical framing protocols include PPP and SLIP.
Service Type	Limits the policy to those clients requesting the specified service.
Tunnel Type	Limits the policy to those clients whose tunnel type matches the policy. Tunnel types include PPTP, SSTP, and L2TP.
Day and Time Restrictions	Limits the policy to only permit or only deny access during specified time periods.
Identity Type	Limits the policy to only those clients identified by the specified mechanism, typically a NAP Statement of Health (SOH)
Calling Station ID	Limits the policy to access clients that dialed in to a specific phone number. (Pattern matching supported.)
Client Friendly Name	Limits the policy to clients whose friendly name matches the condition. (Pattern matching supported.)
Client IPv4 Address	Limits the policy to clients whose IPv4 address name matches the condition. (Pattern matching supported.)
Client IPv6 Address	Limits the policy to clients whose IPv6 address name matches the condition. (Pattern matching supported.)
Client Vendor	Limits the policy to RADIUS clients of the specified vendor names.
Called Station ID	Limits the policy to the specific phone number of the NAS server. (Pattern matching supported.)
NAS Identifier	Limits the policy to the specified named network access device.
NAS IPv4	Limits the policy to the network access server whose IPv4 address matches the policy. (Pattern matching supported.)
NAS IPv6	Limits the policy to the network access server whose IPv6 address matches the policy. (Pattern matching supported.)
NAS Port Type	Limits the policy to the access clients using the specified port type. Typical values include analog phone lines, ISDN, VPN protocols, and IEEE 802.11 wireless.

Configuring network policies for VPN clients

NPS has two sets of policies for all VPNs: connection request policies and network policies. Additionally, if configured to use them, NPS can apply health policies as well (these policies are covered in Objective 4.3).

Connection request policies define which connections are processed on the NPS server and which are processed on remote RADIUS servers. Network policies define who is allowed to connect to the network, how they are authenticated, and what network access is permitted. When you configure the NPS RADIUS server for a VPN connection, the wizard creates both a connection request policy and a network policy. But that default network policy can be further configured, and you can create additional new VPN network policies. Network policies are processed in the processing order defined in the network policies details pane of the NPS server.

Policy processing

When a connection request is processed, the policy conditions must all be met for the policy to succeed. If a condition is not met, NPS processes the next policy in the ordered list of policies. If all the conditions of that policy are met, the policy succeeds. If all the conditions of the second policy are not met, the third policy is processed, and so on until all policies have been processed or a policy succeeds. When a policy succeeds, it either grants access or denies access, based on the setting in the policy. If no policy succeeds, access is denied.

Configuring an existing policy

To configure an existing network policy, follow these steps:

1. In the Network Policy Server console, expand Policies and then click Network Policies.

2. In the details pane, double-click the policy you want to configure.

3. On the Overview tab, you can configure the following settings:

    - **Policy Name**   Sets the name of the policy.

    - **Policy Enabled**   When selected, the policy is processed and evaluated while authorizing. When disabled, the policy is not evaluated.

    - **Grant Access/Deny Access**   When set to Grant Access, access is granted if the policy matches the connection request. When set to Deny Access, the connection request is denied if it matches the policy.

    - **Ignore User Account Dial-in Properties**   When selected, the RADIUS network and connection properties control access regardless of what the dial-in setting is for the user account.

    - **Type of Network Access Server**   Typically set to Remote Access Server (VPN-Dial up) for VPN connections.

4. Click the Conditions tab, shown in Figure 4-36. All network policies must have at least one condition but can also have multiple conditions. When you set conditions on a policy, all the conditions must be met for the policy to succeed. If any condition fails, the policy isn't processed, and the next policy in the processing order is evaluated. Click Add to add additional conditions, Edit to change one of the conditions, or Remove to remove a condition. The conditions for network policies are shown in Table 4-2.

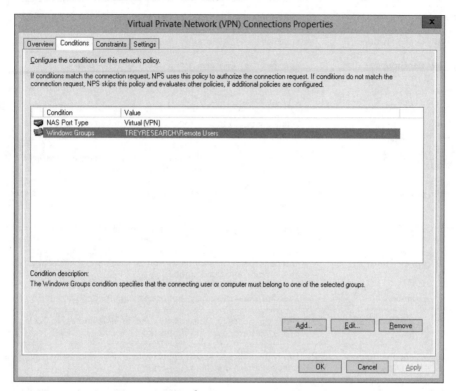

FIGURE 4-36 The Conditions tab of the network policy properties dialog box

5. Click the Constraints tab to set constraints for the network policy. If all constraints are not met by the connection request, access is denied. The constraints are detailed in Table 4-3.

6. Click the Settings tab. If all the conditions and constraints are met and the connection request is authorized, the settings are applied. The settings for network policies are shown in Table 4-4.

7. Click OK; the network policy is updated.

TABLE 4-2 Network policy conditions

Condition	Description
Windows Groups	The connecting user or computer must belong to one of the specified groups.
Machine Groups	The connection computer must belong to one of the specified groups.
User Groups	The connecting user must belong to one of the specified groups
HCAP Location Groups	Specifies the HCAP location groups that match the policy.
HCAP User Groups	Specifies the HCAP user groups that match the policy.
Day and Time Restrictions	Limits the policy to only permit or only deny access during specified time periods.
Identity Type	Limits the policy to only those clients identified by the specified mechanism, typically a NAP statement of health (SoH).
MS-Service Class	The connecting computer must have an IP address from a DHCP scope that matches the specified profile name.
Health policy	The connecting computer must meet the health criteria in the specified health policy
NAP-Capable Computers	The connecting computer either is or is not a NAP-capable computer.
Operating System	The connecting computer meets the specified operating system criteria. Criteria can include version, service pack, role (client or server), architecture, and build number.
Policy Expiration	Specifies when the policy expires and is no longer evaluated by NPS.
Access Client IPv4 Address	Limits the policy to Access Clients with an IPv4 address matching the policy. (Pattern matching supported.)
Access Client IPv6 Address	Limits the policy to Access Clients with an IPv6 address matching the policy. (Pattern matching supported.)
Authentication Type	Specifies the authentication methods that can be used to meet the policy.
Allowed EAP Types	Specifies the EAP types that are allowed for client computer authentication.
Framed Protocol	Limits the policy to clients using specific framing protocols for incoming packets. Typical framing protocols include PPP and SLIP.
Service Type	Limits the policy to those clients requesting the specified service.
Tunnel Type	Limits the policy to those clients whose tunnel type matches the policy. Typical tunnel types include PPTP, SSTP, and L2TP.
Calling Station ID	Limits the policy to access clients that dialed in to a specific phone number. (Pattern matching supported.)
Client Friendly Name	Limits the policy to clients whose friendly name matches the condition. (Pattern matching supported.)

Condition	Description
Client IPv4 Address	Limits the policy to clients whose IPv4 address name matches the condition. (Pattern matching supported.)
Client IPv6 Address	Limits the policy to clients whose IPv6 address name matches the condition. (Pattern matching supported.)
Client Vendor	Limits the policy to RADIUS clients of the specified vendor names.
MS-RAS Vendor	Specifies the vendor identification number of the network access server requesting authentication.
Called Station ID	Limits the policy to the specific phone number of the NAS server. (Pattern matching supported.)
NAS Identifier	Limits the policy to the specified named network access device.
NAS IPv4	Limits the policy to the network access server whose IPv4 address matches the policy. (Pattern matching supported.)
NAS IPv6	Limits the policy to the network access server whose IPv6 address matches the policy. (Pattern matching supported.)
NAS Port Type	Limits the policy to the access clients using the specified port type. Typical values include analog phone lines, ISDN, VPN protocols, and IEEE 802.11 wireless.

TABLE 4-3 Network policy constraints

Constraint	Description
Authentication Methods	Allows access only for those clients using the specified authentication methods.
Idle Timeout	Disconnects the client after the maximum idle time specified.
Session Timeout	Specifies the maximum time a session can be connected. User is disconnected when the time limit is reached.
Called Station ID	Specifies the phone number of the network access server. (Pattern matching supported.)
Day and time restrictions	Specifies the days of the week and hours of the day during which access is permitted.
NAS Port Type	Specifies the acceptable port types. Typical values include Async (Modem), ISDN, VPN protocols, and IEEE 802.11 wireless.

TABLE 4-4 Network policy settings

Setting	Description
RADIUS Attributes Standard	Specifies the RADIUS standard attributes to send to clients. If an attribute isn't configured, it isn't set to the client.
RADIUS Attributes Vendor Specific	Specifies vendor-specific attributes to send to clients. If an attribute isn't configured, it isn't set to the client.
NAP Enforcement	Choose from one of three modes: **Allow Full Network Access** When selected, allows unrestricted network access. Use for reporting mode only. **Allow Full Network Access For A Limited Time** Allows full network access until the specified time. After the specified date and time, the health policy is enforced. **Allow Limited Access** Noncompliant computers are allowed access only to the remediation network. **Remediation Server Group And Troubleshooting URL** When limited time or limited access is selected previously, you can configure the location of the remediation. **Enable Auto-remediation of Client Computers** When selected, computers that don't meet the health policy are automatically remediated
NAP Extended State	Specifies the extended state required to match the policy. Choices are Blank, Transitional, Infected, and Unknown.
Multilink and Bandwidth Allocation Protocol (BAP)	**Multilink**: Select one of three modes: ■ Server Settings Determine Multilink Usage ■ Do Not Allow Multilink Connections ■ Specify Multilink Settings allows you to configure the maximum number of ports a client computer can use. **Bandwidth Allocation Protocol** Specifies the percentage of capacity that must be reached for the specified time to reduce a multilink connection by one line. **Require BAP For Dynamic Multilink Requests** When selected, only BAP-enabled clients are allowed to use dynamic Multilink requests.
IP filters	Specifies IP filters to apply to the interface. (See the following "IP filters" section for details.)
Encryption	Choose accepted encryption settings: ■ Basic Encryption (MPPE 40-bit) ■ Strong Encryption (MPPE 56-bit) ■ Strongest Encryption (MPPE 128-bit) ■ No Encryption (not recommended)
IP Settings	Specifies the IP address assignment rules for this policy: ■ Server must supply an IP address. ■ Client may request an IP address. ■ Server settings determine IP address assignment. ■ Assign a static IPv4 address.

IP filters

You can use IP filters as part of a network policy or a connection request policy to control which input and output packets are allowed for both IPv4 and IPv6. You can configure IP filters individually in the policy, or create a template and apply the template. It makes sense in most cases to create an IP filter template because you can reuse the settings.

To create an IP filter template, follow these steps:

1. In the Network Policy Server, expand the Templates Management pane.

2. Right-click IP Filters and select New from the menu to open the New IP Filters Template dialog box.

3. Enter a name for the template and then click Input Filters in the IPv4 section to start creating the filter.

4. In the Inbound Filters dialog box, shown in Figure 4-37, click New to add a filter.

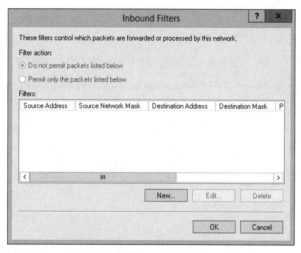

FIGURE 4-37 The Inbound Filters dialog box

5. In the Add IP Filter dialog box, select Destination Mask.

6. Enter an IP address and a subnet mask, and select the protocol, as shown in Figure 4-38. You can choose from the following protocols:

- **TCP**   Enter a Source Port and Destination Port.

- **TCP (established)**   Enter a Source Port and Destination Port.

- **UDP**   Enter a Source Port and Destination Port.

- **ICMP**   Enter an ICMP Type and an ICMP Code.

- **Any**   Includes any protocol and any port.

- **Other**   Specify a Protocol Number.

FIGURE 4-38 The Add IP Filter dialog box

7. Click OK to return to the Inbound Filters dialog box.

8. Select Do Not Permit Packets Listed Below or Permit Only the Packets Listed Below.

9. Click New to add additional Inbound IPv4 Filters. After you finish adding filters, click OK.

10. Repeat the process for IPv4 Output Filters, except select a Source IP Address and Subnet Mask.

11. Repeat for IPv6 Input Filters and IPv6 Output Filters, specifying an IPv6 Address and Prefix Length.

12. Click OK to create the template.

After you have created an IP filter, you can use it to build network policies.

Managing NPS templates

Templates that you create in NPS can be exported to a file. You export the templates to a file by right-clicking Templates Management and selecting Export Templates To A File. Files are exported as XML files that can be backed up as part of normal backup procedures.

After a set of templates has been exported to an XML file, it can then be imported to replace the templates on an NPS server. Importing templates is a destructive process that replaces any existing templates with the templates in the exported XML file.

You can import the templates from a running NPS server by importing them directly. Right-click Templates Management in the console tree and select Import Templates From A Computer. Enter the name or IP address of the remote NPS server and then click OK to import the templates. If the server isn't available online, you can import the settings from a file by selecting Import Templates From A File.

Importing and exporting NPS configuration

You can export the configuration of an NPS server, including policies, templates, NAP configuration, and client information. The exported file includes the shared secrets used between RADIUS clients and the RADIUS server, or between the RADIUS server and remote RADIUS servers. This is sensitive information and should be stored in a secure location except when actually being used to recover a server configuration.

EXAM TIP

Let me emphasize this, since it's very likely to show up on the exam. The exported configuration of an NPS server contains sensitive information. How you use the export, and how you store it, are significant security concerns.

NOTE RADIUS ACCOUNTING

If RADIUS accounting is being logged to a SQL Server database, the exported NPS configuration does not include the SQL Server logging information. After importing this to another server, you must manually reconfigure SQL Server logging.

To export the NPS configuration, follow these steps:

1. Open the Network Policy Server console.

2. Right-click NPS (Local) at the very top of the console tree.

3. Select Export Configuration from the menu.

4. Select I Am Aware That I Am Exporting All Shared Secrets and then click OK.

5. Select the location and file name for saving the XML file and click OK.

You can export the NPS server configuration by using the Export-NpsConfiguration cmdlet; for example:

```
Export-NpsConfiguraton -Path "C:\Temp\NPSConfig.xml"
```

EXAM TIP

While netsh has been deprecated, it's still possible it will show up on the exam. The command to export the NPS server configuration using netsh is:

```
netsh nps export filename=c:\temp\npsconfig.xml exportpsk=yes
```

You can import the configuration from an NPS configuration export. This import includes all policies, shared secrets, templates, RADIUS clients, and remote RADIUS server information. Follow these steps to import the NPS configuration:

1. Open the Network Policy Server console.

2. Right-click NPS (Local) at the very top of the console tree.

3. Select Import Configuration from the menu.

4. Navigate to the location where the exported XML file is stored and select the file.

5. When the import completes, click OK.

You can import the NPS server configuration by using the Import-NpsConfiguration cmdlet; for example:

```
Import-NpsConfiguraton -Path "C:\Temp\NPSConfig.xml"
```

Thought experiment

Copying NPS server configurations

In this thought experiment, apply what you've learned about this objective. You can find answers to these questions in the "Answers" section at the end of this chapter.

You are the network administrator for TreyResearch.net. Company policy requires that all sensitive company data be encrypted, and that all remote access to the corporate network use two-factor authentication (2FA). The current NPS server, remote1, is configured to enforce company policy and is working correctly, but to improve redundancy and increase throughput, you've been tasked with creating a second NPS server, remote2, that will use the same configuration as remote1. You need to accomplish this with the minimum administrative overhead while ensuring that the configuration is replicated accurately.

1. How should you go about copying the configuration of the existing server?

2. What security considerations does this raise?

3. How should you mitigate these security considerations? Describe the alternatives.

Objective summary

- The connection request policy controls the initial connection from a requesting client.
- The connection request policy controls whether NPS acts as a RADIUS server or a RADIUS proxy.
- The network policy is responsible for authorizing and authenticating the client.
- VPN and dial-up use different connection request policies, based on the different types of ports on which they request access.
- Network policies have one or more conditions, and may have constraints.

- Network policies can impose IP filters to control which input and output packets are allowed for both IPv4 and IPv6.

- Use NPS templates to simplify configuring policies, and deploying additional servers.

- Export NPS configuration to store for recovery purposes or to configure a new NPS server.

- Exported NPS configuration files contain unencrypted shared secrets.

Objective review

1. The connection request policy supports which of the following conditions? (Choose all that apply.)

   A. User Groups

   B. User Name

   C. NAS Port Type

   D. MS Service Class

2. You have a Windows Server 2012 R2 server (RAD1) acting as a RADIUS proxy and a RADIUS server group with a single Windows Server 2012 server (RAD2) as a RADIUS server in it. You need to configure a second RADIUS server to distribute the load. What should you do?

   A. Deploy a second Windows Server 2012 R2 server (RAD3) and install the Routing and Remote access service (RRAS) on it. Export the configuration from RAD1 and import it to RAD3.

   B. Deploy a second Windows Server 2012 server (RAD3) and install RRAS on it. Export the configuration from RAD2 and import it to RAD3.

   C. Deploy a second Windows Server 2012 R2 server (RAD3) and install NPS Server on it. Export the configuration from RAD2 and import it to RAD3.

   D. Deploy a second Windows Server 2012 server (RAD3) and install NPS on it. Export the configuration from RAD1 and import it to RAD3.

3. You need to improve the security of your remote access and want to limit the protocols that are used to connect to the RADIUS server. What condition could you use to limit the protocols?

   A. Use a Tunnel Type condition in the connection request policy.

   B. Use a Framed Protocol condition in the connection request policy.

   C. Use an Authentication Type condition in the network policy.

   D. Use an Allowed EAP Types condition in the network policy.

Objective 4.3: Configure Network Access Protection (NAP)

Network Access Protection (NAP) works with NPS server to ensure that clients connecting to the network meet specific health requirements. These requirements are validated by SHVs. NPS health policies work with connection request policies and network polices to enforce NAP health requirements and remediation. NAP is deprecated in Windows Server 2012 R2. This means that NAP is still supported in Windows Server 2012 R2 and Windows 8.1, but will not be supported in future versions of Windows.

This objective covers how to:

- Configure system health validators (SHVs)
- Configure health policies
- Configure NAP enforcement using DHCP and VPN
- Configure isolation and remediation of noncompliant computers using DHCP and VPN
- Configure NAP client settings

Configuring system health validators (SHVs)

The only system health validator (SHV) that ships with Windows Server 2012 R2 is the Windows Security Health Validator (WSHV). You can modify the Default Configuration (ID 0) of the WSHV or you can create new configurations.

To create a new WSHV configuration, follow these steps:

1. Open the Network Policy Server console and expand NPS (Local) in the console tree.

2. In the Network Access Protection pane, expand System Health Validators and then Windows Security Health Validator.

3. Right-click Settings and select New from the menu to open the Windows Security Health Validator dialog box shown in Figure 4-39.

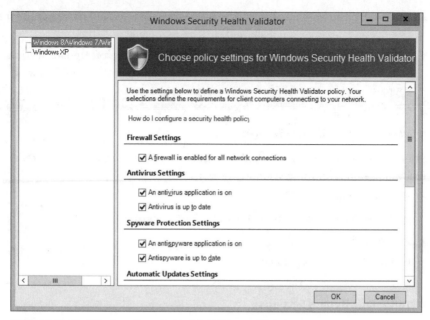

FIGURE 4-39 The Windows Security Health Validator dialog box

4. Select Windows 8/Windows 7/Windows Vista in the console tree to change the following settings for these Windows versions:

- **Firewall Settings**
    - A Firewall Is Enabled For All Network Connections
- **Antivirus Settings**
    - An Antivirus Application Is On
    - Antivirus Is Up To Date
- **Spyware Protection Settings**
    - An Antispyware Application Is On
    - Antispyware Is Up To Date
- **Automatic Update Settings**
    - Automatic Updating Is Enabled
- **Security Update Settings**
    - Restrict access for clients that do not have all available security updates installed
    - Choose from four levels:
    - Critical Only
    - Important And Above
    - Moderate And Above
    - Low And Above

- Specify the minimum number of hours allowed since the client has checked for new security updates (maximum allowed is 72 hours; default is 22 hours).
- By default, clients can receive security updates from Microsoft Update. If additional sources are required for your deployment, select one or both of the following sources:
- Windows Update
- Windows Server Update Services

5. Select Windows 8/Windows 7/Windows Vista in the console tree to change the following settings for these Windows versions:

- **Firewall Settings**
  - A Firewall Is Enabled For All Network Connections
- **Antivirus Settings**
  - An Antivirus Application Is On
  - Antivirus Is Up To Date
- **Automatic Update Settings**
  - Automatic Updating Is Enabled
- **Security Update Settings**
  - Restrict access for clients that do not have all available security updates installed
  - Choose from four levels:
  - Critical Only
  - Important And Above
  - Moderate And Above
  - Low And Above
- Specify the minimum number of hours allowed since the client has checked for new security updates (maximum allowed is 72 hours, default is 22 hours).
- By default, clients can receive security updates from Microsoft Update. If additional sources are required for your deployment, select one or both of the following sources:
- Windows Update
- Windows Server Update Services

6. Click OK to close the Windows Security Health Validator settings dialog box.

7. Right-click Error Codes and select Properties to change the default error codes shown in Figure 4-40.

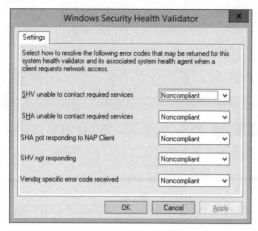

FIGURE 4-40 The Windows Security Health Validator Settings tab for error codes

The error codes can be set to Noncompliant or Compliant. If you want the WSHV to ignore a particular error, set the error code to Compliant.

8. Click OK to close the settings dialog box.

Configuring health policies

You can configure an existing health policy or create a new one. The settings available are the same. To create a new health policy, follow these steps:

1. Open the Network Policy Server console and expand NPS (Local) in the console tree.

2. In the Network Access Protection pane, and expand Policies.

3. Right-click Health Policies and select New.

4. In the Create New Health Policy dialog box, enter a Policy Name.

5. From the Client SHV Checks list, select one of the following:
   - Client Passes All SHV Checks
   - Client Fails All SHV Checks
   - Client Passes One Or More SHV Checks
   - Client Fails One Or More SHV Checks
   - Client Reported AS Transitional By One Or More SHVs
   - Client Reported As Infected By One Or More SHVs
   - Client Reported As Unknown By One Or More SHVs

6. Select an SHV in the SHVs Used In This Health Policy list. If the SHV supports more than one configuration, choose the configuration you want.

7. Click OK to save the policy.

You can save an existing health policy as a template to use to build new health policies. To save a policy as a template, right-click the policy in the Health Policies folder and select Save And Apply As Template, as shown in Figure 4-41.

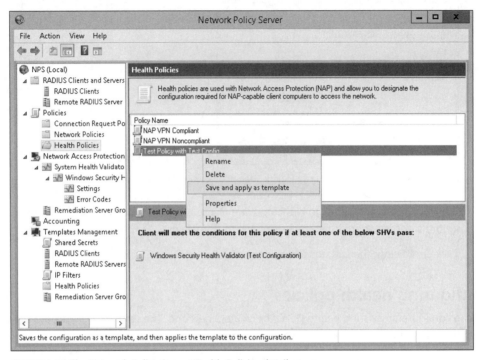

FIGURE 4-41 The Network Policy Server Health Policies details pane

Configuring NAP enforcement using DHCP and VPN

You can configure Network Access Protection enforcement to prevent noncompliant computers from connecting to the main network. They can be configured either to fail the connection or to be placed on a restricted network for remediation. There are multiple scenarios for NAP enforcement, including IEEE 802.1x for either wired or wireless connections, RD Gateway, DHCP, and VPN. The exam covers only the two most common NAP scenarios: DHCP and VPN.

NAP enforcement for DHCP

The DHCP scenario is straightforward and prevents noncompliant computers from getting a DHCP address on the main network. The scenario depends on DHCP either being installed on the main NAP computer or on a remote computer in the network that then gets NPS installed on it in RADIUS Proxy mode.

NAP enforcement by using DHCP is not a secure enforcement method. The knowledgeable user can bypass it by assigning a fixed IP address from the IP address range of the network. This makes the use of the DHCP for NAP enforcement an obvious exam question scenario.

To configure NAP enforcement, use the following process:

- If DHCP is already running on the network, install the Network Policy Server role on the remote computer running DHCP. Configure as a RADIUS proxy, as described in Objective 4.1. Configure the Remote RADIUS Server Group to include the NAP enforcement server as the server to which RADIUS messages are forwarded. If installing DCHP on the NAP enforcement server, this step isn't necessary.

- Create a connection request policy using NAS Port as the condition and set it to the specific types of DHCP clients on which you want NAP enforcement. Configure the connection request policy to forward both authentication and accounting messages to the NAP enforcement computer.

- On the DHCP server, select the properties for the DHCP scope on which you want to enforce NAP and enable Network Access Protection settings for the scope, as shown in Figure 4-42.

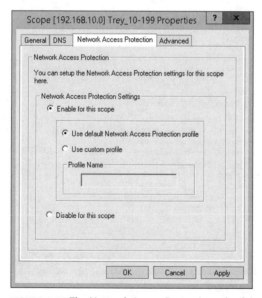

FIGURE 4-42 The Network Access Protection tab of the Properties dialog box for a DHCP scope

- Enable the DHCP server as a RADIUS client, as covered in Objective 4.1.

- To enable authorization by group, create a security group in AD DS and add the users who are authorized to obtain IP addresses via DHCP to that group.

- On NAP–capable client computers, configure as described later in this chapter in the "Configuring NAP clients" section.

- If using remediation servers, configure them as described in the "Configuring isolation and remediation of noncompliant computers using DHCP and VPN" section.

- Configure a health policy, connection request policy, and network policy to enforce NAP for DHCP.

- Configure the constraints in the network policy to allow health checks on DHCP IP address renewal.

- Select the network policy you want to configure in the Network Policy Server console and double-click.

- On the Constraints tab, ensure that Authentication Methods has Perform Machine Health Check Only selected, as shown in Figure 4-43.

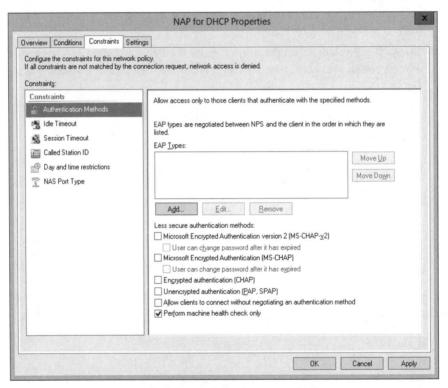

FIGURE 4-43 The Constraints tab of the network policy properties.

NAP enforcement for VPN

The VPN scenario for NAP enforcement follows a similar process to that for DHCP, but with some differences. The process flow for NAP enforcement for VPNs is as follows:

- Create a global security group in AD DS that has as members the users that will be permitted to use VPN.

- Configure the NPS server as a RADIUS server for VPN connections, using PEAP or EAP for authentication (see Objective 4.1 for details).

- Deploy a certification authority (CA) or buy a Server certificate for PEAP-MS-CHAPv2). (See Objective 4.1 for details on setting up certificate autoenrollment.)

- Deploy client computer and user certificates. (See Objective 4.1 for details on setting up certificate autoenrollment.)

- If using multiple VPN servers, configure the NPS server as the primary RADIUS server, with the other servers being RADIUS clients of the NPS server. (See Objective 4.1 for how to configure RADIUS clients.)

- On the NPS server, configure health policies, connection request policies, and network policies for VPN that enforce NAP for those VPN connections.

- On NAP–capable client computers, configure as described later in this chapter in the "Configuring NAP clients" section.

- If using remediation servers, configure them as described in the following section, "Configuring isolation and remediation of noncompliant computers using DHCP and VPN."

- Configure the client computers with a VPN connection, setting the configuration to PEAP or EAP.

Configuring isolation and remediation of noncompliant computers using DHCP and VPN

When creating a NAP enforcement policy, you can choose the following:

- Non-enforcement, allowing you to simply monitor the computers that are noncompliant with the NAP health policy

- Limited enforcement, allowing computers that are noncompliant access to the network for a limited time

- Full enforcement, blocking access to the network for all noncompliant computers

- Full enforcement with remediation, allowing noncompliant computers access to a limited set of servers to correct the noncompliance, including the automatic corrections of some conditions that cause noncompliance.

This last bullet is the one of interest in this section. To configure isolation and remediation, you have to configure a remediation server group and set NAP Enforcement to Allow Limited Network Access Only. You can also enable Auto-remediation to automatically remediate computers that fail the health check.

The first step is to configure a remediation server group and optionally a troubleshooting URL. The remediation server group is a group of one or more servers that have the resources to remediate the noncompliant servers to bring them back into compliance. The trouble-shooting URL should point to a web page with descriptions of what is required for compliance and links to resources to correct noncompliance.

To configure a remediation server group, follow these steps:

1. Open the Network Policy Server console and navigate to Network Access Protection.

2. Click Configure Remediation Server Groups in the details pane shown in Figure 4-44.

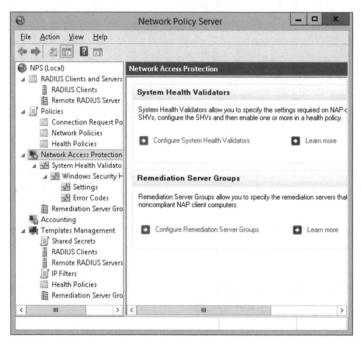

FIGURE 4-44 The Network Policy Server console

3. Right-click Remediation Server Groups and select New from the menu.

4. Select a Remediation Server Group template or create a new group.

5. Enter a Group Name and click Add to open the Add New Server dialog box shown in Figure 4-45.

6. Enter a Friendly Name for the server and type in an IP Address Or DNS Name.

7. Click Resolve. If you used a DNS name, and it resolves to more than one IP address, select the IP address to use and click OK. If you used an IP address and it resolves, click OK.

8. To add additional servers to the Remediation Server Group, click Add and repeat steps 6 and 7 to add servers as required.

9. After you add all the servers that need to be in the group, click OK.

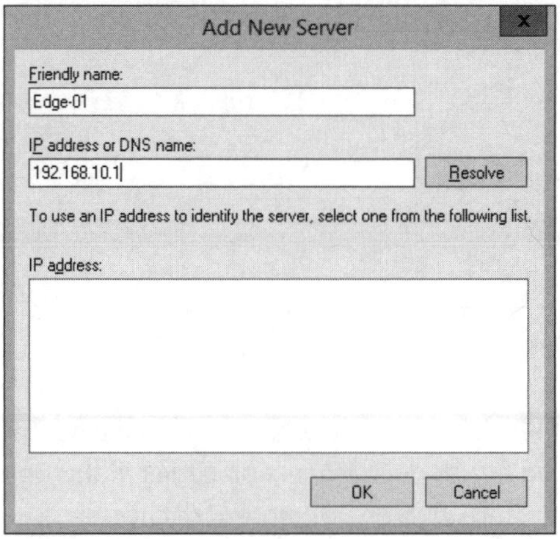

FIGURE 4-45 The Add New Server dialog box

10. You can now use this Remediation Server Group in network policies to allow non-compliant clients to correct the problem and return to compliance.

To create an NPS Remediation Server Group and add an NPS Remediation Server to it, use the New-NpsRemediationServerGroup and New-NpsRemediationServer cmdlets; for example:

```
New-NpsRemediationServerGroup -Name "RemGroup1"
New-NpsRemediationServer -RemediationServerGroup "RemGroup1" -Address "192.168.10.1"
```

To isolate the noncompliant clients, you need to configure a noncompliant NAP policy, as described in the earlier section, "Configuring network policies for VPN clients." The process is similar for both VPN and DHCP policies. To create a new noncompliant network policy, follow these steps:

1. Right-click Network Policies in the Policies folder of the console tree.

2. Select New to open the New Network Policy Wizard.

3. Enter a Policy Name, such as **NAP Noncompliant**.

4. Select the type of Network Access Server, such as DHCP Server or Remote Access Server (VPN-Dial-up).

5. Click Next to open the Specify Conditions page and click Add to add policy conditions.

6. Scroll down and select Health Policies and click Add to open the Health Policies dialog box shown in Figure 4-46.

FIGURE 4-46 The Health Policies dialog box

7. Select a health policy from the Health Policies list or click New to create a new health policy, as described in the "Configuring health policies" section earlier in this objective. The policy should be one of noncompliance with one or more SHV checks.

8. Click OK after you either create a new health policy or select an existing one.

9. Click Add again to select additional conditions (such as user group or machine group), as shown in Figure 4-47.

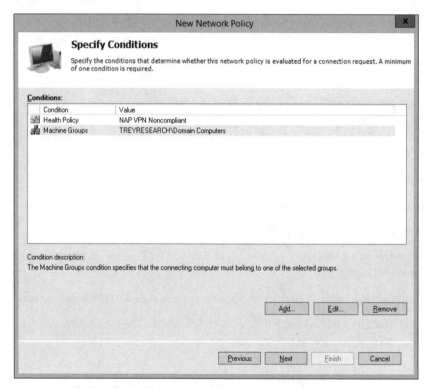

FIGURE 4-47 The Specify Conditions page of the New Network Policy Wizard

10. Click Next and select Access Granted on the Specify Access Permission page.

11. Select Access Is Determined By User Dial-In Properties (Which Overrides NPS Policy) to deny access to users who are not normally allowed remote access rather than continuing to the remediation steps.

12. Click Next to open the Configure Authentication Method. Select Perform Machine Health Check Only for DHCP or the authentication types you support for VPN.

13. Click Next to open the Configure Constraints page. Add constraints here only if your particular network environment requires them.

14. Click Next to open the Configure Settings page.

15. Select NAP Enforcement in the left pane, as shown in Figure 4-48.

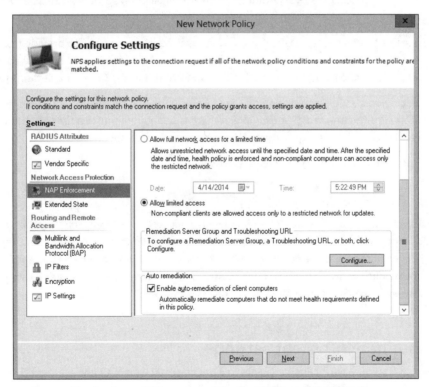

FIGURE 4-48 The Configure Settings page of the New Network Policy Wizard

16. Select Allow Limited Access and click Configure to open the Remediation Servers And Troubleshooting URL dialog box shown in Figure 4-49.

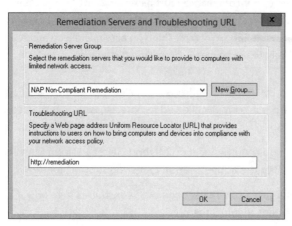

Remediation Servers and Troubleshooting URL   [x]

Remediation Server Group

Select the remediation servers that you would like to provide to computers with limited network access.

NAP Non-Compliant Remediation ▾   New Group...

Troubleshooting URL

Specify a Web page address Uniform Resource Locator (URL) that provides instructions to users on how to bring computers and devices into compliance with your network access policy.

http://remediation

OK   Cancel

FIGURE 4-49 The Remediation Servers And Troubleshooting URL dialog box

17. Select a Remediation Server Group from the list or click New Group to create a new one.

18. Specify a troubleshooting URL if you have (or will have) a web page to provide trouble-shooting information and resources for remediation. This page should be reachable by computers in the restricted network. Click OK to return to the Configure Settings page.

19. Select Enable Auto-Remediation Of Client Computers to have health requirements automatically corrected. (For example, if there is a requirement for a firewall, and the health check fails this requirement, Windows Firewall is enabled.)

20. Click Next and then Finish to create the new policy.

> **NOTE** **STEPS FOR DHCP**
>
> The steps for this procedure are those for creating a network policy for a noncompliant VPN connection. The steps for a noncompliant DHCP connection are slightly different, and you'll be asked to specify the name of the DHCP scope to use. The scope name becomes part of the policy to match the MS-Service Class condition. Exams aren't about exact steps, but what you're configuring, and the basic process is the same.

Configuring NAP client settings

You need to configure NAP-capable clients to work correctly with NAP enforcement. The settings you need to configure are shown in the following steps:

1. Start the Network Access Protection Agent Windows Service.

2. Set the Network Access Protection Agent Windows Service startup type to Automatic.

3. Use the NAP Client Configuration console (Napclcfg.msc) on the client computer to enable the following enforcement clients:

   - DHCP Quarantine Enforcement Agent
   - EAP Quarantine Enforcement Agent

4. Configure Group Policy to enable the Security Center.

5. Edit the Default Domain Policy.

6. Navigate to Computer Configuration/Administrative Templates/Windows Components/Security Center.

7. Double-click Turn On Security Center (Domain PCs Only).

8. Select Enabled. Click OK and exit the Group Policy Management Editor and the GPMC.

Thought experiment

Performing health checks

In this thought experiment, apply what you've learned about this objective. You can find answers to these questions in the "Answers" section at the end of this chapter.

You are the network administrator for TreyResearch.net. As a result of a recent virus attack on the network that originated with an unprotected remote user, you have been asked to immediately implement network access policies to ensure that computers that connect remotely are fully updated and protected.

1. What changes do you need to make to your existing NPS RADIUS infrastructure to support the change?

2. What changes do you need to make on remote client computers? How can you implement them?

3. What transitional steps should you take before locking out noncompliant users?

Objective summary

- NAP uses SHVs to verify that network clients meet specific health requirements.
- NAP health policies work with connection request policies and network policies to determine which clients are allowed to connect to the network.
- NAP enforcement can be set to monitor, limited enforcement, or full enforcement.
- NAP enforcement can use remediation server groups to remediate noncompliant clients.
- NAP clients need configuration to work with NAP enforcement.

Objective review

1. User1 has been on vacation for a week, with his laptop turned off. When he attempted to connect via modem to the Remote Access dial-in bank on day four of the vacation, his dial-in attempt was rejected. However, when he returns home three days later, he initially has a problem when he logs on to his laptop and attempts to connect to the network remotely. When he returns to the office, all is well, although his initial logon seems rather slow. When he goes home that night, he is again able to connect to the network. User1 is authorized for dial-up, and NAP policies are in place for both internal network connections and remote connections. What was a possible cause of the problem?

   A. The connection request policy for dial-up connections has a condition on the Called Station ID that limits callers to the local area code.

   B. The health policy for dial-up and VPN access requires that all client SHV checks must pass.

   C. The health policy for internal network access requires that all client SHV checks must pass.

   D. The network connection policy for dial-up connections is set to enable access.

2. What configuration changes do you need to make on client computers to support NAP?

   A. Set the Network Access Protection Agent to Automatic.

   B. Enable the DHCP Quarantine Enforcement Agent.

   C. Enable the EAP Quarantine Enforcement Agent.

   D. Use Group Policy to set the Turn On Security Center (Domain PCs Only) policy to Enabled.

   E. A, B, D.

   F. B, C, D.

   G. All of the above.

3. When you configure NPS for DHCP, you configure the network policy to enforce the health policy. What settings do you need make in the network policy?

   A. If the client SHV fails one or more SHV checks, deny access.

   B. If the client SHV fails one or more SHV checks, grant access only for EAP clients.

   C. If the client SHV passes one or more SHV checks, deny access.

   D. If the client SHV passes one or more SHV checks, enable access.

Answers

This section contains the solutions to the thought experiments and answers to the lesson review questions in this chapter.

Objective 4.1: Thought experiment

1. You can use the Configure VPN Or Dial-up Wizard to create both VPN and dial-up connection request policies. The dial-up connection request policy works with a separate dial-up network policy to limit users to only members of the Domain Admins security group. It doesn't require a separate NPS server.

2. Configure a network policy for HR that uses their membership in the HR Users security group to then limit access to only those authenticating with EAP Smart Card or other certificate. Because HR staff have access to sensitive data, they should be required to have TPM chips and BitLocker on their laptops, so by installing Windows 8 on their laptops, they can use a virtual smart card.

3. Although it is certainly possible to implement this policy on a single server, distributing it across multiple NPS servers enables you to have different policies for different Remote RADIUS Server Groups. The initial client access is handled by the RADIUS proxy, which distributes the load based on the priorities and weighting.

Objective 4.1: Review

1. **Correct answer:** A

   A. **Correct**. The Network Policy Server role service is required for all RADIUS functionality.

   B. **Incorrect**. The Health Registration Authority (HRA) is used only with the NAP IPsec enforcement method.

   C. **Incorrect**. The Host Credential Authorization Protocol is used only for integration into a Cisco Network Access Control Server.

   D. **Incorrect**. The RRAS role service is now part of the Remote Access role, not NPS.

2. **Correct answers:** B, D

   A. **Incorrect**. Despite its name, the All Purpose certificate type doesn't work for client authentication or server authentication.

   B. **Correct**. The server authentication purpose is needed to authenticate the server to the client.

   C. **Incorrect**. Although a root certificate for the CA used needs to be part of both the client's and server's root certificate store, this certificate is not used for mutual authentication.

   D. **Correct**. The client authentication purpose is needed to authenticate the client to the server.

3. **Correct answer:** D

   A. **Incorrect**. This is not how a RADIUS client works. The authentication happens at the RADIUS server.

   B. **Incorrect**. RADIUS proxy means it acts as a RADIUS client.

   C. **Incorrect**. RADIUS proxy means it acts as a RADIUS client.

   D. **Correct**. As a RADIUS proxy, NPS forwards connections to a RADIUS server group for authentication and authorization.

Objective 4.2: Thought experiment

1. Export the current NPS configuration on remote1, and import it to the new NPS server, remote2. A more limited approach would be to only export and import the templates, but this would not meet the requirement.

2. An export of the NPS configuration of remote1 includes all of the shared secrets in plain text.

3. To mitigate the plain text shared secrets of an NPS export, you need to ensure that the configuration file itself is encrypted. Failure to do so would violate company policy. Two possible solutions, include:

   - Export the NPS configuration file to a shared folder on the network that is encrypted with the EFS file system.

   - Export the NPS configuration file to a USB stick, encrypted with BitLocker To Go.

Objective 4.2: Review

1.   **Correct answers:** B, C

   A.   **Incorrect**. User groups are available only as a condition of the network policy

   B.   **Correct**. The user name is a possible condition for the connection request policy because it is part of a character string that typically includes a realm name.

   C.   **Correct**. The NAS Port Type identifies what port type was used by the client to connect to the RADIUS server.

   D.   **Incorrect**. The MS Service Class is not available in the connection request policy.

2.   **Correct answer:** C

   A.   **Incorrect**. The RRAS service is not a RADIUS server.

   B.   **Incorrect**. The RRAS service is not a RADIUS server.

   C.   **Correct**. NPS is a RADIUS server. Copying the configuration from Windows Server 2012 is not a problem, and you should copy the configuration from another member of the same RADIUS server group.

   D.   **Incorrect**. NPS is a RADIUS server, and this is the same version of the operating system. But copying the configuration from RAD1 would copy the RADIUS proxy configuration, not the RADIUS server configuration.

3.   **Correct answer:** A

   A.   **Correct**. The Tunnel Type condition includes the protocols that are used to connect to the RADIUS server.

   B.   **Incorrect**. The Framed Protocol primarily includes dial-up protocols such as SLIP and PPP.

   C.   **Incorrect**. Authentication Type specifies the authentication methods used, such as CHAP, EAP, and MS-CHAPv2.

   D.   **Incorrect**. Allowed EAP Types specifies which EAP authentication methods are allowed to be used.

Objective 4.3: Thought experiment

1.   You need to enable NAP on your RADIUS servers and implement a health policy that requires users to have their firewall turned on, have all current updates, and be free of infection. You have to implement a remediation server group that you can redirect noncompliant users to, including clients that don't have the NAP agent enabled.

2.   You need to configure the remote computers to support NAP. Part of it can be done via Group Policy, but you'll probably have to use a logon script during the transition phase to set the startup for the Network Access Protection Agent.

3. You need to configure remediation server groups to support remediating your current users who are not infected but just noncompliant. You need to have a separate policy that will lock out a user who is infected.

4. You probably want to start by creating the policies and setting them to monitor mode only, allowing access for noncompliant clients but logging their status. Doing this enables you to work directly with problem users who haven't gotten compliant yet. But the infected users should be locked out anyway to prevent another incident.

Objective 4.3: Review

1. **Correct answer:** B

   A. **Incorrect**. The Called Station ID is the phone number of the dial-up modem on the server, not the client.

   B. **Correct**. The remote laptop fails because it hasn't checked for updates in more than 72 hours.

   C. **Incorrect**. The laptop would fail, but instead automatically routed to a remediation server that autoremediated on the local network. Makes for a slowish logon, however.

   D. **Incorrect**. This would not prevent the remote access on day four of the vacation.

2. **Correct answer:** G

   A. **Incorrect**. This answer forms part of the total answer, but is not sufficient in and of itself. The network access protection agent needs to start automatically.

   B. **Incorrect**. This answer forms part of the total answer, but is not sufficient in and of itself. The DHCP Quarantine Enforcement Agent needs to be enabled.

   C. **Incorrect**. This answer forms part of the total answer, but is not sufficient in and of itself. The EAP Quarantine Enforcement Agent needs to be enabled.

   D. **Incorrect**. This answer forms part of the total answer, but is not sufficient in and of itself. The Group Policy needs to be changed.

   E. **Incorrect**. You need all four of the items A–D.

   F. **Incorrect**. You need all four of the items A–D.

   G. **Correct**. This answer choice includes all four required elements of the correct answer.

3. **Correct answer:** D

   A. **Incorrect**. By denying access, you prevent remediation.

   B. **Incorrect**. EAP is a remote access protocol.

   C. **Incorrect**. By denying access, you prevent remediation.

   D. **Correct**. Allows the client to be forwarded to the remediation server group.

CHAPTER 5

Configure and manage Active Directory

Active Directory Domain Services (AD DS) is the fundamental building block for building Windows enterprise networks, so it plays a crucial role in Windows Server exams. The basic installation and administration of AD DS is covered in Exam 70-410, but the configuration and management of AD DS is covered in Exam 7-411, including service accounts, read-only domain controllers, domain controller cloning, backup and restore, and account policies.

Objectives in this chapter:

- Objective 5.1: Configure service authentication
- Objective 5.2: Configure domain controllers
- Objective 5.3: Maintain Active Directory
- Objective 5.4: Configure account policies

Objective 5.1: Configure service authentication

Since their introduction in Windows Server 2003, service accounts have played an important role in isolating services and their authentication. *Service accounts* are user accounts used to provide authentication and authorization for services or applications running on the Windows server. Service accounts were originally only available as local accounts that required significant ongoing maintenance and administrative effort. Service accounts have matured and now include group Managed Service Accounts (MSAs) and virtual accounts that provide simplified service principal name (SPN) management and automatic password management.

This objective covers how to:

- Create and configure service accounts
- Create and configure Managed Service Accounts (MSAs)
- Create and configure group Managed Service Accounts (gMSAs)
- Configure Kerberos delegation
- Configure virtual accounts
- Manage service principal names (SPNs)

Creating and configuring service accounts

You create a service account exactly the same way as you create any user account. You can create a service account as a local account or as an Active Directory account. Service accounts should be created with user-level permissions and should not be members of the Domain Admins group or the local Administrators group on the server they are for.

Windows Server 2008 R2 introduced Managed Service Accounts (MSAs), and Windows Server 2012 introduced group Managed Service Accounts (gMSAs). Both are preferable to using a regular user account for services and are described later in this objective.

To create a local service account, use Computer Management and select the Users folder of Local Users And Groups in the console tree. Or open the Local Users And Groups console directly by typing **lusrmgr.msc** at a command prompt. Then follow these steps:

1. Right-click Users in the console tree and select New User from the Action menu.

2. Enter a User Name, Full Name, and Description for the account.

3. Enter a Password and Confirm the password.

4. Clear the User Must Change Password At Next Logon check box. Set any additional options and then click Create to create the account.

To create a domain service account, use Active Directory Users and Computers to create the account by following these steps:

1. Right-click the organizational unit (OU) where you want the service account created and select New, User from the Action menu.

2. Enter a Full Name and User Logon Name and then click Next.

3. Enter and confirm a password and then clear the User Must Change Password At Next Logon check box. Set any additional options, click Next, and then click Finish to create the account.

Services or applications that require a service account typically configure the associated application permissions to run the application and associated services with the minimum and appropriate permissions to start and run the service. SQL Server, for example, sets different permissions on the service accounts it uses, depending on exactly which features and capabilities of SQL Server are installed.

Creating and configuring Managed Service Accounts

Managed Service Accounts (MSAs) were introduced in Windows Server 2008 R2 and Windows 7. MSAs are Active Directory accounts that are tied to a specific computer. MSAs have long complex passwords, and they are maintained automatically. MSA passwords are changed on the same schedule as the computer account and through the same mechanism.

In addition to complex passwords that are automatically maintained, MSAs can't be used for interactive logon, nor can they be locked out. Normally, the MSA password is generated and set automatically, but it can be set to an explicit value by an administrator. However, they can be reset on demand to a new generated value.

EXAM TIP

The password associated with an MSA is automatically updated every 30 days. This is likely to find its way into the conditions for an exam question, so it's good to remember that number.

Creating an MSA

MSAs are created in the Manage Service Accounts container of Active Directory and have an object class of msDS-ManagedServiceAccount. MSAs require a minimum Active Directory domain functional level of Windows Server 2008 R2 to allow for automatic management of the Service Principal Name and password of the MSA, and can be installed only on Windows Server 2008 R2, Windows 7, and later releases of Windows and Windows Server. If your domain is not at least Windows Server 2008 R2 level, but your schema is updated to Windows Server 2008 R2, automatic password management works, but automatic SPN management does not.

MSAs can be created only by using the ActiveDirectory module of Windows PowerShell. This module requires Windows PowerShell version 2.0 or later and can be installed on Windows Server 2008 R2 or later servers, or Windows 7 or later clients with Remote Server Administration Tools (RSAT) installed.

You can create an MSA by following these steps:

1. Open a Windows PowerShell prompt with elevated privilege.

2. Import the ActiveDirectory module. (This step is required only on Windows Server 2008 R2 and Windows 7. Later releases automatically load the module.)

    ```
    Import-Module ActiveDirectory
    ```

3. Create the MSA account (Windows Server 2012 R2).

    ```
    New-ADServiceAccount -Name <MSAAccountName> -RestrictToSingleComputer -Enabled $True
    ```

4. Associate the MSA with the computer on which you want to use it.

```
Add-ADComputerServiceAccount -Identity <computername> -ServiceAccount <MSAName>
```

5. Log on to the computer where the MSA will be used and install the MSA to the target computer with this:

```
Install-ADServiceAccount -Identity <MSAName>
```

> **NOTE DEPENDENCIES**
>
> This requires installing the ActiveDirectory Windows PowerShell module and .NET Framework 3.5 or later on the target computer.

Associating an MSA with a service

After the MSA has been assigned to a computer, you can associate it with a service account by using either the GUI or Windows PowerShell. To use the GUI, open services.msc and edit the properties of the service you want to associate with the MSA. Set the Log On value for the service to *DOMAIN\MSA$*, where *MSA* is the account name you installed on the local computer. Make sure that the Password and Confirm Password boxes are empty.

To do the same with Windows PowerShell requires a bit of scripting. You need to use Windows Management Instrumentation (WMI) to set the account for a service:

SetMSA.ps1

```
$MSA = "TREYRESEARCH\TestMSA$"
$SvcName = "MSATestSvc"
$Password = $Null
$Svc = Get-WMIObject Win32_Service -filter "Name=$SvcName"
$InParams = $Svc.psbase.getMethodParameters("Change")
$InParams["StartName"] = $MSA
$InParams["StartPassword"] = $Password
$Svc.invokeMethod("Change",$InParams,$null)
```

You can edit the preceding script to change the values of $MSA and $SvcName as appropriate to your environment.

Removing an MSA

You can remove an MSA from a computer by using Windows PowerShell. You can remove it from the current computer by using the Uninstall-ADServiceAccount cmdlet on the local computer where it was installed. Then remove the assignment to the computer by using the Remove-ADComputerServiceAccount cmdlet. This process leaves the MSA in place in Active Directory but not assigned to a specific computer, allowing you to reuse the account on another computer. To remove the MSA entirely from Active Directory, use the Remove-ADServiceAccount cmdlet.

Creating and configuring group Managed Service Accounts (gMSAs)

The group Managed Service Account (gMSA), introduced in Windows Server 2012, takes the functionality of the stand-alone MSA and extends that functionality across multiple servers. This change allows gMSAs to be used for services that span multiple hosts and also extends the basic MSA to allow it to be used for scheduled tasks, Internet Information Services (IIS) application pools, SQL 2012, and Microsoft Exchange.

To enable automatic password management across multiple computers, gMSAs use the Key Distribution Services (KDS) running on a Windows Server 2012 or Windows Server 2012 R2 domain controller to distribute keys.

Creating a gMSA

Before you can create a gMSA, you need to create the KDS root key. This step is required only once per domain. Use the following command:

```
Add-KDSRootKey –EffectiveImmediately
```

Even though you specified that the root key should be effective immediately, it actually takes 10 hours before the key is effective, which ensures that the key is fully deployed to all domain controllers in the domain.

To simplify managing a gMSA and the computers that can use it, it's useful to have the computers that will use the gMSA in a security group. However, if you create a new security group and assign computers to it, you have to restart the computers before the group membership is recognized.

To create a gMSA, you need to use the New-ADServiceAccount cmdlet. For a gMSA, you need to specify the -Name parameter and the -DNSHostName parameter at a minimum. For example:

```
New-ADServiceAccount -Name ServiceAccount1 -DNSHostName ServiceAccount1.treyresearch.net
```

The list of available options you can specify when creating a gMSA is long. For full details, see *http://go.microsoft.com/fwlink/p/?linkid=291076*. You can also use an existing gMSA as a template to create a new gMSA, setting only the changed properties for the new instance of the gMSA. For example:

```
$svcAcct1 = Get-ADServiceAccout -Identity ServiceAccount1
New-ADServiceAccount -Name SvcAcct2 `
                     -DNSHostName SvcAcct2.treyresearch.net `
                     -PrincipalsAllowedToDelegateToAccount "Domain Controllers" `
                     -Instance $svcAcct1
```

Installing a gMSA

You install a gMSA on a host just as you install an MSA on a host: with the Install-ADServiceAccount cmdlet. Before you can install a gMSA on a host, however, you need to set the -PrincipalsAllowedToRetrieveManagedPassword value for the gMSA to include the host. This process is usually done by adding the hosts that will be allowed to install the gMSA to a security group and then using the Set-ADServiceAccount cmdlet. So, for example:

```
Set-ADServiceAccount -Identity $svcAcct1 `
                       -PrincipalsAllowedToRetrieveManagedPassword "Domain Controllers"
Install-ADServiceAccount -Identity #svcAcct1
```

You can test whether the gMSA has successfully been installed to the host with the Test-ADServiceAccount cmdlet:

```
Test-ADServiceAccount ServiceAccount1
```

Test-ADServiceAccount returns $True if the gMSA has been installed, and returns $False if it is not installed on the host.

Using a gMSA to run a scheduled task

One of the useful improvements of Group Managed Service Accounts as compared with stand-alone Managed Service Accounts is the ability to use the account to run a scheduled task. You can run the task with administrative privileges without creating an account that needs to be managed. So, for example, you can use the gMSA to run a routine backup task:

```
$bkAction = New-ScheduledTaskAction \\server\scriptshare\backup.ps1
$bkTrigger = New-ScheduledTaskTrigger -At 21:00 -Weekly -DaysOfWeek Friday
$bkAcct = NewScheduledTaskPrincipal -UserID ServiceAccount1$ -LogonType Password
```

Configuring Kerberos delegation

Windows Server implements Kerberos v5 with the authentication client implemented as a security support provider (SSP). Initial user authentication is integrated with the Winlogon single sign-on (SSO) architecture. The Kerberos Key Distribution Center (KDC) is integrated in the domain controller. The KDC uses AD DS as its security account database. In Windows 8x and Windows Server 2012 and Windows Server 2012 R2, Kerberos authentication is proxied through DirectAccess or Remote Desktop Services.

New Group Policy settings

Windows Server 2012 and Windows Server 2012 R2 include a new Kerberos administrative template policy with GPO settings to configure Kerberos. These settings are shown in Table 5-1.

TABLE 5-1 New administrative template policy settings

Policy	Description
Set maximum Kerberos SSPI context token buffer size	Sets the return value for applications that request the maximum size of the authentication context token buffer. The recommended size is 48,000 bytes.
Warning events for large Kerberos tickets	Sets the warning threshold for large Kerberos tickets. The default is 12,000 bytes to issue an Event ID 31 if this policy is not enabled.
KDC support for claims, compound authentication, and Kerberos armoring	Enables a domain controller to support claims and compound authentication for Dynamic Access Control (DAC) and Kerberos armoring.
Kerberos client support for claims, compound authentication, and Kerberos armoring	Enables configuration of devices running Windows 8x to support claims and compound authentication. When enabled, devices fail authentication if they can't reach a domain controller.
Support compound authentication	When configured, you can set to Never, Automatic, or Always.
Fail authentication requests when Kerberos armoring is not available	When enabled, client computers require that Kerberos message exchanges be armored when communicating with a domain controller.

In Windows Server 2012 and Windows Server 2012 R2, resource–based Kerberos constrained delegation can be used to provide constrained delegation when front-end services and back-end resources are not in the same domain. Constrained delegation restricts a server to act on behalf of a user for only specific services. To configure a resource service to allow a front-end server to act on behalf of users, use the -PrincipalsAllowedToDelegateToAccount parameter of the New and Set verbs of the ADComputer, ADServiceAccount, and ADUser cmdlets. Use the Get verb for the cmdlets with the -PrincipalsAllowedToDelegateToAccount parameter to retrieve a list of principals.

Configuring virtual accounts

Another kind of service account is the *virtual account*. Virtual accounts require no configuration to access local resources. To use a virtual account for a service, simply enter **NT SERVICE\<ServiceName>** for the account name, and leave the password blank.

Virtual accounts can be used for services that require network access, but it isn't recommended. To give the virtual accounts access to network resources, you need to give the computer account for the computer where the service is located permission to access the resource. Instead, it's recommended to use gMSAs for services that require network access.

You can use virtual accounts with IIS. The user is called IIS AppPool\<*apppoolname*> (for example, IIS AppPool\DefaultAppPool).

Managing service principal names

A service principal name (SPN) is the name by which a client uniquely identifies an instance of a service. If there are multiple instances of a service on computers throughout a forest, each instance must have its own SPN. One service instance can have multiple SPNs where there are multiple names that clients might use for authentication. For example, an SPN always includes the name of the host computer on which the service instance is running, so a service instance might register an SPN for each name or alias of its host.

SPNs are of the format: `serviceclass/host:port servicename` where *serviceclass* and *host* are required, but *port* and *service* name are optional. The colon between *host* and *port* is only required when a value for port is present.

The elements of an SPN are described in Table 5-2.

TABLE 5-2 The elements of an SPN

Element	Description
serviceclass	A string that identifies the general class of service; for example, "SqlServer". There are well-known service class names, such as "www" for a Web service or "ldap" for a directory service. In general, this can be any string that is unique to the service class. The SPN syntax uses a forward slash (/) to separate elements, so this character cannot appear in a service class name.
host	The name of the computer on which the service is running. This can be a fully-qualified DNS name or a NetBIOS name. Be mindful that NetBIOS names are not guaranteed to be unique in a forest, so an SPN that contains a NetBIOS name may not be unique.
port	An optional TCP or UDP port number to distinguish between multiple instances of the same service class on a single host computer. Omit this element if the service uses the default port for its service class.

Element	Description
accountname	An optional name used in the SPNs of a replicable service to identify the data or services provided by the service or the domain served by the service. This element can have one of the following formats: ■ The distinguished name or objectGUID of an object in Active Directory Domain Services, such as a service connection point (SCP). ■ The DNS name of the domain for a service that provides a specified service for a domain as a whole. ■ The DNS name of an SRV or MX record.

Some examples of SPN registrations include:

- **HTTP/www.treyresearch.net:8080**   Any page on the website on the non-standard TCP port 8080 for www.treyresearch.net, that is *http://www.treyresearch.net*.

- **HOST/WORKSTATION5**   Any service running on the computer with NetBIOS name WORKSTATION5

- **HOST/SERVER7.treyresearch.net**   Any service running on the computer with hostname SERVER7.treyresearch.net

- **TERMSRV/FRONTRM.treyresearch.net**   The Remote Desktop Protocol (RDP) service running on the computer with hostname FRONTRM.treyresearch.net

- **MSSQLSvc/SQLSERVER2.tailspintoys.com:1433**   The SQL Server listening on SQLSERVER2.tailspintoys.com, port 1433.

- **cifs/KHWIN7.tailspintoys.com**   The file share on the computer with hostname KHWIN7.tailspintoys.com

When creating an SPN for a well-known service, you do not need to specify the port for the SPN when the service uses the default port. The default SPNs are registered by the NetLogon service. They are refreshed every 22 minutes after startup.

Thought experiment
Running batch jobs as an administrator

In this thought experiment, apply what you've learned about this objective. You can find answers to these questions in the "Answers" section at the end of this chapter.

You are the network administrator for TreyResearch.net. Your environment requires administrative privilege to perform periodic backup and cleanup operations. You want to automate these operations without adding an administrative account that could create a potential security exposure. You create a Windows PowerShell script, Start-myDailyCleanup.ps1, to run the tasks. and it works when run interactively by an administrator.

1. What kind of account should you use to run the script automatically?

    A. Regular user account with Run as Batch permissions

    B. MSA

    C. Virtual account

    D. gMSA

2. Which commands do you use to initialize the environment for your chosen account?

3. What other considerations are there for running the script as a scheduled task?

Objective summary

- Service accounts are local or domain accounts created for and used by local applications and services.
- MSAs are Active Directory accounts that are tied to a specific computer.
- MSAs use a complex generated password that is maintained automatically.
- gMSAs extend MSAs to support multiple servers with a single account.
- gMSAs can be used for scheduled tasks, IIS application pools, SQL Server, and Microsoft Exchange.
- Kerberos delegation is improved in Windows Server 2012 and Windows Server 2012 R2 to provide resource–based Kerberos delegation.
- Virtual accounts are automatically created when you assign them to a service or IIS AppPool. They require no additional management and are a good solution for services that don't require network access to resources.

Objective review

1. What tool or command do you use to create a MSA?

    A. Computer management with the Users folder of Local Users and Groups

    B. Active Directory Users and Computers

    C. New-ADServiceAccount

    D. Install-ADServiceAccount

    E. Add-ADComputerServiceAccount

2. What command should you use to add a gMSA on a computer?

    A. Add-ADGroupMember

    B. Install-ADServiceAccount

    C. Add-ADServiceAccount

    D. Install-ADComputerServiceAccount

3. You want to use a virtual account for the TestService on computer Server1. What commands or tools would you use? (Choose all that apply.)

    A. Set-Service -computername Server1

    B. Services.msc

    C. Lusrmgr.msc

    D. Add-ADComputerServiceAccount

Objective 5.2: Configure domain controllers

The core of the Windows domain system is the domain controller. Exam 70-410 covered the basics of installing and configuring Active Directory and domain controllers. Exam 70-411 covers more advanced topics for domain controllers and Active Directory.

This objective covers how to:

- Configure universal group membership caching (UGMC)
- Transfer and seize operations master
- Install and configure a read-only domain controller (RODC)
- Configure domain controller cloning

Configuring universal group membership caching

When a user logs on to a domain in a multidomain forest, the user's group membership is ascertained by querying a global catalog server. Only global catalog servers store the memberships of universal groups in the forest. If a global catalog is not available in the local site, the domain controller needs to contact a global catalog in another site. When a global catalog is not available at the local site, universal group membership caching (UGMC) can be used to reduce the load on slow (wide area network) WAN connections and speed up user logons.

When UGMC is enabled, the user's initial logon to the domain requires contacting a global catalog, but for subsequent logons, the local domain controller stores (caches) the user's universal group memberships.

To enable universal group members caching for a site, follow these steps:

1. Open Active Directory Sites And Services (dssite.msc) and select the site on which you want to enable UGMC.

2. Right-click NTDS Site Settings in the details pane and select Properties.

3. In the NTDS Site Settings Properties dialog box, shown in Figure 5-1, select Enable Universal Group Membership Caching and then specify the Refresh Cache From setting.

FIGURE 5-1 The NTDS Site Settings Properties dialog box

Transferring and seizing operations master

Windows Server domains have five operations master roles (also known as flexible single master operations or FSMO) that support the operations of the domain. Each role resides on only a single domain controller. You can transfer one or more roles to a different server in the domain to balance the operations across available domain controllers. Transferring a role requires both the original domain controller and the target domain controller to be online and able to communicate.

If a domain controller is permanently unavailable, you can seize any operations master roles that it held to another domain controller. You should seize roles only when the original holder of the role is not available and can't be restored. After a role has been seized from a domain controller, that domain controller should never be reintroduced into the domain.

Two of the operations master roles are forest-wide roles, and the remaining three are domain-wide roles, as follows:

- **Schema master** Responsible for performing updates to the AD DS schema. The schema master role is a forest-wide role. The domain controller that holds the schema master role is the only domain controller that can perform write operations to the directory schema. Transferring or seizing the schema master role requires the Change Schema Master right. By default, only members of the Schema Administrators group have this right.

- **Domain naming master** Responsible for the addition and removal of all domains and directory partitions in the forest. The domain naming master role is a forest-wide role. Transferring or seizing the domain naming master role requires the Change Domain Master right. By default, only members of the Enterprise Admins group have this right.

- **RID master** Allocates blocks of relative identifiers (RIDs) to each domain controller in the domain. The RID master role is a domain-wide role. When a domain controller creates a new security principal, such as a user, group, or computer object, the object is assigned a globally unique security identifier (SID). The SID is a combination of the domain SID plus an RID for the object. Transferring or seizing the RID master role requires the Change RID Master right. By default, only members of the Domain Admins group have this right.

- **PDC emulator master** Receives preferential replication of password changes in the domain and is the definitive source for password information. The primary domain controller (PDC) emulator in the forest root domain is the Windows Time Service time source for the forest. The PDC emulator master role is a domain-wide role. Transferring or seizing the PDC emulator role requires the Change PDC right. By default, only members of the Domain Admins group have this right.

- **Infrastructure master** Responsible for updating object references in its domain to objects in another domain and replicating changed references to other domain controllers in the domain. The infrastructure master role is a domain-wide role. Transferring or seizing the infrastructure master role requires the Change Infrastructure Master right. By default, only members of the Domain Admins group have this right.

There are three methods for transferring operations master roles in Windows Server 2012 and Windows Server 2012 R2, and two of them can be used for seizing operations master roles if it is required. The three methods are as follows:

- **Graphical**   Only for transferring roles; requires three different consoles to transfer the five roles.

- **Ntdsutil.exe**   Can be used for both transferring and seizing roles; supported on all versions of Windows Server.

- **Move-ADDirectoryServerOperationMasterRole**   Can be used for both transferring and seizing roles; supported on Windows Server 2012 and Windows Server 2012 R2, and on Windows 8.x with RSAT installed.

Transferring roles graphically

Three different consoles are required to transfer all five roles:

- Active Directory Users and Computers is used to change the three domain-wide roles.

- Active Directory Domains And Trusts is used to change the forest-wide domain naming master role.

- Active Directory Schema is used to change the forest-wide schema master role.

Before you can use the Active Directory Schema console, you need to register the schema management DLL. Follow these steps to transfer the schema master role:

1. Open an elevated command or Windows PowerShell window with an account that has the Change Schema Master right. By default, only members of the Schema Admins group have this right.

2. Type **regsvr32 schmmgmt.dll** to register the schema management dll.

3. Type **mmc** to open a blank management console and select Add/Remove Snap-in from the File menu.

4. Select Active Directory Schema from the Available Snap-ins list, as shown in Figure 5-2.

5. Click Add and then click OK to open the Active Directory Schema console.

6. Select Active Directory Schema in the console tree and right-click.

7. Select Operations Master from the Action menu to open the Change Schema Master dialog box shown in Figure 5-3.

8. Click Change to move the schema master role from to the new domain controller.

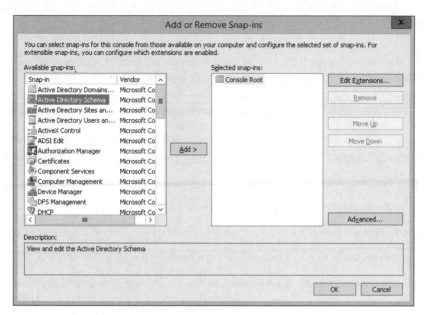

FIGURE 5-2 The Add Or Remove Snap-ins dialog box

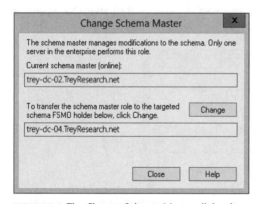

FIGURE 5-3 The Change Schema Master dialog box

To transfer the domain naming operations master role, open the Active Directory Domains And Trusts console. Right-click Active Directory Domains And Trusts and select Operations Master from the Action menu.

To transfer the three domain-wide roles, open Active Directory Users And Computers, right-click the domain in the console tree, and select Operations Masters to open the Operations Masters dialog box. This dialog box has three tabs, one each for RID, PDC, and Infrastructure.

Transferring roles by using Ntdsutil.exe

The Ntdsutil.exe utility is the legacy way to transfer or seize roles with Windows Server domains. If your current operations master roles reside on versions of Windows Server prior to Windows Server 2012, you must use Ntdsutil.exe to transfer or seize the role. The steps to transfer the PDC Emulator role from trey-dc-02.TreyResearch.net to trey-dc-04.TreyResearch.net are the following:

1. Log on to the target domain controller (trey-dc-04) with an account that has the Change PDC right. By default, members of the Domain Admins group have this right.

2. Open a command or Windows PowerShell window with Run As Administrator.

3. At the elevated prompt, type **Ntdsutil** to open the Ntdsutil.exe shell.

4. Type **Roles** to move to the fsmo maintenance prompt.

5. Type **Connections** to move to the server connections prompt.

6. Type **connect to domain treyresearch.net** to bind to the domain and the local server.

7. Type **Quit** to return to the fsmo maintenance prompt.

8. Type **Transfer PDC** and click Yes on the Role Transfer Confirmation Dialog shown in Figure 5-4.

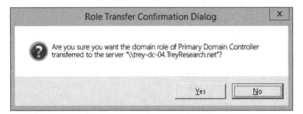

FIGURE 5-4 The Role Transfer Confirmation Dialog

9. Type **Quit** to return to the Ntdsutil.exe prompt, and then **Quit** again to exit Ntdsutil. Figure 5-5 shows the complete sequence.

> ***NOTE*** **USE CORRECT SERVER AND DOMAIN NAMES FOR YOUR ENVIRONMENT**
>
> The example shown in Figure 5-5 and in the steps immediately preceding uses a domain of TreyResearch.net and the target server of trey-dc-04.TreyResearch.net. Substitute the correct values for your environment.

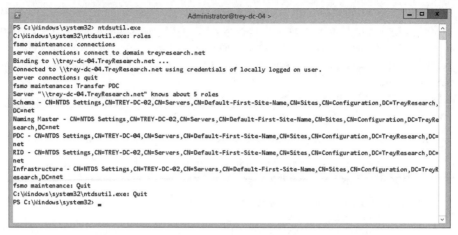

```
PS C:\Windows\system32> ntdsutil.exe
C:\Windows\system32\ntdsutil.exe: roles
fsmo maintenance: connections
server connections: connect to domain treyresearch.net
Binding to \\trey-dc-04.TreyResearch.net ...
Connected to \\trey-dc-04.TreyResearch.net using credentials of locally logged on user.
server connections: quit
fsmo maintenance: Transfer PDC
Server "\\trey-dc-04.TreyResearch.net" knows about 5 roles
Schema - CN=NTDS Settings,CN=TREY-DC-02,CN=Servers,CN=Default-First-Site-Name,CN=Sites,CN=Configuration,DC=TreyResearch,
DC=net
Naming Master - CN=NTDS Settings,CN=TREY-DC-02,CN=Servers,CN=Default-First-Site-Name,CN=Sites,CN=Configuration,DC=TreyRe
search,DC=net
PDC - CN=NTDS Settings,CN=TREY-DC-04,CN=Servers,CN=Default-First-Site-Name,CN=Sites,CN=Configuration,DC=TreyResearch,DC=
net
RID - CN=NTDS Settings,CN=TREY-DC-02,CN=Servers,CN=Default-First-Site-Name,CN=Sites,CN=Configuration,DC=TreyResearch,DC=
net
Infrastructure - CN=NTDS Settings,CN=TREY-DC-02,CN=Servers,CN=Default-First-Site-Name,CN=Sites,CN=Configuration,DC=TreyR
esearch,DC=net
fsmo maintenance: Quit
C:\Windows\system32\ntdsutil.exe: Quit
PS C:\Windows\system32>
```

FIGURE 5-5 THE Ntdsutil.exe sequence for transferring the PDC role

The steps to transfer the other roles are the same as for transferring the PDC Emulator role.

Transferring by using Windows PowerShell ActiveDirectory module

Beginning with Windows Server 2012 (and Windows 8 with RSAT), you can use the Move-ADDirectoryServerOperationMasterRole cmdlet to transfer or seize the FSMO roles. Unlike ntdsutil.exe, you can transfer multiple roles with a single command. For example, to transfer the PDC and RID FSMO roles from trey-dc-04 to trey-dc-02, use the following command:

```
Move-ADDirectoryServerOperationMasterRole -Identity trey-dc-02 -OperationMasterRole
RIDMaster,PDC
```

To seize the roles when the original holder is no longer available, use the -Force parameter with the Move-ADDirectoryServerOperationMasterRole cmdlet.

Installing and configuring a read-only domain controller

Windows Server 2008 introduced the read-only domain controller (RODC), which hosts read-only partitions of the AD DS database. Because changes can't be made to the RODC, it is an appropriate solution for deployment to sites in which physical security is less able to be controlled, such as branch offices. Deploying an RODC to sites connected with poor network bandwidth improves the logon time and the time required to access network resources when password caching is configured.

To simplify deployment of RODCs to remote sites, you can stage the deployment of the RODC. A staged deployment creates the account for the RODC; when the computer is actually deployed, it is promoted to an RODC. To reduce the network load, a staged deployment can be done with the AD DS database on physical media, enabling the RODC deployment to use the Install from Media (IFM) feature.

When using a prestaged RODC account, the server that will become the RODC should *not* be joined to the domain where it will be an RODC prior to attaching to the RODC account. If you use the Active Directory Domain Services Installation Wizard or begin the deployment from the Active Directory Administrative Center, you have to prepare the domain with adprep.exe /rodcprep.

Installing an RODC by using Windows PowerShell

Follow these steps to first stage the RODC and then install it on the target computer:

1. From an elevated Windows PowerShell prompt, create the staging account for the RODC. The basic command is this:

```
Add-ADDSReadOnlyDomainControllerAccount `
    -DomainControllerAccountName "trey-rodc-03" `
    -DomainName "TreyResearch.net" `
    -SiteName "Default-First-Site-Name"
```

For a full list of available options, see *http://go.microsoft.com/fwlink/?LinkId=291137*.

2. On the target server, complete the installation of Windows Server 2012 R2. You can use a full installation or a core installation.

3. Set the name of the target server to the name used to create the staging account.

4. Assign static IPv4 and IPv6 addresses to all adapters on the target server.

5. On the target server, install AD DS by using this command:

```
Install-WindowsFeature `
    -Name AD-Domain-Services `
    -IncludeAllSubFeature `
    -IncludeManagementTools
```

6. Connect to the domain and promote the RODC by using the following commands:

```
$myCred = Get-Credential -Message "Enter your domain credentials"
Install-ADDSDomainController `
    -DomainName "TreyResearch.net" `
    -Credential $myCred `
    -UseExistingAccount:$True
```

7. You'll be prompted for the SafeModeAdministrorPassword on the command line and then to confirm the password. Make sure that you enter a password that meets the length and complexity requirements for the domain.

When the domain controller promotion completes, the new RODC restarts.

If the RODC is not prestaged, you can still install it by using Windows PowerShell. Follow these steps:

1. Install Windows Server 2012 R2, either full or core installation.

2. Install the AD DS server role, including the management tools and Windows PowerShell cmdlets, by using this command:

```
Install-WindowsFeature `
    -Name AD-Domain-Services `
    -IncludeAllSubFeature `
    -IncludeManagementTools
```

3. Assign the server fixed IPv4 and IPv6 addresses for all network adapters and set the server's name.

4. Promote the server to an RODC and install DNS with the following commands:

```
$myCred = Get-Credential -Message "Enter your domain credentials"
Install-ADDSDomainController `
    -DomainName "TreyResearch.net" `
    -Credential $myCred `
    -InstallDNS `
    -ReadOnlyReplica:$True
```

5. You'll be prompted for the SafeModeAdministrorPassword on the command line and then to confirm the password. Make sure that you enter a password that meets the length and complexity requirements for the domain.

   When the domain controller promotion completes, the new RODC restarts.

For the full syntax and options for the Install-ADDSDomainController cmdlet, see *http://go.microsoft.com/fwlink/?LinkId=291139.*

Installing a RODC graphically

You can install an RODC graphically, whether it is prestaged or not. If the first RODC you install is not a staged RODC, you don't need to prepare the domain for the RODC because the wizard does it for you. However, if the first RODC is a staged RODC, you have to manually run adprep.exe /rodcprep one time to prepare the domain.

To stage an RODC, follow these steps:

1. Open the Active Directory Administrative Center. You can select it from the Tools menu of Server Manager or by typing **dsac.exe** in a shell.

2. In the left pane, select the domain in which you want to create the RODC and click Domain Controllers, as shown in Figure 5-6.

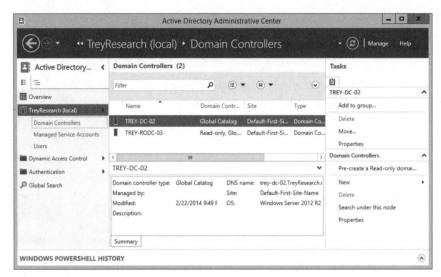

FIGURE 5-6 The Active Directory Administrative Center Domain Controllers page

3. In the Tasks pane, under Domain Controllers, click Pre-create A Read-only Domain Controller Account.

4. On the Welcome page, select Use Advanced Mode Installation and then click Next.

5. On the Network Credentials page, select My Current Logged On Credentials or select Alternate Credentials. The credentials you use must be a member of the Domain Admins or Enterprise Admins groups. Click Next.

6. On the Specify The Computer Name page, shown in Figure 5-7, enter the computer name you want to use for the RODC and then click Next.

7. On the Select A Site page, specify the site in which the new RODC will reside and click Next.

8. On the Additional Domain Controller Options page shown in Figure 5-8, specify whether the new RODC will be a DNS Server and a Global Catalog server. The default in domains with AD-integrated DNS is for both to be selected. Click Next.

FIGURE 5-7 The Specify The Computer Name page

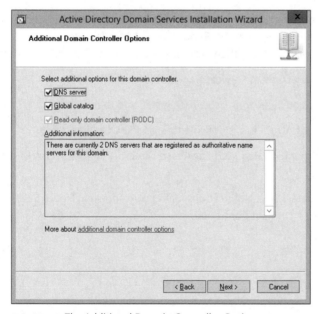

FIGURE 5-8 The Additional Domain Controller Options page

9. On the Delegation Of RODC Installation And Administration page, specify a group or individual user to have local administrative access to the RODC, as well as be able to attach the RODC to the account you're creating. If you don't specify any additional names or groups, only a member of the Domain Admins group can attach the RODC to the account. Click Next.

10. On the Summary page, you see all the settings of the wizard and you can then export the settings to an answer file for use with unattended installations. Click Next and then click Finish to close the wizard.

After the account is created, you can attach a server to the account either graphically or by using the Install-ADDSDomainServer cmdlet, as described earlier. To attach it graphically, follow these steps:

1. Install Windows Server 2012 R2 on the target computer.

2. Open Server Manager and click Configure This Local Server.

3. Assign fixed IPv4 and IPv6 addresses for all adapters and set the Computer Name value to the name chosen when you prestaged the RODC.

4. Select Add Roles And Features from the Manage menu. Click Next, Select Role-based Or Feature-based Installation, and click Next twice.

5. On the Select Server Roles page, select Active Directory Domain Services. Click Add Features when the Add Features That Are Required For Active Directory Domain Services page opens. Click Next and then click Next again on the Select Features page.

6. Read the Active Directory Domain Services page and click Next.

7. On the Confirm Installation Selections page, click Install and then Close.

8. In Server Manager, select AD DS in the console tree, as shown in Figure 5-9.

9. Click More in the Configuration Required For Active Directory Domain Services At warning bar.

10. In the All Server Task Details And Notifications dialog box, shown in Figure 5-10, click Promote This Server To A Domain Controller.

FIGURE 5-9 The AD DS section of Server Manager

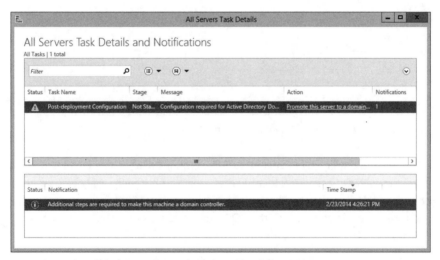

FIGURE 5-10 The All Servers Task Details And Notifications page

11. In the Active Directory Domain Services Configuration Wizard shown in Figure 5-11. Specify the domain to connect to and the credentials to use to attach to the RODC domain account.

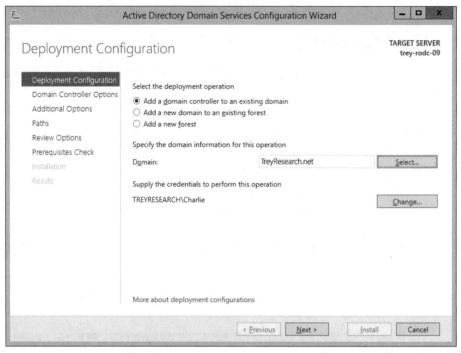

FIGURE 5-11 The Deployment Configuration page

12. Click Next to display the Domain Controller Options page, as shown in Figure 5-12. The precreated RODC account is identified as shown by the yellow banner. Complete the options, including a Directory Services Restore Mode (DSRM) password. Click Next and complete the wizard to attach the RODC to the computer account you prestaged in AD DS.

13. On the Prerequisites Check page shown in Figure 5-13, verify that all prerequisites have been met. If there are anomalies identified, correct them and click Rerun Prerequisites Check until you get a green check mark. Then click Install to promote the RODC.

14. Click Install; the computer is promoted to an RODC and restarts to complete the promotion.

The steps for installing an RODC that you haven't prestaged are essentially similar, except that you need to specify the information that you specified during the staging process.

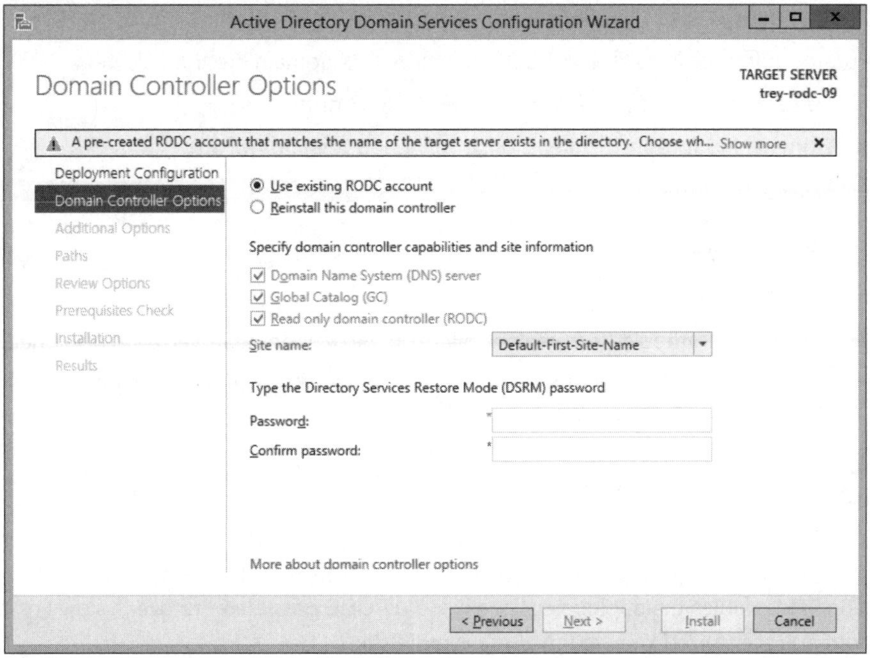

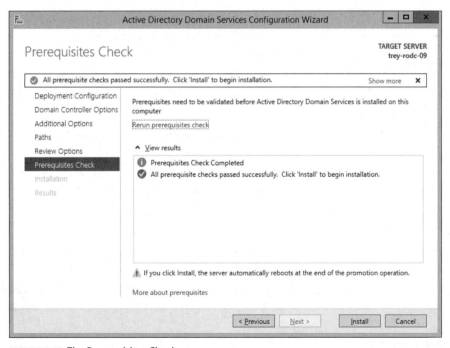

FIGURE 5-12 The Domain Controller Options page

FIGURE 5-13 The Prerequisites Check page

RODC prerequisites

The prerequisites for installing an RODC in your AD DS domain are the following:

- Forest functional level of Windows Server 2003 or higher.

- Domain and forest prep steps (*once only* per domain or forest).

  ```
  adprep /forestprep
  adprep /domainprep /gpprep
  adprep /rodcprep
  ```

- AD DS installed.

- At least one writable domain controller running Windows Server 2008 or higher. The domain controller must also be a DNS server and have a registered name server (NS) resource record.

Installing a domain controller from media

When deploying a domain controller at a remote location, you can speed up the process of initial replication by installing the AD DS database from disk: IFM. When combined with staging, IFM enables the deployment of a remote RODC possible even over a slow link and without any specialized knowledge at the remote site.

To create the media, use the Ntdsutil.exe ifm command. You can also create the installation media by restoring a critical-volume backup of a domain controller in the same domain. The requirements for IFM are these:

- You can't use IFM to create the first domain controller in a domain; there must be a Windows Server 2008 or later domain controller.

- The IFM media must be taken from the same domain as the new domain controller.

- If you're creating a global catalog server, the IFM must be from a domain controller that is also a global catalog.

- To install a domain controller that is also a DNS server, the IFM must be from a domain controller that is also a DNS server.

- To create installation media for a writable domain controller, you must create the IFM on a writeable domain controller that is running Windows Server 2008 or later.

- To create installation media for an RODC, you can create the IFM on either a writeable domain controller or an RODC.

- To create installation media that includes SYSVOL, you must create the IFM on a domain controller running Windows Server 2008 Service Pack 2 or later.

To create the installation media, open a command shell or Windows PowerShell window with Run As Administrator. In the shell, use the following commands to create the media:

```
Ntdsutil
activate instance ntds
ifm
create [Sysvol] <full/RODC> <pathtomediafolder>
```

The installation media can be saved to a network shared folder or to removable media. For example, to create RODC installation media that includes the SYSVOL on the D:\IFM folder, use create sysvol RODC "D:\IFM" to replace the last command in the preceding sequence.

After you have the installation media, create a new domain controller by specifying the media source as part of the Install-ADDSDomainController cmdlet. Use the -InstallationMediaPath parameter. For example:

```
$myCred = Get-Credential -Message "Enter your domain credentials"
Install-ADDSDomainController `
    -DomainName "TreyResearch.net" `
    -Credential $myCred `
    -InstallDNS `
    -InstallationMediaPath "D:\IFM" `
    -ReadOnlyReplica:$True
```

EXAM TIP

The -InstallationMediaPath parameter is quite fussy. The path must be on a local drive, not a mounted remote share. The path must *not* include a trailing "\", and should not include the final "Active Directory" portion of the path. So, "D:\IFM" is acceptable, but "D:\IFM\" or "D:\IFM\Active Directory" is not.

Configuring domain controller cloning

Windows Server does not support cloning of virtualized domain controllers by simply copying the .vhd or .vhdx files (virtual hard disk [VHD] files). You need to follow the supported cloning process to ensure that domain integrity and data are maintained. The process for cloning a domain controller is the following:

1. Verify that the environment meets the requirements.

2. Prepare the source domain controller.

3. Create the cloned domain controller.

Verifying the environment

The support for cloning a virtualized domain controllerwas introduced with Windows Server 2012. The environment for cloning must meet the following requirements:

- PDC emulator FSMO role hosted on Windows Server 2012 or Windows Server 2012 R2 domain controller
- PDC emulator available during the cloning operation
- Clone source and target of Windows Server 2012 or Windows Server 2012 R2
- Virtualization host platform supports VM-Generation ID (VMGID)

- Supported Microsoft virtualization host platforms:

  - Microsoft Windows Server 2012 with Hyper-V feature

  - Microsoft Windows Server 2012 R2 with Hyper-V feature

  - Microsoft Windows Server 2012 Hyper-V Server

  - Microsoft Windows Server 2012 R2 Hyper-V Server

  - Microsoft Windows 8 with Hyper-V client feature

  - Microsoft Windows 8.1 with Hyper-V client feature

> **IMPORTANT   UNSUPPORTED RESTORES**
>
> Virtualized domain controllers do *not* support safe restores or cloning by manual copying of VHDs over existing files or by VHD file restore using file backup or full disk backup software.

Preparing the source domain controller

After you verify that the environment meets the minimum requirements, you need to prepare the source domain controller. The domain controller needs to be authorized for cloning by making it a member of the Cloneable Domain Controllers security group in Active Directory. You can use the Active Directory Administrative Center console, Active Directory Users and Computers, or the Windows PowerShell ActiveDirectory module to assign the source domain controller to the security group. The Windows PowerShell for this is the following:

```
Get-ADComputer <sourcedc> | Foreach-Object `
    {Add-ADGroupMember -Identity "Cloneable Domain Controllers" $_.SamAccountName }
```

Identify any applications that will prevent cloning by running the Get-ADDCCloningExclusionApplicationList cmdlet. Any applications or services identified must be either removed or added to the CustomDCCloneAllowList.xml file. After you remove any services or applications that don't support cloning, you can use the -GenerateXML parameter to create the CustomDCCloneAllowList.xml file. For example, on trey-rodc-03, I got the following:

```
Get-ADDCCloningExcludedApplicationList
Name                                        Type
----                                        ----
Vim 7.3                                     Program
HyperSnap 7                                 WoW64Program
```

Both programs are simple utilities used in writing this chapter: one to edit files and the other to take screen shots. Neither one poses an issue with cloning, so I know I'm safe to add them to the CustomDCCloneAllowList.xml file. So I ran the cmdlet again:

```
Get-ADDCCloningExcludedApplicationList -GenerateXML
The inclusion list was written to 'C:\Windows\NTDS\CustomDCCloneAllowList.xml'.
```

For applications that are flagged by the Get-ADDCCloningExcludedApplicationList cmdlet, a good rule of thumb is that if they are Microsoft applications or services, such as the DHCP Server role, they really should be removed, not added to the CustomDCCloneAllowList.xml file. For third-party applications, such as the two on my server, verify with the vendor or remove them to be safe.

Remove any stand-alone MSAs from the source server. Group MSAs (gMSAs) support cloning, but stand-alone ones do not. Use Get-ADComputerServiceAccount to identify any MSAs and use Uninstall-ADServiceAccount to remove the accounts. You can read the accounts after you finish the offline cloning operation by using the Install-ADServiceAccount cmdlet.

Create the DCCloneConfig.xml file by using the New-ADDCCloneConfig cmdlet, which creates the XML file based on the options you specify in the command. Table 5-3 shows the arguments to New-ADDCCloneConfig.

TABLE 5-3 New-ADDCCloneConfig parameters

Parameter	Description
None	Creates a blank DCCloneConfig.xml file.
-CloneComputerName	Specifies the clone (target) computer name.
-Path	Specifies a custom path for the DCCloneConfig.xml file. Default value is $env:windir\ntds.
-SiteName	The Active Directory site name for the target domain controller.
-IPv4Address	The static IPv4 address of the cloned computer.
-IPv4SubnetMask	The static IPv4 subnet mask of the cloned computer.
-IPv4DefaultGateway	The static IPv4 default gateway address of the cloned computer.
-IPv4DNSResolver	The static IPv4 DNS entries of the cloned computer. It is an array data type of up to four entries in a comma-separated list.
-PreferredWINSServer	The static IPv4 address of the primary Windows Internet Name Service (WINS) server.
-AlternateWINSServer	The static IPv4 address of the secondary WINS server.
-IPv6DNSResolver	The static IPv6 DNS entries of the cloned computer. It is an array data type in a comma-separated list.
-Offline	Overwrites any existing DCCloneConfig.xml file and does not perform any validation tests.
-Static	Required if you specify static IP address arguments.

EXAM TIP

Domain controller cloning is a new feature that is likely to get solid coverage in the exam. Make sure you know the file names and commands for the clone process; and which items will definitely prevent a successful clone, such as DHCP.

The results of running New-ADDCCloneConfigFile on trey-rodc-03 are shown in Figure 5-14.

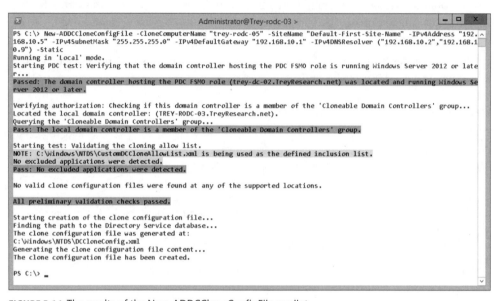

```
Administrator@Trey-rodc-03 >
PS C:\> New-ADDCCloneConfigFile -CloneComputerName "trey-rodc-05" -SiteName "Default-First-Site-Name" -IPv4Address "192.
168.10.5" -IPv4SubnetMask "255.255.255.0" -IPv4DefaultGateway "192.168.10.1" -IPv4DNSResolver ("192.168.10.2","192.168.1
0.9") -Static
Running in 'Local' mode.
Starting PDC test: Verifying that the domain controller hosting the PDC FSMO role is running Windows Server 2012 or late
r...
Passed: The domain controller hosting the PDC FSMO role (trey-dc-02.TreyResearch.net) was located and running Windows Se
rver 2012 or later.

Verifying authorization: Checking if this domain controller is a member of the 'Cloneable Domain Controllers' group...
Located the local domain controller: (TREY-RODC-03.TreyResearch.net).
Querying the 'Cloneable Domain Controllers' group...
Pass: The local domain controller is a member of the 'Cloneable Domain Controllers' group.

Starting test: Validating the cloning allow list.
NOTE: C:\Windows\NTDS\CustomDCCloneAllowList.xml is being used as the defined inclusion list.
No excluded applications were detected.
Pass: No excluded applications were detected.

No valid clone configuration files were found at any of the supported locations.

All preliminary validation checks passed.

Starting creation of the clone configuration file...
Finding the path to the Directory Service database...
The clone configuration file was generated at:
C:\Windows\NTDS\DCCloneConfig.xml
Generating the clone configuration file content...
The clone configuration file has been created.

PS C:\> _
```

FIGURE 5-14 The results of the New-ADDCCloneConfigFile cmdlet

The final step to prepare the source computer for cloning is to gracefully shut it down. You can use the GUI, the legacy shutdown.exe command, the Stop-Computer cmdlet, or the Stop-VM cmdlet.

Creating the cloned domain controller

After the source domain controller is gracefully shut down, you can copy its VHDs by using File Explorer, Xcopy.exe, or Robocopy.exe to the new location; or use Hyper-V export. Whichever method you use, you should remove any snapshots prior to cloning, and merge any differencing disks prior to importing or creating the clone domain controller. After the files for the cloned domain controller are copied, you can restart the source domain controller.

Create the new target virtual machine (VM) by using whatever method you prefer. For single-disk VMs with a single network adapter, it's probably easiest to rename the copied VHD and create a new VM that uses it.

Start the target cloned VM, and the cloning operation automatically completes (see Figure 5-15), based on the settings in the DCCloneConfig.xml file.

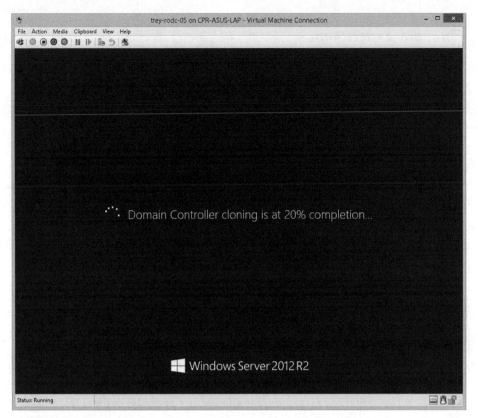

FIGURE 5-15 The Virtual Machine Connection to a domain controller being cloned

When the cloning is complete, both the original source domain controller and the new cloned domain controller are in the Cloneable Domain Controllers security group. They should be removed from this group except during active cloning operations.

Thought experiment

Supporting a new branch office

In this thought experiment, apply what you've learned about this objective. You can find answers to these questions in the "Answers" section at the end of this chapter.

You are the network administrator for TreyResearch.net, and the company has decided to expand operations to include an East Coast branch office. Initially, this office will be in shared space and be limited to sales and administrative staff, with no full-time IT staff onsite and only a limited bandwidth connection to the main data center.

1. Should you create a separate subdomain for the new office?

2. Does the office need a domain controller? If it does, what kind should it have?

3. Should one of the administrative staff be assigned as a Domain Administrator to support the operations at the new office?

Objective summary

- UGMC can speed up local user logons and reduce loads on slow WAN connections where a global catalog server isn't available.

- AD DS uses five operations master roles to support the operation of the forest and domain.

- FSMO roles can be transferred to a different domain controller if both the source and target domain controllers are available and communicating.

- When a domain controller that holds an operations master role becomes permanently unavailable, the role can be seized by another domain controller.

- RODCs enable an improved user experience at remote sites.

- RODCs can be prestaged for deployment, allowing them to be automatically promoted without administrator intervention.

- In virtual environments, domain controllers can be cloned to quickly create multiple domain controllers that have a known and consistent configuration.

Objective review

1. What commands should you use to prepare a clone of domain controller trey-dc-03? (Choose all that apply.)

   A. Get-ADDCCloningExcludedApplicationList -GenerateXML

   B. Get-ADDCCloningAllowedList -GenerateXML

   C. Get-ADComputer trey-dc-03 | Foreach-Object {Add-ADGroupMember -Identity "Cloneable Domain Controllers" $_.SamAccountName }

   D. Get-ADDomainController trey-dc-03 | Foreach-Object {Add-ADGroupMember -Identity "Cloneable Domain Controllers" $_.SamAccountName }

   E. New-ADDCCloneConfigFile

2. Server trey-dc-02 hosts all the forest-wide operations master roles. You want to transfer the roles to server trey-dc-04, and are logged in to trey-dc-04 with an account that is a member of the Schema Admins group. What commands can you use to transfer the roles?

   A. Move-ADDirectoryServerOperationMasterRole -Identity trey-dc-02 -OperationMasterRole SchemaMaster,InfrastuctureMaster

   B. Move-ADDirectoryServerOperationMasterRole -Identity trey-dc-04 -OperationMasterRole SchemaMaster,DomainNamingMaster

   C. Move-ADDirectoryServerOperationMasterRole -Identity trey-dc-02 -OperationMasterRole SchemaMaster,DomainNamingMaster

   D. Move-ADDirectoryServerOperationMasterRole -Identity trey-dc-04 -OperationMasterRole SchemaMaster,InfrastructureMaster

3. What command can you use to stage an RODC?

   A. New-ADDSDomainControllerAccount

   B. Install-ADDSDomainController

   C. Add-ADDSReadOnlyDomainControllerAccount

   D. New-ADDSReadOnlyDomainControllerAccount

Objective 5.3: Maintain Active Directory

Like most features of Windows Server, Active Directory requires routine maintenance to ensure that it performs optimally and is recoverable. This objective covers basic maintenance and backup procedures that are likely to be on the exam.

This objective covers how to:

- Back up Active Directory and SYSVOL
- Manage Active Directory offline
- Optimize an Active Directory database
- Clean up metadata
- Configure Active Directory snapshots
- Perform object- and container-level recovery
- Perform Active Directory restore
- Configure and restore objects by using the Active Directory Recycle Bin

Backing up Active Directory and SYSVOL

Use the standard Windows Server Backup and the backup command-line tools to create backups that can restore Active Directory and the SYSVOL folder. Windows Server 2012 and Windows Server 2012 R2 support system state, critical-volumes, and full-server backups from the following:

- GUI with the Windows Server Backup (wbadmin.msc)
- Command line with the wbadmin.exe utility
- Windows PowerShell with the WindowsServerBackup module

The Windows Server Backup feature is not installed by default. Use Add Roles And Features in Server Manager or the Install-WindowsFeature cmdlet to add the Windows Server Backup feature. The three key backup types are these:

- **System state backup**   A system state backup can be used to recover registry and directory service configuration and data, along with the SYSVOL.
- **Critical-volumes backup**   A critical-volumes backup or bare-metal backup can be used to restore in a fail-to-boot scenario as well as to recover Active Directory and the SYSVOL.
- **Full server backup**   A full server backup can be used to fully restore a failed server to new hardware. It can also be used for Active Directory restore and SYSVOL restore.

The Wbadmin.exe command line and the WindowsServerBackup Windows PowerShell commands can be used to configure and initiate backups, including system state backups. The Wbadmin.exe syntax is this:

```
wbadmin.exe /?
wbadmin 1.0 - Backup command-line tool
(C) Copyright 2013 Microsoft Corporation. All rights reserved.

---- Commands Supported ----

ENABLE BACKUP              -- Creates or modifies a daily backup schedule.
DISABLE BACKUP             -- Disables the scheduled backups.
START BACKUP               -- Runs a one-time backup.
STOP JOB                   -- Stops the currently running backup or recovery
                              operation.
GET VERSIONS               -- Lists details of backups that can be recovered
                              from a specified location.
GET ITEMS                  -- Lists items contained in a backup.
START RECOVERY             -- Runs a recovery.
GET STATUS                 -- Reports the status of the currently running
                              operation.
GET DISKS                  -- Lists the disks that are currently online.
GET VIRTUALMACHINES        -- Lists current Hyper-V virtual machines.
START SYSTEMSTATERECOVERY  -- Runs a system state recovery.
START SYSTEMSTATEBACKUP    -- Runs a system state backup.
DELETE SYSTEMSTATEBACKUP   -- Deletes one or more system state backups.
DELETE BACKUP              -- Deletes one or more backups.
```

The Windows Server Backup Windows PowerShell cmdlets can also be used to configure a backup by creating a WBPolicy object and then modifying it. For a list of the commands in the WindowsServerBackup module, run this:

```
Get-Command -Mod WindowsServerBackup | Sort Noun,Verb | ft -auto Verb,Noun
```

Managing Active Directory offline

Some Active Directory tasks can be performed offline, including offline promotion to domain controller and offline defragmentation of the AD DS database. Offline defragmentation is covered in the following "Optimizing an Active Directory database" section.

You can promote a server to be a domain controller by using the Install From Media (IFM) option. First, create the installation media by using Ntdsutil.exe:

```
Ntdsutil
activate instance ntds
ifm
create [Sysvol] <full/RODC> <pathtomediafolder>
```

Run the previous commands from an elevated shell with Domain Admin privileges. You can create installation media for an RODC from either a full domain controller or another RODC. However, you can create installation media for a full domain controller only from a full domain controller. You must create the installation media from the same version of Windows Server as the version you want to promote to a domain controller.

After you have the installation media for the IFM option, use the following to promote the server to a domain controller:

```
$myCred = Get-Credential -Message "Enter your domain credentials"
Install-ADDSDomainController `
    -DomainName "TreyResearch.net" `
    -Credential $myCred `
    -InstallDNS `
    -InstallationMediaPath "D:\IFM"
```

If you are logged in with an account that has Domain Admin privileges, you can skip the credentials. If you are promoting a domain controller that is also a DNS server, the installation media has to be created on a domain controller that is also a DNS server.

Optimizing an Active Directory database

You can optimize an Active Directory database by defragmenting it. Normally, defragmentation automatically occurs online. However, you can do an offline defragmentation to recover space in the AD DS database and optimize it. The tool for offline defragmentation is Ntdsutil. exe. Use the following sequence from an elevated command prompt with Domain Admin credentials on the domain controller where you want to defragment the database:

```
Net stop NTDS
Ntdsutil.exe
activate instance ntds
files
compact to "<location>"
quit
quit
```

If the compaction occurred without error, ntdsutil reports success and lists the remaining steps, as shown in Figure 5-16.

Once back at the command prompt, copy the existing C:\Windows\ntds\ntds.dit file to a temporary location, just in case, and then delete the log files, as described by the Ntdsutil. exe shell, and copy the compacted ntds.nit file back to C:\Windows\ntds. Use the following Ntdsutil.exe sequence to verify the integrity of the compacted database:

```
Ntdsutil.exe
activate instance ntds
files
Integrity
```

If there are no integrity problems with the Active Directory database, ntdsutil.exe reports success and you can type **quit** and then **quit** again to exit Ntdsutil.exe. Restart the ntds service by typing **net start NTDS**.

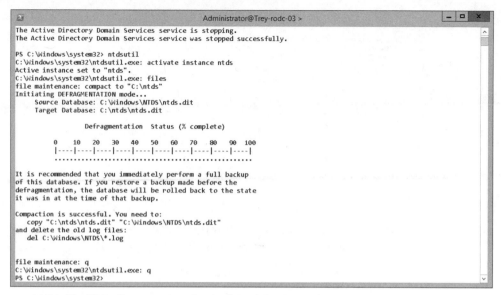

The following image contains a terminal window titled "Administrator@Trey-rodc-03 >" with the following content:

```
The Active Directory Domain Services service is stopping.
The Active Directory Domain Services service was stopped successfully.

PS C:\Windows\system32> ntdsutil
C:\Windows\system32\ntdsutil.exe: activate instance ntds
Active instance set to "ntds".
C:\Windows\system32\ntdsutil.exe: files
file maintenance: compact to "C:\ntds"
Initiating DEFRAGMENTATION mode...
    Source Database: C:\Windows\NTDS\ntds.dit
    Target Database: C:\ntds\ntds.dit

              Defragmentation  Status (% complete)

     0    10   20   30   40   50   60   70   80   90  100
     |----|----|----|----|----|----|----|----|----|----|
     ....................................................

It is recommended that you immediately perform a full backup
of this database. If you restore a backup made before the
defragmentation, the database will be rolled back to the state
it was in at the time of that backup.

Compaction is successful. You need to:
    copy "C:\ntds\ntds.dit" "C:\Windows\NTDS\ntds.dit"
and delete the old log files:
    del C:\Windows\NTDS\*.log

file maintenance: q
C:\Windows\system32\ntdsutil.exe: q
PS C:\Windows\system32>
```

FIGURE 5-16 The Ntdsutil.exe sequence for database defragmentation

Cleaning up metadata

With each new version of Windows Server, Active Directory has gotten better at cleaning up lingering metadata from decommissioned domain controllers. With Windows Server 2012 R2, deleting a domain controller that is no longer available usually doesn't leave any lingering server metadata, but this cleanup requires intervention in some circumstances.

Using Active Directory Users and Computers

If you have to forcibly remove a domain controller that is no longer available, you can use Active Directory Users and Computers to do metadata cleanup. To clean up metadata with Active Directory Users and Computers, follow these steps:

1. Select Domain Controllers in the console tree, right-click the computer object of the domain controller for which you want to clean up the metadata, and click Delete.

2. Click Yes to confirm the deletion.

3. The Deleting Domain Controller dialog box (see Figure 5-17) warns you that you should run the Remove Roles And Features Wizard in Server Manager to remove the domain controller from the domain.

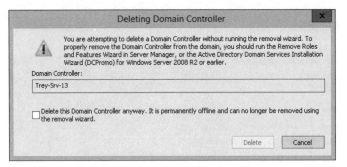

FIGURE 5-17 The Deleting Domain Controller dialog box

4. If the domain controller is no longer available and can't be restored, select the Delete The Domain Controller Anyway. It Is Permanently Offline And Can No Longer Be Removed Using The Removal Wizard box and click Delete.

5. If the domain controller is a global catalog, you are warned again. Click Yes.

6. If one or more FSMO roles is hosted on the server, you are warned that the roles will be moved to a specific domain controller, as shown in Figure 5-18. You can't change where the role will be moved to during this process. If you want the role on a different domain controller, transfer the role after the domain controller deletion is complete.

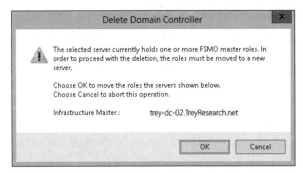

FIGURE 5-18 The Delete Domain Controller dialog box, showing that the Infrastructure master role will be moved

7. Click OK; the domain controller is gone, along with its metadata.

Using Active Directory Sites and Services

You can also use the Active Directory Sites and Services console to clean up metadata. To clean up metadata with ADSS, follow these steps:

1. In the Active Directory Sites and Services console, expand the site where the server is located; then expand the Servers container and select the server name you want to remove.

2. Expand the server name container. If there is an NTDS Settings container, select the container and right-click.

3. Select Delete. In the Active Directory Domain Services dialog box, click Yes to confirm the NTDS Settings deletion.

4. In the Deleting Domain Controller dialog box, if the domain controller is no longer available and can't be restored, select the Delete The Domain Controller Anyway. It Is Permanently Offline And Can No Longer Be Removed Using The Removal Wizard box and click Delete.

5. If the domain controller is a global catalog server, click Yes to confirm the deletion.

6. If the domain controller currently holds one or more operations master roles, click OK to move the role to the domain controller that is shown.

7. Right-click the domain controller that was forcibly removed and click Delete.

8. In the Active Directory Domain Services dialog box, shown in Figure 5-19, click Yes to confirm the deletion.

FIGURE 5-19 The Active Directory Domain Services dialog box

Using Ntdsutil.exe

The third way to clean up metadata is by using the Ntdsutil.exe shell. The exact steps will depend on exactly what vestiges remain and what you're trying to clean up, but the basic process is this:

1. Start Ntdsutil.exe with an account that has Domain Admin privileges.

2. Enter **metadata cleanup** to change to the metadata cleanup: prompt.

3. Enter **connections** to change to the server connections: prompt where you can set the server and domain you're connected to.

4. Enter **connect to domain <fqdn>** where <fqdn> is replaced with the fully qualified domain name (FQDN), such as TreyResearch.net.

5. Enter **quit** to return to the metadata cleanup: prompt.

6. Enter **select operation target** to change to the select operation target: prompt.

7. From this point on, your path will vary depending on what you're trying to clean up. You can see a list of current commands at any level of Ntdsutil.exe by pressing **?**. And you can exit the current level and return to the previous one by typing **quit** or simply **q**.

Configuring Active Directory snapshots

Active Directory snapshots are a point-in-time view of Active Directory, which are created by using the Volume Shadow Copy Service (VSS). You can create a snapshot by using Ntdsutil.exe and then mount it to view the objects and their properties.

To create a snapshot, run the following command from an elevated cmd or Windows PowerShell prompt:

```
ntdsutil snapshot "activate instance ntds" create "list all" quit quit
```

This command creates a snapshot of the ntds database and then lists all available snapshots (see Figure 5-20).

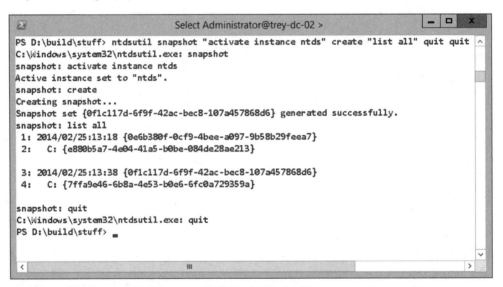

FIGURE 5-20 The elevated Windows PowerShell showing Active Directory snapshot creation

You can mount a specific snapshot from its GUID or its index number by using the following command:

```
Ntdsutil snapshot "activate instance ntds" "list all"  "mount 2" quit quit
```

The result of this command shows that the database was mounted on the C drive at: C:\$SNAP_*datetime*_VOLUMEC$ where *datetime* is the date and time of the snapshot you're mounting. You can now connect to the mounted database using the Dsamain.exe utility:

```
Dsamain -dbpath "C:\$SNAP_201402251635_VOLUMEC$\Windows\NTDS\ntds.dit" -ldapport 45000
```

You can now use Active Directory Users and Computers and other tools to view the content of the snapshot and have a view into Active Directory at the moment it was taken. To connect with Active Directory Users and Computers, for example, follow these steps:

1. Open Active Directory Users And Computers.

2. Select the Active Directory Users And Computers [*servername*].

3. Right-click and select Change Domain Controller from the context menu.

4. In the Change Directory Server dialog box, click <Type a Directory Server name[port] here> and enter the name of the domain controller and the ldap port number you used with Dsamain (see Figure 5-21). Click OK.

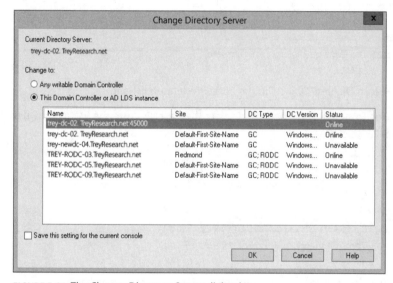

FIGURE 5-21 The Change Directory Server dialog box

5. You now have a complete view of Active Directory Users and Computers at the moment of the snapshot.

Performing object- and container-level recovery

You can use the Ldp.exe utility or Windows PowerShell ADObject cmdlets to restore deleted objects in Active Directory.

To restore a deleted object using Ldp.exe, follow these steps:

1. Open Ldp.exe from an elevated prompt.

2. Select Connect from the Connection menu and enter the name of the server that hosts the forest root domain of your Active Directory. Use port 389.

3. Select Bind from the Connections menu and click OK.

4. Select Controls from the Options menu to open the Controls dialog box shown in Figure 5-22.

FIGURE 5-22 The Controls dialog box of Ldp.exe

5. Select Return Deleted Objects in the Load Predefined list and click OK.

6. Select Tree from the View menu and select the BaseDN from the list, as shown in Figure 5-23. Click OK.

FIGURE 5-23 The Tree View dialog box of Ldp.exe

7. In the console tree, navigate to CN=Deleted Objects and expand it.

8. Select the deleted object you want to recover and select Modify from the Browse menu.

9. In the Modify dialog box, do the following:

   A. In the Edit Entry Attribute box, type **isDeleted** (see Figure 5-24).

   B. Select Delete in the Operation area.

   C. Click Enter to move the [Delete]isDeleted item to the Entry List box.

   D. In the Edit Entry Attribute box, type **distinguishedName**.

   E. In the Values box, type the original DN of the Active Directory Object.

   F. Select Replace in the Operation area and select Extended.

   G. Click Enter and then click Run to restore the deleted object.

To restore an object with Windows PowerShell, use the Get-ADObject and Restore-ADObject cmdlets. Use Get-ADObject with the -IncludeDeletedObjects parameter to find and restore deleted objects.

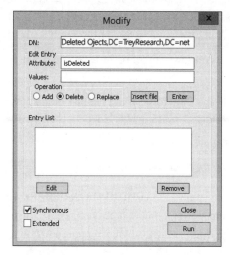

FIGURE 5-24 The Modify dialog box

Performing Active Directory restore

There are two types of Active Directory restore: authoritative and non-authoritative. In an authoritative restore, the Active Directory that you restore becomes the authoritative AD for the domain. In a non-authoritative restore, the Active Directory you restore accepts replication changes from the other domain controllers in the domain. The restored Active Directory acts as a seed rather than as the final result. Both types of restore follow a similar set of steps, but in an authoritative restore, the version number of the restored database is set higher than that on other domain controllers.

Performing an authoritative restore

An authoritative restore recovers the Active Directory database to a specific point in time. You can restore the entire database, an entire container, or a single object. Once restored, that data is replicated to all other domain controllers in the domain. Usually an authoritative restore is used to recover from a serious mistake or corruption. In all cases of an authoritative restore, any changes to Active Directory since the snapshot was taken are lost.

Another concern with authoritative restores is the domain trust relationships between workstations and the domain. Computer account passwords are changed automatically every seven days, and a restoration to a snapshot older than seven days can result in workstations being unable to connect to the domain.

To perform an authoritative restore, follow these steps:

1. Power on the domain controller you want to restore and interrupt the boot process to boot to the Advanced Boot Options menu. Or from an elevated prompt on the running domain controller, type **bcdedit /set safeboot dsrepair** and then reboot the server. This will cause the server to boot into Directory Services Repair mode until changed.

2. Choose Directory Services Repair mode. Windows Server restarts in Safe mode without loading Active Directory.

3. Log on to the Administrator account with the Directory Services Repair mode password and open an elevated command or Windows PowerShell window.

4. Identify the version of backup you want to restore with:

   ```
   Wbadmin get versions -backuptarget:<backupdrive> -machine:<DCName>
   ```

5. After you identify the version identifier for the version you want to restore, use the following command to restore the system state:

   ```
   Wbadmin start systemstaterecovery -version:<versionID> -backuptarget:<backupdrive>
   -machine:<DCName>
   ```

6. After the restore is complete, open Ntdsutil.exe and type **activate instance ntds**; then type **authoritative restore**.
   - To restore the entire database, type **restore database**.
   - To restore a container, type **restore subtree <ObjectDN>** where *<ObjectDN>* is the distinguished name of the container to restore,
   - To restore an individual object, type **restore object <ObjectDN>** where *<ObjectDN>* is the distinguished name of the object to restore.

7. Quit out of Ntdsutil.exe, change the bcdedit sequence with **bcdedit /deletevalue safeboot** if you altered it, and restart the server.

Performing a non-authoritative restore

The steps to perform a non-authoritative restore are the same as the authoritative restore, except that you don't run Ntdsutil.exe. All your items will now be restored, but any items that have been modified since the time of the backup are overwritten when replication occurs. The primary use case for a non-authoritative restore is when there has been a hardware or software failure on the server, and you need to restore the server and the Active Directory database. In this case, the restored Active Directory database acts as a seed, reducing the amount of replication that has to occur from other domain controllers.

Configuring and restoring objects by using the Active Directory Recycle Bin

Before you can use the Recycle Bin to recover deleted Active Directory objects, you need to first enable the Recycle Bin. The AD DS Recycle Bin requires a Forest functional level of at least Windows Server 2008 R2.

Enabling the Active Directory Recycle Bin is a one-way, one-time process and is not reversible. Enabling the feature requires membership in the Enterprise Admins group or equivalent. You can enable the Recycle Bin by using the Active Directory Administrative Center, by using Ldp.exe, or by using the Enable-ADOptionalFeature cmdlet. The Windows PowerShell command to enable it on the TreyResearch.net domain is the following:

```
Enable-ADOptionalFeature `
    -Identity "Recycle Bin Feature" `
    -Scope  ForestOrConfigurationSet `
    -Target "TreyResearch.net"
```

To enable it in the Active Directory Administrative Center, select the domain in the left pane and then click Enable Recycle Bin in the right Tasks pane. When prompted, click OK.

To restore a deleted object in the Recycle Bin, select it in the Deleted Objects container of the Active Directory Administrative Center, and select Restore from the Tasks menu, as shown in Figure 5-25.

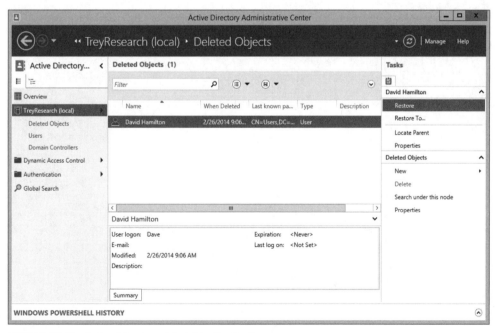

FIGURE 5-25 The Active Directory Administrative Center

Alternately, you can use Windows PowerShell to locate and restore a deleted object. To restore that same David Hamilton user shown in Figure 5-25, use the following:

```
Get-ADObject -Filter {Name -like "David*"} -IncludeDeletedObjects | Restore-ADObject
```

As shown in Figure 5-26, if you search for the David Hamilton object, you don't find it until you use the -IncludeDeletedObjects parameter. After you restore it with Restore-ADObject, the user object is found.

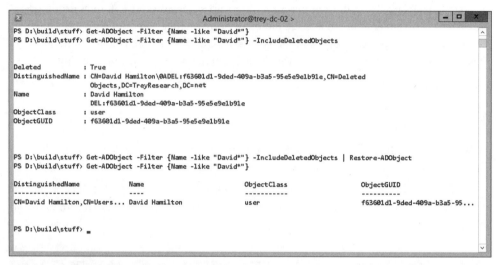

FIGURE 5-26 The Windows PowerShell Restore-ADObject

Thought experiment

Developing a comprehensive Active Directory backup and recovery plan

In this thought experiment, apply what you've learned about this objective. You can find answers to these questions in the "Answers" section at the end of this chapter.

You are the network administrator for TreyResearch.net. You have been asked to develop a comprehensive Active Directory backup and recovery plan for the company. You need to include recommendations on backup types and details on how to restore backups in a variety of use cases.

After a series of meetings, you've identified several recovery use cases, including major disaster recovery to a new location; total failure of a domain controller, including one holding one or more operations master roles; inadvertent or deliberate deletion of a major portion of Active Directory; and inadvertent or deliberate deletion of individual objects in Active Directory.

1. What solutions would you propose for the total failure of a domain controller that doesn't hold operations master roles?

2. What solutions would you propose for the recovery of an entire Active Directory container?

3. What solutions would you propose for the recovery of individual objects in Active Directory?

Objective summary

- Windows Server Backup can be used to create system state backups as well as critical files and full server backups. All three types can be used to restore Active Directory.

- The legacy command line for Windows Server Backup is wbadmin.exe, and there is a full set of Windows PowerShell cmdlets as well.

- Use Install From Media to do an offline domain controller promotion. Create the media in Ntdsutil.exe and use Install-ADDSDomainController with the -InstallationMediaPath parameter.

- Use offline defragmentation to optimize the Active Directory database.

- Use Active Directory snapshots to take a point-in-time view of Active Directory.

- Use Ldp.exe or the ADObject cmdlets to perform an object-level or container-level recovery.

- Use an authoritative Active Directory restore to recover to a specific point in time.

- Use a non-authoritative Active Directory restore to recover from hardware or software failure.

- Enable and use the Active Directory Recycle Bin to restore deleted objects or containers.

Objective review

1. What command or tool do you use to enable the Active Directory Recycle Bin?

   A. Ntdsutil.exe

   B. Active Directory Users and Computers

   C. Active Directory Sites and Services

   D. Enable-ADOptionalFeature

2. What tools or commands do you use to create and mount an Active Directory snapshot? (Choose two.)

   A. ntdsutil snapshot "activate instance ntds" create "list all" quit quit

   B. ntdsutil create snapshot "activate instance ntds" "list all" quit quit

   C. Ntdsutil snapshot "activate instance ntds" "list all" "mount 2" quit quit

   D. Ntdsutil snapshot "activate instance ntds" " mount 2" quit quit

3. You accidentally delete a user account in Active Directory. What can you do to correct the problem and provide the user full access to their files?

   A. Do a non-authoritative restore of Active Directory.

   B. Enable the Active Directory Recycle Bin and restore the deleted user object.

   C. Re-create the user with the exact same name, email, and SAM account name.

   D. Restore the deleted object with Ldp.exe.

Objective 5.4: Configure account policies

Windows Server has traditionally had a single password policy and a single account lockout policy for an entire domain, but with Windows Server 2008, Microsoft introduced fine-grained account policies, making it possible to assign different policies to different sets of users in a domain. In Windows Server 2012, these policies can be set by using the graphical Active Directory Administrative Center or by using Windows PowerShell.

> **This objective covers how to:**
> - Configure domain user password policy
> - Configure and apply Password Settings Objects (PSOs)
> - Delegate password settings management
> - Configure local user password policy
> - Configure account lockout settings
> - Configure Kerberos policy settings

Configuring domain user password policy

The domain user password policy applies to all users in the domain except where specific Password Settings Objects (PSOs) have been assigned. You can set the Default Domain Password Policy by using the Group Policy Management Console (GPMC) or the Set-ADDefaultDomainPasswordPolicy cmdlet.

To set the Default Domain Password Policy by using the GPMC, follow these steps:

1. Open the GPMC and select Default Domain Policy in the Group Policy Objects container for the domain.

2. Click the Settings tab to see the current settings.

3. Right-click the Default Domain Policy and select Edit from the menu to open the Group Policy Management Editor.

4. Navigate to Computer Configuration\Policies\Windows Settings\Security Settings\ Account Policies\Password Settings.

The six settings are shown in Table 5-4.

TABLE 5-4 Default Domain Password Policy settings

Policy	Description
Enforce Password History	Sets the number of unique passwords associated with an account before one can be repeated. Default is 24 in Windows Server 2012 R2. Minimum value is 0; maximum is 24.
Maximum Password Age	Sets the maximum time a password can be used, in days. When set to 0, passwords never expire. Maximum value is 999 days. The value of Maximum Password Age must be greater than the value of Minimum Password age. The default value is 42 days.
Minimum Password Age	The minimum time between password changes, in days. If it is set to 0, users can change passwords immediately after they have changed their password. The Minimum Password Age must be set to less than the Maximum Password Age unless the Maximum Password Age is set to 0, meaning that passwords never expire. The default value is one day.
Minimum Password Length	Sets the minimum number of characters in a password. If set to 0, no password is required. The minimum password length can be set from 0 to 14 characters. The default on domain controllers is 7 characters and 0 on stand-alone servers.
Passwords Must Meet Complexity Requirements	Enabled by default. When enabled, passwords must meet the following requirements: ■ No more than two consecutive characters of the user's account name or full name ■ At least six characters long ■ Contain characters from each of the four categories: uppercase (A-Z), lowercase (a-z), digits (0-9), non-alphanumeric ($, #, %, !)
Store Passwords Using Reversible Encryption	Disabled by default. When enabled, passwords are stored in plain text. Some applications might require this setting, but should be enabled only when security is less important than the application.

To set the Default Domain Password Policy by using Windows PowerShell, use the Set-ADDefaultDomainPasswordPolicy cmdlet. For example, to set the Default Domain Password Policy to a minimum of 10 characters without changing other policies, use this:

```
Get-ADDefaultDomainPasswordPolicy `
  | Set-ADDefaultDomainPasswordPolicy -MinPasswordLength 10
```

Configuring and applying Password Settings Objects

Password Settings Objects (PSOs) are part of the fine-grained account policies introduced in Windows Server 2008. The Active Directory Administrative Center was introduced in Windows Server 2008 R2 and provides a graphical way to configure and apply PSOs. PSOs can also be configured and applied by using the ADFineGrainedPasswordPolicy and ADFineGrainedPasswordPolicySubject sets of cmdlets.

Creating a PSO

To create a PSO by using the Active Directory Administrative Center, follow these steps:

1. Select the Domain (Local) node in the console tree and then double-click the System object in the details pane.

2. Select the Password Settings Container in the System details pane and then click New, Password Settings (as shown in Figure 5-27).

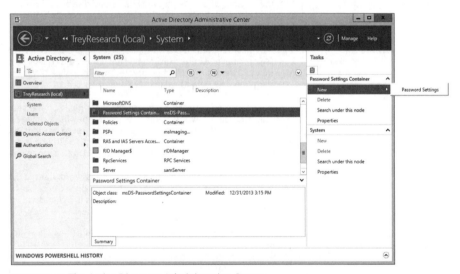

FIGURE 5-27 The Active Directory Administrative Center

3. On the Create Password Settings page, shown in Figure 5-28, enter the specific settings for this password policy. The items that are required are identified by large asterisks.

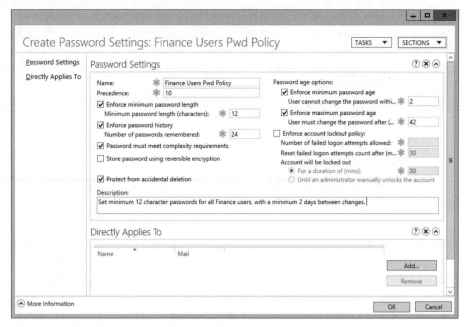

FIGURE 5-28 The Create Password Settings page

4. Optionally, click Add to apply the new PSO to one or more specific security groups.

5. Click OK to create the PSO.

To see the Windows PowerShell for the PSO creation, click Windows PowerShell History at the bottom of the Active Directory Administrative Center. The Windows PowerShell for the PSO creation shown in Figure 5-28 is the following:

```
New-ADFineGrainedPasswordPolicy `
    -ComplexityEnabled:$true `
    -description:"Set minimum 12 character passwords for all Finance users, with a
minimum 2 days between changes." `
    -LockoutDuration:"00:30:00" `
    -LockoutObservationWindow:"00:30:00" `
    -LockoutThreshold:"0" `
    -MaxPasswordAge:"42.00:00:00" `
    -MinPasswordAge:"2.00:00:00" `
    -MinPasswordLength:"12" `
    -Name:"Finance Users Pwd Policy" `
    -PasswordHistoryCount:"24" `
    -Precedence:"10" `
    -ReversibleEncryptionEnabled:$false `
    -Server:"trey-dc-02.TreyResearch.net"
```

Note that when capturing the Windows PowerShell used for an action in the Active Directory Administrative Center, a verbose version of the command is captured. You can use the New-ADFineGrainedPasswordPolicy cmdlet by setting only the items you want to change from the Default Domain Policy. So, for example, you could create a new "Domain Admins Policy" with the following command:

```
New-ADFineGrainedPasswordPolicy `
    -Name "Domain Admins Policy" `
    -MinPasswordLength 10 `
    -Precedence 20 `
    -LockoutThreshold 5
```

If you want to use an existing PSO as a template for a new policy, use Get-ADFineGrainedPasswordPolicy and pipe it to New-ADFineGrainedPasswordPolicy.

Applying a PSO

After you have a PSO, you can apply it to sets of users as appropriate. For example, I created a Domain Admins Policy previously, but it doesn't actually apply the policy to Domain Admins. For that you have to use the Active Directory Administrative Center or the Add-ADFineGrainedPasswordPolicySubject cmdlet.

To add a group to an existing PSO, follow these steps:

1. Open the Active Directory Administrative Center and select Domain (Local) in the left pane.

2. Navigate to the container or OU where the group resides and then double-click the container or OU.

3. Select the group in the details pane and then click Properties in the Tasks pane to open the page for the group.

4. Click Password Settings in the left pane, as shown in Figure 5-29, and then click Assign.

5. Click Assign to open the Select Password Settings Object dialog box and enter the PSO to assign to the group, or click Advanced to search for the PSO.

6. Click OK and then click OK again to add the PSO to the group.

To add a policy called "Domain Users Policy" to the global security group "Domain Users", use the following command:

```
Add-ADFineGrainedPasswordPolicySubject `
    -Subjects "Domain Users" `
    -Identity (Get-ADFineGrainedPasswordPolicy `
    -Filter {name -eq "Domain Users Policy" }).DistinguishedName
```

FIGURE 5-29 The Domain Admins page of the Active Directory Administrative Center

Resultant password settings

You can view the results of fine-grained password policies by selecting the user in the Active Directory Administrative Center and clicking View Resultant Password Settings, or us the Get-ADUserResultantPasswordPolicy cmdlet. This cmdlet accepts a variety of forms for the -Identity parameter, or you can use Get-ADUser and pipe the result to the Get-ADUserResultantPasswordPolicy cmdlet:

```
Get-ADUser -Identity "Charlie" | Get-ADUserResultantPasswordPolicy
```

```
AppliesTo                   : {CN=Domain Admins,CN=Users,DC=TreyResearch,DC=net}
ComplexityEnabled           : True
DistinguishedName           : CN=Domain Admins Policy,CN=Password Settings Container,CN=
System,DC=TreyResearch,DC=net
LockoutDuration             : 00:30:00
LockoutObservationWindow    : 00:30:00
LockoutThreshold            : 5
MaxPasswordAge              : 42.00:00:00
MinPasswordAge              : 1.00:00:00
MinPasswordLength           : 10
Name                        : Domain Admins Policy
ObjectClass                 : msDS-PasswordSettings
ObjectGUID                  : 89a03866-756d-4bd1-9835-5553b6e221de
PasswordHistoryCount        : 24
Precedence                  : 20
ReversibleEncryptionEnabled : False
```

The lower the precedence of the PSO, the higher the priority. If a user is subject to two PSOs, one with a precedence of 50 and one with a precedence of 100, the PSO with a precedence of 50 will be the password setting that is applied to the user.

Removing a PSO

You can remove a PSO with Remove-ADFineGrainedPasswordPolicy or by using the Active Directory Administrative Center. When you remove a policy, any groups that have the policy assigned to them revert to the appropriate GPO policy (usually the Default Domain Policy) or to the lowest-precedence PSO if the group had multiple PSOs assigned to it.

Delegating password settings management

To delegate the ability to set passwords, follow these steps:

1. Open Active Directory Users and Computers.

2. Select the OU or container for which you want to delegate control.

3. Right-click and choose Delegate Control to open the Delegation of Control Wizard.

4. Click Next on the opening screen and then click Add on the Users Or Groups page.

5. In the Select Users, Computers, Or Groups dialog box, enter the group to which you want to delegate control. Click Check Names to verify that it is typed correctly, or click Advanced to search for the user or group of users.

6. Click OK to return to the Users Or Groups page of the Delegation Of Control Wizard.

7. Click Next to open the Tasks To Delegate page, as shown in Figure 5-30.

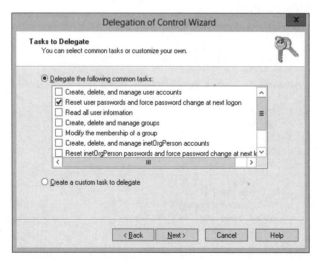

FIGURE 5-30 The Tasks To Delegate page of the Delegation of Control Wizard

8. Select Reset User Passwords And Force Password Change At Next Logon, click Next, and then click Finish.

Configuring local user password policy

The local user password policy is inherited from the Default Domain Policy and can't be overridden for domain joined computers. If you have to set a different local user password policy for a subset of computers, place those computers in a separate OU and define the password policy for that OU. For example, TreyResearch.net has an OU named Win81 with two computers in it. I defined a password policy and linked it to that OU, as shown in Figure 5-31.

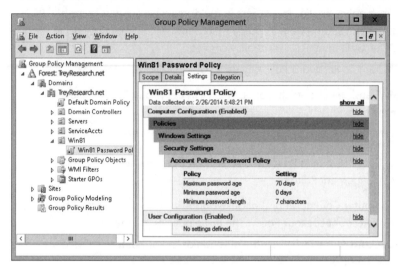

FIGURE 5-31 The Group Policy Management console

The Win81 Password Policy has a more relaxed password policy with a Maximum Password Age of 70 days, a Minimum Password Age of 0 days, and a Minimum Password Length of 7 characters. All other settings it inherits from the Default Domain Policy. As shown in Figure 5-32, this policy has been set on computers in the Win81 OU.

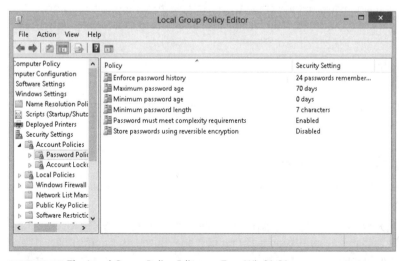

FIGURE 5-32 The Local Group Policy Editor on Trey-Win81-21

The password policies set on the computer trey-win81-21, a member of the Win81 OU, are a combination of the Default Domain Policy (where the policy is Not Defined in the Win81 Password Policy) and the policies of the Win81 Password Policy (where they were Enabled).

Configuring account lockout settings

You configure the default account lockout settings as part of the Default Domain Policy. The domain account lockout policy applies to all users in the domain except where specific PSOs have been assigned. You can set the Default Domain Account Lockout Policy by using the GPMC or the Set-ADDefaultDomainPasswordPolicy cmdlet.

To set the Default Domain Password Policy by using GPMC, follow these steps:

1. Open the GPMC and select Default Domain Policy in the Group Policy Objects container for the domain.

2. Click the Settings tab to see the current settings.

3. Right-click the Default Domain Policy and select Edit from the menu to open the Group Policy Management Editor.

4. Navigate to Computer Configuration\Policies\Windows Settings\Security Settings\ Account Policies\Account Lockout Policy. The three policies are these:

   - **Account Lockout Duration** Sets the duration of lockout before an account automatically unlocks.

   - **Account Lockout Threshold** Configures the number of failed logon attempts before the account is locked. When set to 0, the account will never be locked out.

   - **Reset Lockout Counter** The time before the failed account logon counter is reset to 0. Must be set to less than or equal to the account lockout duration.

To set the Default Domain Account Lockout Policy by using Windows PowerShell, use the Set-ADDefaultDomainPasswordPolicy cmdlet. For example, to set the Default Domain Account Lockout Policy to a threshold of 10 failed logon attempts to lockout accounts, use this command:

```
Get-ADDefaultDomainPasswordPolicy `
| Set-ADDefaultDomainPasswordPolicy -LockoutThreshold 10
```

You can also set fine-grained account lockout policies as part of creating and applying PSOs.

Configuring Kerberos policy settings

The default Kerberos policy settings are set as part of the Default Domain Policy. There are five Kerberos policy settings:

   - **Enforce User Logon Restrictions** When enabled, the Kerberos V5 Key Distribution Center (KDC) validates every session ticket request against the user rights policy. The default value is Enabled.

- **Maximum Lifetime For Service Ticket**   The maximum time (in minutes) that a service ticket is valid to access a particular service. The default is 600 minutes.
- **Maximum Lifetime For User Ticket**   The maximum time (in hours) that a ticket granting ticket is valid. The default is 10 hours.
- **Maximum Lifetime for User Ticket Renewal**   The maximum amount of time (in days) that a ticket granting ticket can be renewed. The default is seven days.
- **Maximum Tolerance For Computer Clock Synchronization**   The maximum difference (in minutes) between a client clock and a domain controller clock that is allowed before a timestamp is considered not authentic. The default is five minutes.

Thought experiment
Enabling fine-grained password policies

In this thought experiment, apply what you've learned about this objective. You can find answers to these questions in the "Answers" section at the end of this chapter.

You are the network administrator for TreyResearch.net. The Default Domain Password Policy is for a minimum 8-character password with enforced complexity that is changed at least once per quarter. Management determines that this policy is insufficient for users with access to sensitive information, including Human Resources, Finance, and Administration users, as well as key management personnel in Engineering. It has mandated that a minimum password length of 15 characters and a maximum age of 35 days is necessary and appropriate while further research is done on the cost and suitability of moving to two-factor authentication (TFA). You need to implement these changes without affecting other users.

1. What options do you have for giving these users password policies different from the default policy?

2. How would you implement this change?

Objective summary

- The Default Domain Policy sets the baseline for all other password policies.
- Individual PSOs can be assigned to security groups in Active Directory.
- You can see the resultant password setting for an object with the Active Directory Administrative Center.
- Account lockout policies are set with the Default Domain Policy and any additional PSOs that apply.
- Use the Delegation of Control Wizard in the Active Directory Users and Computers to delegate password resetting permission.

Objective review

1. What commands or tools would you use to set a default lockout setting?

   A. From an elevated prompt on the PDC Emulator, type **GPEdit.msc**.

   B. From an elevated prompt on the client computer, type **GPEdit.msc**.

   C. From an elevated Windows PowerShell prompt, run Set-ADDefaultDomainPasswordPolicy.

   D. From an elevated Windows PowerShell prompt, run Set-ADAccountExpiration.

2. Some users are reporting that they can't log on to the domain. You suspect a Kerberos issue. What settings can you change to temporarily alleviate the problem?

   A. Set the Default Domain Policy for Maximum Tolerance For Computer Clock Synchronization to 10.

   B. Set the Default Domain Policy for Maximum Tolerance For Computer Clock Synchronization to 0.

   C. Change the Enforce User Logon Restrictions policy to Disabled.

   D. Change the Computer Configuration\Policies\Windows Settings\Security Settings\ Account Policies\Account Lockout Policy\Lockout Threshold to 0.

3. Remote sales users complain that they frequently need to run with a local account on their laptops, but they are still subject to the Domain Password Policy that requires them to change their password every 40 days. Upon consultation with management, there is agreement that a 70-day policy for salespeople is appropriate. How would you implement this new policy? (Choose all that apply.)

   A. Create a Sales OU and then use the Set-ADAccountExpiration cmdlet.

   B. Create a Sales OU and then use the Set-ADFineGrainedPasswordPolicy cmdlet

   C. Create a Sales security group and then use the Set-ADFineGrainedPasswordPolicy cmdlet.

   D. Create a Sales security group and then use the New-ADFineGrainedPasswordPolicy and Add-ADFineGraintPasswordPolicySubject cmdlets.

Answers

This section contains the solutions to the thought experiments and answers to the lesson review questions in this chapter.

Objective 5.1: Thought experiment

1. **Correct answer:** D. Because you want to run this as a scheduled task, it needs to run as a gMSA, not a stand-alone MSA. Virtual accounts would not have access to network resources without giving the entire computer account access.

2. Because you're running a gMSA, you have to initialize the KDS root key with Add-KDSRootKey, if it hasn't been done already. If it has been done, no additional initialization needs to be done.

3. Because the script will run as a scheduled job, it won't have access to the console. You need to ensure that output is redirected appropriately and that no user input is required. Also, ensure that you explicitly set any necessary environmental variables inside the script.

Objective 5.1: Review

1. **Correct answer:** C
   A. **Incorrect**. This tool could be used to create a local service account only.
   B. **Incorrect**. This tool could be used to create a domain service account.
   C. **Correct**. This command creates a new MSA with the -Standalone parameter.
   D. **Incorrect**. This command installs the service account on a computer, but doesn't create it.
   E. **Incorrect**. This command assigns a service account to a computer, but doesn't create it.

2. **Correct answer:** B
   A. **Incorrect**. This command adds an object to an Active Directory group.
   B. **Correct**. This command installs the service account onto the computer that will use it.
   C. **Incorrect**. This command doesn't exist. Instead of simply adding the account, you're actually installing it.
   D. **Incorrect**. This command doesn't exist. There is a Windows PowerShell Add-ADComputerServiceAccount cmdlet, but it only assigns the account as available to the computer; it doesn't actually install it on the computer.

3.   **Correct answer:** B

   A.   **Incorrect**. The Set-Service cmdlet does not allow you to set the account that the service runs as.

   B.   **Correct**. In the Services console, you can set the Log On As property for the service.

   C.   **Incorrect**. You do not need to create an account; it already virtually exists.

   D.   **Incorrect**. You don't need to assign an account to the computer; it already virtually exists.

Objective 5.2: Thought experiment

1.   No. Creating a separate subdomain would increase the administrative overhead for a small office. Without local IT support, you'd also likely need to assign a Domain Administrator in the branch office, increasing the security risks.

2.   Maybe. Depending on the number of users, the level of connectivity, and the users' tolerance for delays, there are several possible scenarios for the branch office running in shared space, including using a Remote Desktop Session Host (RDSH) server. But in most cases, having a local domain controller improves the overall responsiveness perception of the users. The domain controller should be configured as an RODC because of the shared space and lack of a local administrator.

3.   No. You can give delegated authority to manage the RODC to one of the administrative staff without promoting them to a Domain Administrator. They can log on locally to the RODC to perform maintenance operations, but any Active Directory write operations are redirected to the domain controllers in the main datacenter.

Objective 5.2: Review

1.   **Correct answers:** A, C, E

   A.   **Correct**. This command generates the CustomDCCloneAllowList.xml file.

   B.   **Incorrect**. This command doesn't exist. The Windows PowerShell Get-ADDCCloningExcludedApplicationList cmdlet is used to identify applications to exclude from testing by adding to the CustomDCCloneAllowList.xml file.

   C.   **Correct**. This command adds the computer account to the Cloneable Domain Controllers group, allowing it to be cloned.

   D.   **Incorrect**. The Get-ADDomainController command does not provide the correct input object to the Add-ADGroupMember cmdlet.

   E.   **Correct**. This command generates the DCCloneConfig.xml file that is used to control the cloning of the domain controller.

2. **Correct answer:** B

   A. Incorrect. This command has the source domain controller in the Identity parameter; it should be the target. And it is moving the Infrastructure Master role, which is a domain-wide role.

   B. Correct. This command moves the two forest-wide roles to server trey-dc-04.

   C. Incorrect. This command has the source domain controller in the Identity parameter, it should be the target.

   D. Incorrect. This command has the correct target domain controller, but is moving the Infrastructure master role, which is a domain-wide role, not a forest-wide role.

3. **Correct answer:** C

   A. Incorrect. This command doesn't exist.

   B. Incorrect. This command is used to do an online install of a domain controller, including an RODC controller. It is not used with a staged RODC.

   C. Correct. This is the correct command to create a new staging account for an RODC.

   D. Incorrect. This command doesn't exist.

Objective 5.3: Thought experiment

1. The full server backup of a domain controller can be restored as a non-authoritative restore when it doesn't hold the operations master roles. You can do a full, bare-metal restore of the server and let normal replication complete the restoration by updating any Active Directory objects that have changed since the backup was made. If the server holds operations master roles, especially if you have had to seize the roles since the backup was made, you should rebuild the server from scratch and promote it to a domain controller again. You should never try to restore a server that has had the roles seized.

2. The easiest solution is an authoritative restore of the domain controller, in which you restore the subtree of Active Directory that was deleted. Alternately, restoring from the Active Directory Recycle Bin is a good alternative if it is enabled.

3. For individual objects, using the Active Directory Recycle Bin is the easiest solution if you've enabled it in your environment. If you haven't enabled the Recycle Bin, you can use Ldp.exe or the ADObject cmdlets. Use Get-Help ADObject to get a list of the available ADObject cmdlets.

Objective 5.3: Review

1. **Correct answer:** D

   A. **Incorrect.** Ntdsutil.exe can't be used to enable the Active Directory Recycle Bin.

   B. **Incorrect.** Active Directory Users and Computers can't be used to enable the Active Directory Recycle Bin.

   C. **Incorrect.** ADSS can't be used to enable the Active Directory Recycle Bin.

   D. **Correct.** Enable-ADOptionalFeature can be used to enable the Active Directory Recycle Bin. Ldp.exe and Active Directory Administrative Center at the other two ways to enable it.

2. **Correct answers:** A, C

   A. **Correct.** This command will create a new snapshot and list all of the snapshots of the ntds database.

   B. **Incorrect.** This command doesn't work because you can't create a snapshot until you are in the snapshot context.

   C. **Correct.** This command enters the snapshot context, activates the NTDS instance, lists the available snapshots, and then mounts the most recent with "mount 2". The list command is required to establish the index number.

   D. **Incorrect.** This command doesn't work because the mount command doesn't know what the index is to mount without a list command.

3. **Correct answer:** D

   A. **Incorrect.** A non-authoritative restore sees the restored object overwritten by the deleted object because the current update sequence number (USN) of the restored object is lower than the current objects.

   B. **Incorrect.** If the Recycle Bin were already enabled, you could use it to restore the deleted object. But the Recycle Bin doesn't know about deleted objects that were deleted before it was enabled.

   C. **Incorrect.** The re-created user will be a new user with a different SID.

   D. **Correct.** You can use Ldp.exe or Windows PowerShell to restore the deleted object.

Objective 5.4: Thought experiment

1. You have two ways to accomplish the mandated change.

   ■ You could create a new domain with a new Default Domain Policy. But doing this creates significant additional overhead and requires additional server resources. It is also likely to be more than a little disruptive.

   ■ Create a PSO and apply it to the users.

2. Assuming that the users are currently each in their own security groups based on their department, you could simply apply the PSO to each of the security groups. But a cleaner solution might be to create an Enhanced Password Security group with the users in it. You then have a single place to manage this policy and the users, and it gives you a good test group for the new TFA policy if that's what you decide to implement.

Objective 5.4: Review

1. **Correct answer:** C

    A. **Incorrect**. This command enables you to change the local security policy on the domain controller.

    B. **Incorrect**. This command enables you to change the local security policy on the local computer.

    C. **Correct**. This command enables you to change the Default Domain Policy for the domain.

    D. **Incorrect**. Controls account expiration for an individual account; it has nothing to do with domain lockout policies.

2. **Correct answer:** A

    A. **Correct**. This changes the amount of time a client computer can be out of sync with the domain controller to 10 minutes instead of 5 minutes. That should be enough time to resolve the issue temporarily, but you have to determine what the root cause is for computers getting out of sync.

    B. **Incorrect**. This makes the problem worse. Setting to 0 doesn't disable the policy.

    C. **Incorrect**. This doesn't affect the clock settings.

    D. **Incorrect**. This has nothing to do with the Kerberos settings and only sets the number of failed logon attempt before the account is locked out.

3. **Correct answer:** D

    A. **Incorrect**. Creating a Sales OU is a possible first step, but then you would need to create a specific password expiration policy that was linked to that OU.

    B. **Incorrect**. Creating a Sales OU is a possible first step, but then you would need to create a specific password expiration policy that was linked to that OU.

    C. **Incorrect**. Creating a Sales security group is a possible first step, but you can't attach a fine-grained password policy by using the New-ADFineGrainedPasswordPolicy, and then Set-ADFineGrainedPasswordPolicy.

    D. **Correct**. After you create the Sales security group and assign the Sales users to the group, you can create a new fine-grained password policy with New-ADFineGrainedPasswordPolicy and then assign the Sales security group to that policy with Add-ADFineGraintPasswordPolicySubject.

CHAPTER 6

Configure and manage Group Policy

Group Policy is at the core of computer and user management in the Active Directory domain environment. With each release of Windows Server, the options and flexibility of Group Policy have improved. This chapter covers the configuration and management of Group Policy and how to ensure that it does what you want it to.

Objectives in this chapter:

- Objective 6.1: Configure Group Policy processing
- Objective 6.2: Configure Group Policy settings
- Objective 6.3: Manage Group Policy Objects (GPOs)
- Objective 6.4: Configure Group Policy Preferences (GPP)

Objective 6.1: Configure Group Policy processing

The processing order and the filtering of Group Policy control which policies are applied to which users and computers. By understanding and controlling the processing order, you can understand and control which policies have the final impact on a given Active Directory object. Local Group Policy is processed first; then each Active Directory level is processed from the farthest away from the object (the site) to the closest to the object (the organizational unit [OU]). This processing order is known as LSDOU: Local, Site, Domain, Organizational Unit.

This objective covers how to:

- Configure processing order and precedence
- Configure blocking of inheritance
- Configure enforced policies
- Configure security filtering and Windows Management Instrumentation (WMI) filtering
- Configure loopback processing
- Configure and manage slow-link processing and Group Policy caching
- Configure client-side extension (CSE) behavior
- Force Group Policy updates

Configuring processing order and precedence

Multiple Group Policy Objects (GPOs) can be linked to the same site, domain, or organizational unit (OU), and OUs inherit GPOs from higher-level containers. GPOs are processed serially, with local computer Group Policy processed first. Inherited GPOs are then processed, unless they are blocked or enforced (see the sections entitled "Configuring blocking of inheritance" and "Configuring enforcement of inheritance" later in this chapter). The GPOs linked directly to the domain or OU are processed in the order they are linked; then enforced GPOs are processed. Where multiple GPOs are configuring the same Group Policy setting, the last one processed controls the setting. You can control the order of linking for an OU or domain, as well as controlling inheritance to some extent. You can block inheritance at the domain or OU level, but where the higher-level link to the GPO is set to Enforced, the inheritance can't be blocked and enforced links are the last processed—again, in the reverse link order.

To see the order of linked GPOs, use the Group Policy Management Console (GPMC). Select the domain or OU for which you want to see the link order in the console tree, and then select the Linked Group Policy Objects tab in the details pane, as shown in Figure 6-1.

To change the link order, select a link in the Linked Group Policy Objects pane and then use the arrow buttons on the left to move the order up or down, as desired. Move a linked GPO to a lower Link Order number to have it processed later. Thus a GPO with a Link Order of 1 will be processed after a GPO with a Link Order of 2; and if both GPOs have a policy configuration for the same setting, the GPO with a Link Order of 1 will be the controlling GPO.

Remember that policy settings can also be inherited. To see all the GPOs that affect a given OU or domain, use the GPMC and follow these steps:

1. Expand the console tree of the GPMC and select the OU or domain for which you want to see the GPOs.

2. In the details pane, select the Group Policy Inheritance tab, as shown in Figure 6-2.

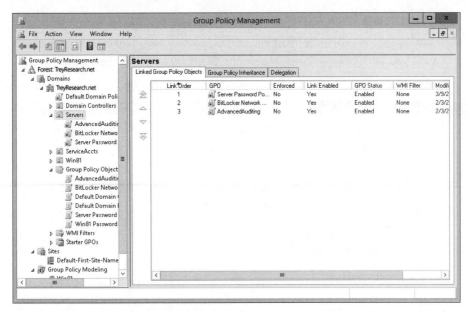

FIGURE 6-1 The Group Policy Management Console

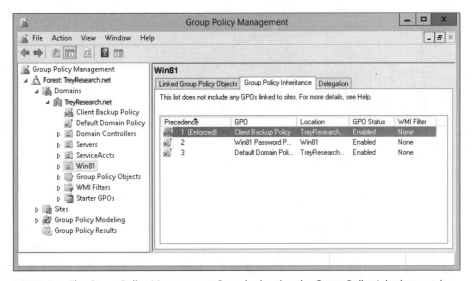

FIGURE 6-2 The Group Policy Management Console showing the Group Policy Inheritance tab

3. The GPOs are shown in the order of precedence, with the inherited but not enforced GPO at the bottom of the list, and the enforced GPO at the top of the list.

Configuring blocking of inheritance

Normally, organizational units (OUs) inherit Group Policy from higher sites, domains, or OUs. However, you can block this inheritance in the GPMC by following these steps:

1. Open the GPMC and expand the console tree to display the domain for which you want to change inheritance.

2. To block inheritance for the entire domain and all its OUs, right-click the domain name and select Block Inheritance from the menu.

3. To block inheritance for an OU, expand the domain and then right-click the OU and select Block Inheritance from the context menu, as shown in Figure 6-3.

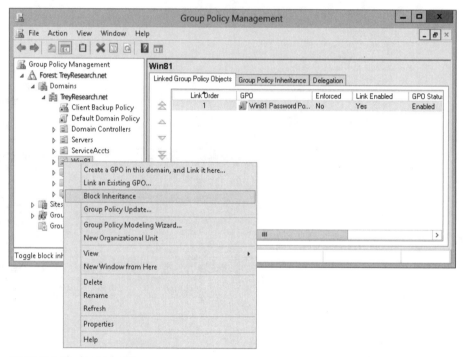

FIGURE 6-3 Blocking inheritance

NOTE **ENFORCED GPOS**

GPO links that are set to Enforced can't be blocked from inheritance. When you block inheritance to a domain or OU, unenforced GPOs are not inherited by the domain or OU, but GPOs that are set to Enforced are still inherited.

Configuring enforced policies

Typically, GPOs are processed in their link order, and if two GPOs configure the same setting, the GPO that is processed last will control the setting. But when a GPO is set to Enforced, it is always processed and can't be blocked.

To set a GPO to Enforced, select the link in the GPMC, either in the console tree or in the Linked Group Policy Objects tab in the details pane, and select Enforced from the context menu, as shown in Figure 6-4.

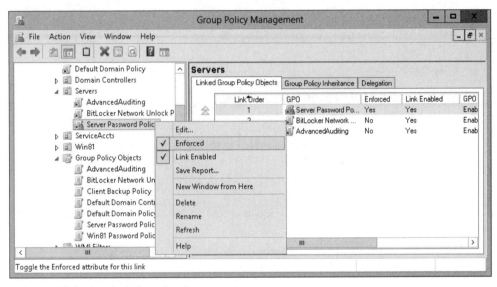

FIGURE 6-4 Selecting the Enforced option

Configuring security filtering and Windows Management Instrumentation filtering

A GPO usually applies to all members of the object it is linked to, but you can filter which objects are affected by the GPO by using a security filter or by using a WMI filter. The filter is applied to the GPO, not to the link.

To apply a security filter to a GPO, follow these steps:

1. Open the GPMC and expand the console tree to display the domain for which you want to set a security filter on a GPO.

2. Select the GPO to which you want to apply the filter.

3. In the details pane, select the Scope tab.

4. Click Add in the Security Filtering section to open the Select User, Computer, Or Group dialog box.

5. Enter the object names to select or click Advanced to search for them, as shown in Figure 6-5.

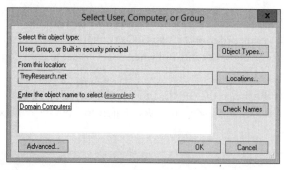

FIGURE 6-5 The Select User, Computer, Or Group dialog box

6. Click OK after you enter the security group, user, or computer to apply the filter to.

7. Select Authenticated Users and click Remove.

To link a WMI filter to a GPO, follow these steps:

1. Open the GPMC and expand the console tree to display the domain for which you want to link a WMI filter to a GPO.

2. Select the GPO you want to filter.

3. Select the WMI filter from the This GPO Is Linked To The Following WMI Filter drop-down list.

Before you can use a WMI filter, you need to create it. You can do the following:

- **Create a new filter** You can create a new filter by following these steps:

    1. In the GPMC, expand the console tree for the domain and forest in which you want to create the filter.

    2. Right-click the WMI Filters container and select New from the menu.

    3. Type a name and description for the new WMI filter and then click Add.

    4. Enter the Namespace to use or Browse to select one.

    5. Type the query you want to use, as shown in Figure 6-6. Click OK and then click Save to save the WMI filter.

- **Export a filter** You can export a WMI filter by right-clicking the filter and selecting Export from the menu. Filters are saved as .mof files.

- **Import a filter** You can import a previously saved filter by right-clicking the WMI Filters container of the domain where it resides in the console tree of the GPMC and selecting Import from the menu.

- **Copy a filter** You can use Copy and Paste with WMI filters by selecting the filter, right-clicking, and selecting Copy. Then right-click the WMI Filters container for the domain you want to copy the filter to and selecting Paste from the menu.

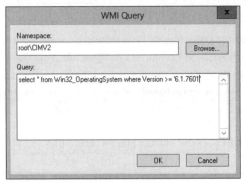

FIGURE 6-6 The WMI Query dialog box

Configuring loopback processing

Normal GPO processing follows the LSDOU rule—Local, Site, Domain, OU. Loopback processing allows different GPO user settings to apply based on which computer the user logs on to.

You can enable loopback processing of user mode settings by setting the Computer Configuration/Policies/Administrative Templates/System/Group Policy/Configure User Group Policy Loopback Processing Mode policy. When set to Enabled, you can choose one of two modes:

- **Merge mode** When set, user settings in the Computer Configuration section of the GPO are combined with settings in the User Configuration section of the GPO. When there is a conflict, the Computer Configuration setting takes precedence.

- **Replace mode** When set, user settings in the Computer Configuration section of the GPO replace any user settings normally applied to the user in the User Configuration section.

Configuring and managing slow-link processing and Group Policy caching

When you log on to a domain-joined computer and a network is present, the computer contacts a domain controller to get the latest GPOs. If the computer is connected by a typical fast network connection, all the GPO settings are processed by the client. However, if the client detects that the link to the domain controller is a slow link, only the most important GPO settings are processed. By default, a slow link is defined as a connection speed of 500 Kbps per second or less. You can configure this threshold by setting the Computer Configuration/ Policies/Administrative Templates/System/Group Policy/Configure Group Policy Slow Link Detection setting.

The settings that are not downloaded when a slow link is detected are these:

- Disk quotas
- Scripts
- Folder redirection
- Software installation
- Network policies for wired and wireless networks
- Internet Explorer maintenance extension

Not included in this list in Windows 8.1 and Windows Server 2012 R2 are drive mappings. They used to be processed as foreground client-side extensions (CSEs), but are now processed in the background, allowing logon to occur without all the Group Policy drive mapping preferences being completed before the logon is allowed to complete.

Group Policy caching is new in Windows Server 2012 R2 and Windows 8.1, and is enabled by default. Group Policy caching stores a copy of policies on the local machine to speed up synchronous foreground processing of GPOs. Caching affects only Windows 8.1; it does not change processing in Windows Server 2012 R2. Windows Server always processes synchronously and never caches unless the Computer Configuration/Administrative Templates/System/Group Policy/Enable Group Policy Caching For Servers policy is enabled.

Group Policy caching doesn't affect asynchronous or background processing. You can disable Group Policy caching by setting the Computer Configuration/Policies/Administrative Templates/System/Group Policy/Configure Group Policy Caching policy to Disabled. If left Not Configured, caching is enabled. If set to Enabled, you can set the value to detect a slow link, and the timeout value before Group Policy will decide that you're not connected to the domain network.

Configuring client-side extension (CSE) behavior

CSEs run on the Windows computer to interpret some of the Group Policy Preferences. CSEs (typically .dll files) do the actual processing and applying of preferences at the destination computer. You can configure the processing of CSEs by configuring the applicable policies in Computer Configuration/Policies/Administrative Templates/System/Group Policy. The policies that control CSEs are shown in Table 6-1.

TABLE 6-1 Group Policy settings for CSEs

Setting	Default State
Change Group Policy processing to run asynchronously when a slow network connection is detected	Not configured
Configure Applications preference extension policy processing	Not configured
Configure Data Sources preference extension policy processing	Not configured
Configure Devices preference extension policy processing	Not configured
Configure Direct Access connections as a fast network connection	Not configured
Configure disk quota policy processing	Not configured
Configure Drive Maps preference extension policy processing	Not configured
Configure Encrypting File System (EFS) recovery policy processing	Not configured
Configure Environment preference extension policy processing	Not configured
Configure Files preference extension policy processing	Not configured
Configure Folder Options preference extension policy processing	Not configured
Configure folder redirection policy processing	Not configured
Configure Folders preference extension policy processing	Not configured
Configure Group Policy caching	Not configured
Configure Group Policy slow link detection	Not configured
Configure Ini Files preference extension policy processing	Not configured
Configure Internet Explorer Maintenance policy processing	Not configured
Configure Internet Settings preference extension policy processing	Not configured
Configure IP security policy processing	Not configured
Configure Local Users And Groups preference extension policy processing	Not configured
Configure Logon Script Delay	Not configured
Configure Network Options preference extension policy processing	Not configured
Configure Network Shares preference extension policy processing	Not configured
Configure Power Options preference extension policy processing	Not configured
Configure Printers preference extension policy processing	Not configured
Configure Regional Options preference extension policy processing	Not configured
Configure registry policy processing	Not configured
Configure Registry preference extension policy processing	Not configured

Setting	Default State
Configure Scheduled Tasks preference extension policy processing	Not configured
Configure scripts policy processing	Not configured
Configure security policy processing	Not configured
Configure Services preference extension policy processing	Not configured
Configure Shortcuts preference extension policy processing	Not configured
Configure software installation policy processing	Not configured
Configure Start Menu preference extension policy processing	Not configured
Configure user Group Policy loopback processing mode	Not configured
Configure wired policy processing	Not configured
Configure wireless policy processing	Not configured

Forcing Group Policy updates

New in Windows Server 2012 is the capability to force a Group Policy update on a remote computer without having to log on to that computer. You can do this from Windows PowerShell with the Invoke-GPUpdate cmdlet or directly in the GPMC.

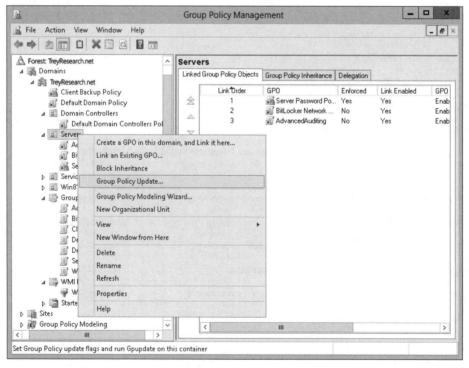

FIGURE 6-7 Invoking a Group Policy update

The Invoke-GPUpdate cmdlet accepts a -Computer parameter that enables you to specify the specific computer on which to force the update. So to force a synchronous update at the next user logon of only the User Configuration preferences on server trey-wds-11, for example, use the following command:

```
Invoke-GPUpdate -Computer trey-wds-11 -Target User -Sync -LogOff
```

To force a Group Policy update from the GPMC, right-click the OU for which you want to trigger the update and select Group Policy Update from the menu, as shown in Figure 6-7.

Click Yes at the confirmation screen, and the policy will be updated on the computers in that OU.

Thought experiment
Configuring drive maps

In this thought experiment, apply what you've learned about this objective. You can find answers to these questions in the "Answers" section at the end of this chapter.

You are the network administrator for TreyResearch.net. Mobile users have a mix of Windows 7, Windows 8, and Windows 8.1 computers. The company has a legacy application that is used by the entire sales force, as well as selected others. The application is configured to expect sales data to be located on drive S:\, although it can work from cached data. Updates to the cached data have previously required trips to the main office or one of the branch offices.

At your suggestion, TreyResearch implemented DirectAccess to improve the overall experience of remote users, especially the sales team. It has generally worked well, but users complain that they still sometimes need to come into one of the offices to update their cached data for the legacy application.

1. Your first attempt to correct the issue is to enable the Change Group Policy Processing To Run Asynchronously When A Slow Network Connection Is Detected Group Policy setting. Doing so makes the problem worse, however. Why does that happen?

2. You quickly disable the problem setting in Group Policy. What other Group Policy settings might improve the situation?

3. After enabling the Configure Direct Access Connections As A Fast Network Connection setting, some users report the problem resolved, whereas others complain that they are still experiencing intermittent problems. Why?

Objective summary

- Although the basic order of GPO processing is LSDOU: Local, Site, Domain, and OU, you can control the order of linked policies.
- You can block inheritance of policies, but Enforced policies can't be blocked.
- You can fine-tune which computers or users a policy is applied to by using security or WMI filters.
- To ensure a consistent and predictable user experience in lab or kiosk environments, use loopback processing.
- Some policies are not processed over slow links.
- Group Policy caching is a new feature of Windows 8.1 and Windows Server 2012 R2 designed to improve logon times for some instances.
- Beginning in Windows Server 2012 and Windows 8, you can now force a remote Group Policy update.

Objective review

1. You need to configure training lab computers to allow users to log on with their own accounts, but still provide a consistent look and experience for the lab, regardless of departments the users are normally in. What Group Policy settings should you use?

   A. Set Computer Configuration/Policies/Administrative Templates/System/Group Policy/Configure User Group Policy Loopback Processing Mode to Merge Mode. and configure the Computer Configuration/Preferences/Windows Settings and Control Panel Settings.

   B. Set Computer Configuration/Policies/Administrative Templates/System/Group Policy/Configure User Group Policy Loopback Processing Mode to Merge Mode, and configure the User Configuration/Preferences/Windows Settings and Control Panel Settings.

   C. Set Computer Configuration/Policies/Administrative Templates/System/Group Policy/Configure User Group Policy Loopback Processing Mode to Replace Mode, and configure the Computer Configuration/Preferences/Windows Settings and Control Panel Settings.

   D. Set Computer Configuration/Policies/Administrative Templates/System/Group Policy/Configure User Group Policy Loopback Processing Mode to Replace Mode, and configure the User Configuration/Preferences/Windows Settings and Control Panel Settings.

2. How do you force a remote Group Policy update on the Computer Configuration of Trey-Srv-12?

   A. Force-GPUpdate -Computer -Sync -Target Trey-Srv-12

   B. Force-GPUpdate -Computer Trey-Srv-12 -Target Computer

   C. Invoke-GPUpdate -Computer -Sync -Target Trey-Srv-12

   D. Invoke-GPUpdate -Computer Trey-Srv-12 -Target Computer

3. You are the network administrator for TreyResearch.net. You have to enforce special policies on the Engineering OU in which the users work with highly sensitive information while ensuring that the Domain Password Policy is used. What Group Policy settings should you use?

   A. Configure Block Inheritance on the OU and set the Domain Password Policy to Enforced.

   B. Configure Block Inheritance on the Domain and configure an OU Password Policy.

   C. Configure Block Inheritance on the Domain, and add a link to the Domain Password Policy to the OU.

   D. Configure Block Inheritance off at the OU, and set the Domain Password Policy to Enforced.

Objective 6.2: Configure Group Policy settings

The basic aim of Group Policy is to configure the settings that control users and computers. By using these settings, you can control what software is installed, where folders are located, what the startup and shutdown experience is, and which individual settings control access and rights to a wide variety of Windows objects.

> **This objective covers how to:**
>
> - Configure settings, including software installation, folder redirection, scripts, and administrative template settings
> - Import security templates
> - Import custom administrative template files
> - Configure property filters for administrative templates

Configuring settings

You can use Group Policy to configure the settings for users and computers to provide a predictable experience for all users. The settings you can configure include these:

- Software installation
- Folder redirection
- Scripts
- Administrative template settings

> **MORE INFO POLICY SETTINGS**
>
> For a complete list of policy settings included in the Administrative template files for Windows Server 2003 SP2 through Windows Server 2012 R2, see *http://www.microsoft.com/en-us/download/details.aspx?id=25250*.

Software Installation

You can use Group Policy to deploy software to groups of users based on their needs and roles, or to deploy software to specific computers. The steps for deploying software are these:

- **Create a shared folder**   A shared folder accessible by all users or computers you want to distribute the software to.
- **Create a GPO**   Using the GPMC, create a GPO for the software distribution.
- **Assign the software package**   Edit the GPO to assign the software package to the computers or users covered by the GPO. This process causes the software to be automatically installed.
- **Publish the software package**   Edit the GPO to publish the software package to the computers or users covered by the GPO. This process causes the software to be listed as available to be installed from the network.

Using Group Policy to deploy software has some limitations. The most basic limitation is that you can deploy only software that uses Microsoft Installer (.msi) or Zero Administration for Windows Downlevel Application Package (.zap) files. Software that uses an executable file (.exe) can't be installed directly from Group Policy, although you can use startup scripts to install the software or use third-party products to package .exe installations as .msi installations.

You can edit the GPO that installs the software to specify whether it is assigned or published to computers or users. If you want the software to be assigned to computers, edit the Computer Configuration/Policies/Software Settings policy. To assign or publish the software to users, edit the User Configuration/Policies/Software Settings policy.

When you add software to the user or computer configuration, you need to specify the location from which the software is being installed. Always use a Universal Naming Convention (UNC) path, not a drive letter path. For example, to add the MyApp application as a published application for users in the HR security group, follow these steps:

1. Open the GPMC and create a new HR Software Deployment GPO.

2. Set the Security Filtering to TREYRESEARCH\HR Users, as shown in Figure 6-8.

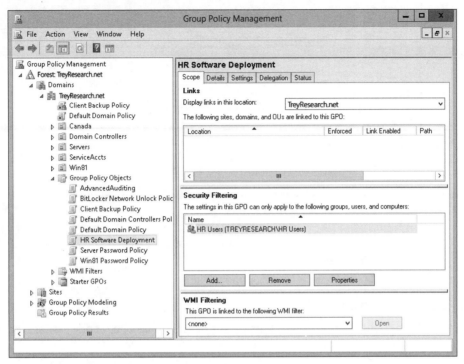

FIGURE 6-8 The HR Software Deployment GPO in the GPMC

3. Right-click the HR Software Deployment policy and select Edit.

4. In the Group Policy Management Editor, expand the Policies container in the User Configuration section and then expand Software Settings.

5. Right-click Software Installation and select New and then Package.

6. In the Open dialog box enter **\\trey-dc-02\software\myapp.msi**, as shown in Figure 6-9, and click Open.

7. In the Deploy Software dialog box, select Published and click OK.

   Now the application will appear in the list of applications that are available to be installed from the network in the Control Panel Programs and Features (appwiz.cpl).

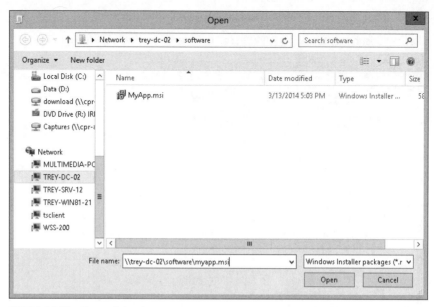

FIGURE 6-9 The Open dialog box

Folder redirection

You can use Group Policy to redirect the folders of user profiles. To modify the user profile folders, follow these steps:

1. In the GPMC, right-click the GPO in which you want to configure folder redirection. It can be an existing GPO linked to the site, domain, or OU containing the users you want to target; or it can be a new GPO you create for folder redirection.

2. Select Edit to open the Group Policy Management Editor.

3. Expand the User Configuration node and navigate to User Configuration/Policies/Windows Settings/Folder Redirection.

4. Right-click the folder you want to redirect and select Properties from the menu.

5. On the Target tab, choose Basic to redirect the folder of every user for whom the GPO applies in the same way. Select Advanced to create multiple redirection rules depending on security group membership. The choices for Target Folder Location are these:

   - **Create A Folder For Each User Under The Root Path**   Each user's profile folder is in a user-specific path below a common root folder (for example, Documents would be \\server\root\%USERNAME%\Documents).

   - **Redirect Everyone's Folder To The Same Location**   All the profile folders are located beneath the same root path.

- **Redirect To The Local Userprofile Location**   The profile folder is redirected back to the local location.

- **Follow The Documents Folder**   Applies only to Music, Pictures, and Videos. When this setting is specified, the relocation of these folders is beneath the Documents folder.

6. On the Settings tab, you can specify the following:

- **Grant The User Exclusive Rights To** *<foldername>*   Only the user has access to the redirected folder.

- **Move The Contents Of** *<foldername>* **To The New Location**   If selected, all the current contents are moved to the new location when implementing the policy.

- **Also Apply Redirection Policy To Windows 2000, Windows 2000 Server, Windows XP, And Windows Server 2003 Operating Systems**   When selected, the equivalent folder for the specified operating systems are redirected.

- **Policy Removal**   By default, folders are left in the redirected location when the policy is removed. You can specify that the folders revert to the local userprofile location when the policy is removed.

7. Click OK to close the Folder Properties dialog box.

8. Exit the Group Policy Management Editor.

Scripts

You can run four types of scripts from Group Policy, triggered by the following:

- Computer startup
- Computer shutdown
- User logon
- User logoff

The scripts run by Group Policy can be Windows PowerShell or any other scripting language supported on the client computers. Any Windows Script Host (WSH) language is supported. You can set up the scripts on a domain controller and then copy them to the Netlogon shared folder on the domain controller. You can also specify the scripts in the Group Policy Management Editor. Logon and logoff scripts are located in User Configuration/Policies/Windows Settings/Scripts. Startup and shutdown scripts are located in Computer Configuration/Policies/Windows Settings/Scripts.

You can have multiple scripts for each of the four scripts folders, both PowerShell and non-PowerShell scripts. You can specify the order in which the scripts run and you can specify that all PowerShell scripts run first or last.

Administrative template settings

Administrative templates are used to edit registry-based policies for users and computers. By default, all language-neutral administrative templates (.admx files) are stored in %systemroot%\PolicyDefinitions, with language-specific templates (.adml files) stored in the appropriate subdirectory (%systemroot%\PolicyDefinitions\en-us for U.S. English). When you add a template to the store, it is available for use in the Group Policy Management Editor. If you're on a local computer and you run gpedit.msc, you're editing the local Group Policy, and it will read from that location.

By default, when you run GPMC and edit a GPO, it opens the Group Policy Management Editor and automatically loads the administrative templates located on the local computer, as shown in Figure 6-10. This process can create a problem if you have different versions of Windows on the network and different sets of Administrative templates. Plus, if there's an update to a template, it might not be migrated to every computer in the network.

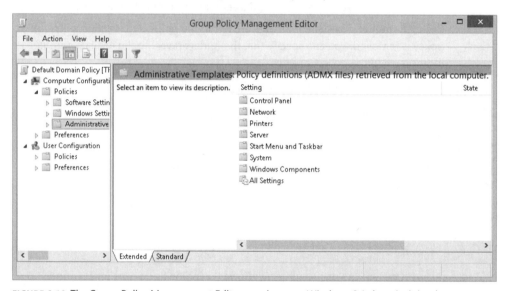

FIGURE 6-10 The Group Policy Management Editor running on a Windows 8.1 domain-joined computer with local policy definitions

You can create a central store of administrative templates that are replicated throughout the domain. When you do, the Group Policy Management Editor loads those files instead of the local store, as shown in Figure 6-11.

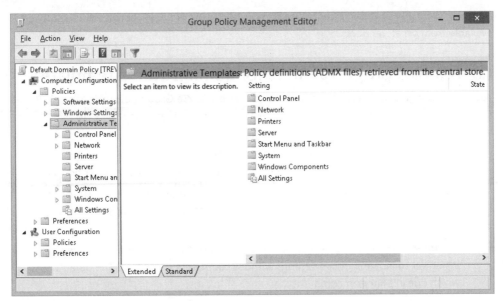

FIGURE 6-11 The Group Policy Management Editor running on Windows 8.1 domain-joined computer with centralized policy definitions.

Importing security templates

You can import security templates directly into a GPO by using the Group Policy Management Editor. Security templates are .inf files that contain specific security settings. One way to create security templates is to create a template policy by configuring the security settings you want to be part of the template and then export the template by using secpol.msc. Another way is to use one of the starter GPOs to create a new policy and then export it.

To import a policy, follow these steps:

1. In the GPMC, right-click the policy that you want to apply the template to and select Edit to open the Group Policy Management Editor.

2. Expand the Computer Configuration node in the console tree and select Computer Configuration/Policies/Windows Settings/Security Settings.

3. Right-click Security Settings and select Import Policy. (The default location for security template policies is in the Documents\Security\Templates folder of the logged-on user.)

4. Select the policy you want to import and click Open.

Importing custom administrative template files

Windows includes a full set of administrative templates, and these templates are automatically available. However, you can install additional administrative templates for other versions of Windows, available from the Microsoft Download Center; for Microsoft Office, also available from the Microsoft Download Center; or for non-Microsoft Windows hardware and software, available from other vendors.

Configuring property filters for administrative templates

You can filter which administrative templates are visible in the Group Policy Management Editor by using filters on the administrative templates. These filters affect only Administrative templates. There are three basic property filters:

- **Managed** Managed settings are those that the Group Policy Client service governs, and the settings are removed when they fall out of scope for a computer or user.

- **Configured** There are three states for administrative template settings: Not Configured, Enabled, or Disabled. When you filter by Configured, only those changed from Not Configured are shown.

- **Commented** When set to Yes, only those settings that have comments are shown. When set to No, only those settings without comments are shown. The default is Any, which doesn't filter on comments.

You can also filter by keyword, as shown in Figure 6-12. For example, you could search on the keyword "Password" and see only policies that related to password policies.

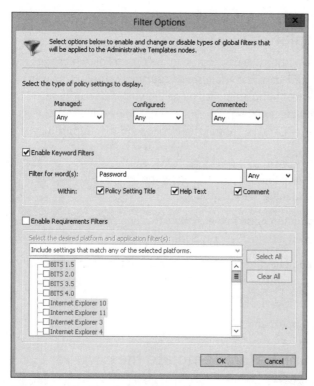

FIGURE 6-12 The Filter Options dialog box

The filtered view of the administrative template settings, as shown in Figure 6-13, shows only settings that are related to passwords.

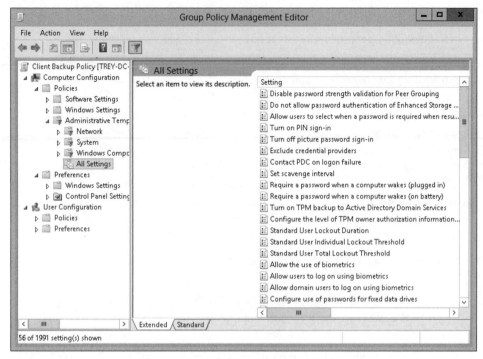

FIGURE 6-13 The Group Policy Management Editor with filtering on

Finally, you can filter by specific product by selecting the Enable Requirements Filters check box and then selecting the product and versions you want to filter on.

You can combine any combination of these filters to get a view of the administrative templates that makes it easy to isolate what you're looking for.

In this thought experiment, apply what you've learned about this objective. You can find answers to these questions in the "Answers" section at the end of this chapter.

You are the network administrator for TreyResearch.net. Company policy allows users to work remotely two days per week; to facilitate, users are issued laptops for working remotely, and DirectAccess is configured and working for all remote computers. You need to ensure that users have access to their work-related documents, including Corporate templates, across both their desktop computers and their remote laptops. You need to do this in a way that minimizes data storage and backup requirements, while recognizing that the remote laptop will likely get used for at least some personal use. Users' computers are running a mix of Windows 7 and Windows 8.1, although the goal is to move all users to 8.1 by the end of the year.

1. One suggestion is to implement Roaming Profiles. Will this meet the needs? If so, what are the key implementation considerations? If not, explain why not.

2. A second suggestion is to implement Folder Redirection. Will this meet the needs? If so, what are the key implementation considerations? If not, explain why not.

3. What other solutions can you think of, and what are the pluses and minuses of each?

4. What Group Policy settings can you use to implement the solution you've decided on?

Objective summary

- Use Group Policy settings to manage software installation and folder redirection.
- Control the four stages of startup and shutdown with Group Policy scripts: Startup, Logon, Logoff, and Shutdown.
- Use Administrative templates to control registry-based policies for users and computers.
- Use security templates to jump-start the configuration of various Administrative template settings and to ensure a consistent experience across multiple GPOs.
- Custom templates can aid in the management of third–party hardware and software, as well as other versions of Windows.

- Manage the view of Group Policy to show only those Administrative settings that you want to see, simplifying the management process by using property filters on Administrative templates.

Objective review

1. You need to ensure that the ABC software application is deployed to all users in the HR department. The installer for ABC is AbcInstall.msi. What steps should you take? (Choose all that apply.)

    A. Create a GPO specifically for Software Distribution.

    B. Use the Default Domain Policy and add Software Distribution to the policy.

    C. Create a distribution point of C:\Software on Trey-Srv-12. Create a share of Software and give Read privileges to all HR users.

    D. Publish the software package to all HR users.

    E. Assign the software package to all HR users.

    F. Configure the GPO to use c:\Software\AbcInstall.msi as the Package.

    G. Configure the GPO to use \\Trey-Srv-12\Software\AbcInstall.msi as the Package.

2. You need to limit the HR Device Use policy that is linked to the Domain. The policy should apply only to HR Users who are part of the HR OU. What should you do?

    A. Use the Set-GPPermission cmdlet with the -Replace and -Target parameters to limit the GPO to HR Users only.

    B. Use the Set-GPLink cmdlet with the -Enforced and the -Target parameters to link the HR Device Policy to the Domain.

    C. Configure Property Filters to block the Computer Configuration container.

    D. Configure Security Filtering on the HR Device Policy by removing Authenticated Users and adding HR Users.

3. You need to ensure that GPOs are consistent across the domain and that new versions of Administrative Templates are fully propagated. What should you do?

    A. Configure the Startup script to include Gpupdate /force.

    B. Configure Logon script to include Gpupdate /force.

    C. Configure a central store of Administrative templates and copy updated templates to that store.

    D. Configure the Startup scripts to copy the .admx files to \\trey-dc-02\Policies, where trey-dc-02 holds the PDC Emulator role.

Objective 6.3: Manage Group Policy Objects (GPOs)

Because Group Policy is critical to the way computers and users can do their work in your enterprise, you need to be able to back up and restore GPOs to known good states. And when things go really wrong, you can reset the default GPOs to their shipping state. When you want to copy GPOs to a new domain environment, use a Migration Table to manage the changes. Finally, you can delegate management of portions of Group Policy to users who are not full domain administrators.

> **This objective covers how to:**
> - Back up, import, copy, and restore GPOs
> - Create and configure a Migration Table
> - Reset default GPOs
> - Delegate Group Policy management

Backing up, importing, copying, and restoring GPOs

You can back up and restore GPOs as well as make copies of them. You can also import the settings from a backed-up GPO without changing the other settings of the GPO, and you can copy GPOs, either within a domain or across domain boundaries.

Backing up and restoring GPOs

When you back up a GPO, the GPO is saved, but the settings that are external to the GPO, such as WMI filters, are not saved. To back up a GPO, open the GPMC and right-click the GPO you want to back up. Select Back Up from the menu to open the Back Up Group Policy Object dialog box shown in Figure 6-14.

FIGURE 6-14 The Back Up Group Policy Object dialog box

The location you use to store backed-up GPOs should have permissions set to prevent unauthorized access to the GPOs.

To back up all GPOs in the domain, right-click the Group Policy Objects container in the console tree and select Back Up All from the menu.

If you have a backup of a GPO, you can quickly recover if you modified the GPO and the results were not quite what you expected. You can restore the backup of the GPO by following these steps:

1. Open the GPMC and navigate to the Group Policy Objects container that hosts the GPO you want to restore.

2. Right-click the GPO and select Restore From Backup.

3. Read the Welcome screen in the Restore Group Policy Object Wizard and then click Next.

4. Specify the location of the backed-up GPO on the Backup Location page and click Next.

5. Select the version of the GPO you want to restore, as shown in Figure 6-15.

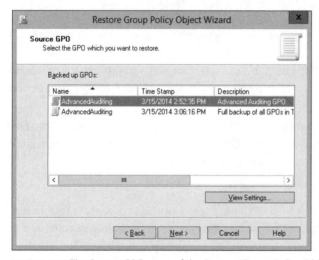

FIGURE 6-15 The Source GPO page of the Restore Group Policy Object Wizard

6. You can view the settings of any version shown in the Source GPO page to ensure that you are restoring the correct version by clicking View Settings.

7. Select the version of the GPO you want to restore, click Next, and then click Finish.

8. When the GPO is restored, click OK.

You can manage your backed-up GPOs. Right-click the Group Policy Objects container in the GPMC and select Manage Backups from the menu to open the Manage Backups dialog box (see Figure 6-16).

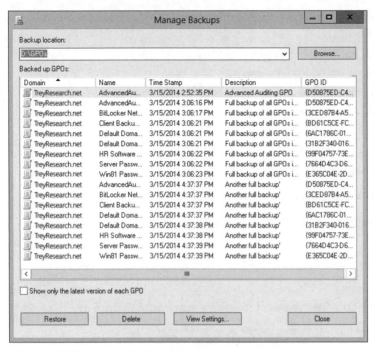

FIGURE 6-16 The Manage Backups dialog box

In the Manage Backups dialog box, you can select a backup to restore, you can delete a backup, or you can view the backup settings. You can also browse for other locations where GPOs are backed up.

You can use the GroupPolicy module of Windows PowerShell to back up and restore GPOs. Use the Backup-GPO cmdlet to back up GPOs. To back up all the GPOs in the domain of the current user, use the following command:

```
Backup-GPO -All -Path <path to GPO backups>
```

To restore a previously backed–up GPO, use the Restore-GPO cmdlet. To restore the most recently backed-up version of the Default Domain Policy, use the following command:

```
Restore-GPO -Name "Default Domain Policy" -path <path to GPO backups>
```

Importing GPO settings

You can import the settings from a backed-up GPO into any other GPO. When you import the settings of a GPO, you import only the settings. The existing attributes of the target GPO, such as security filtering, delegation, links, and WMI filtering, are left untouched. To import GPO settings, follow these steps:

1. Open the GPMC and navigate to the Group Policy Objects container for the domain you want to import settings to.

2. Right-click the target GPO and select Import Settings.

3. Click Next on the Welcome page.

4. On the Backup GPO page, click Backup to make a backup of the current GPO before you make changes to it.

5. Enter the backup location if the correct one isn't already entered, click Back Up, and then click OK when the backup completes.

6. Click Next, enter the GPO Backup location if it isn't shown correctly, and click Next again.

7. Select the source GPO backup whose settings you want to import.

8. On the Scanning Backup page, read the Scan Results. You might have references that you need to address. If not, skip the next step.

9. On the Migrating References page, you can choose to copy the references or use a Migration Table. (See the section, "Creating and configuring a Migration Table" for details on how to make a Migration Table.)

10. Click Next and then Finish to import the settings.

> **IMPORTANT** **IMPORT OVERWRITES EXISTING SETTINGS**
>
> When you import settings from a backed-up GPO, the imported settings overwrite any existing settings in the target GPO. Make sure this is what you want before you commit and always make a backup of the target GPO before you do the import.

To import a GPO, use the Import-GPO cmdlet. The command to import a ClientBackupGPO from the TreyResearch.net domain using a Migration Table is this:

```
Import-GPO -Domain TreyResearch.net `
        -BackupGpoName ClientBackupGPO `
        -TargetName "Client Backup" `
        -Path "D:\GPOs" `
        -MigrationTable "D:\MigTables\ClientBackupToTailspinToys.migtable" `
        -CreateIfNeeded
```

This command imports the most recent backup of the ClientBackupGPO to a new GPO called "Client Backup" in the TailspinToys.com domain. The target GPO is created if it doesn't already exist, and a migration table is used to migrate domain specific settings in the source GPO backup.

Copying GPOs

You can copy an existing GPO within a domain, preserving the existing permissions, or giving the target GPO the default permissions for a new GPO. Or you can copy a GPO across domain boundaries by using the Cross-Domain Copying Wizard. To copy a GPO within a domain, follow these steps:

1. Open the GPMC and navigate to the Group Policy Objects container for the domain you want copy a GPO of.

2. Right-click the source GPO and select Copy.

3. Right-click the Group Policy Objects container and select Paste.

4. In the Copy GPO dialog box, select Use The Default Permissions For New GPOs or choose Preserve The Existing Permissions.

5. Click OK and then OK again.

6. Rename the GPO as appropriate.

To copy a GPO across domain boundaries, follow these steps:

1. Open the GPMC and navigate to the Group Policy Objects container for the domain you want copy a GPO of.

2. Right-click the source GPO and select Copy.

3. In the target domain, right-click the Group Policy Objects container and select Paste.

4. In the Cross-Domain Copying Wizard, click Next on the Welcome page.

5. On the Specifying Permissions page, select Use The Default Permissions For New GPOs or chose Preserve The Existing Permissions.

6. Click Next. On the Scanning Original GPO page, read the Scan Results. You might have references that you need to address. If not, skip the next step.

7. On the Migrating References page, you can choose to copy the references or use a Migration Table. (See the following section, "Creating and configuring a Migration Table" for details on how to make a Migration Table.) In most cases, you have to create or edit a Migration Table to address differences between the two domains.

8. On the Migrating References page, if you choose to use a migration table, you can use one you already created as is, edit it to adjust any settings, or select New to create a new Migration Table from scratch.

9. Click Next, click Finish, and then click OK.

To copy a GPO, use the Copy-GPO cmdlet from the GroupPolicy module. As with other GPO commands, you can specify a Migration Table if copying across domain boundaries.

Creating and configuring a Migration Table

A Group Policy Migration Table is used to migrate GPOs from one domain to another. You generally can't directly copy GPOs from one domain to another without creating problems because GPOs contain domain-specific information. Instead, you create a Migration Table that enables you to map a domain-specific item in the source domain to its equivalent item in the target domain.

To create a Migration Table, follow these steps:

1. Right-click Domains in the GPMC console tree for the source forest.

2. Select Populate From GPO from the Tools menu to populate the source table from the currently active GPOs or select Populate From Backup from the Tools menu to populate the source table.

3. You see three columns in the Migration Table Editor, as shown in Figure 6-17:

   - **Source Name** The name of the source item that needs to be migrated.

   - **Source Type** The type of source item. It can be a user- or group name, DNS address, security ID (SID), or free text.

   - **Destination Name** The equivalent name in the target domain. Edit this value as appropriate for the new domain.

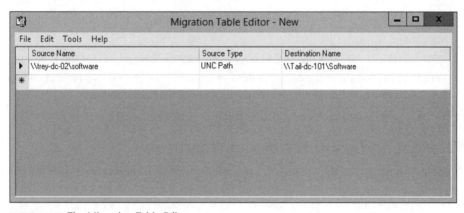

FIGURE 6-17 The Migration Table Editor

4. Select Validate from the Tools menu to validate the migration table entries.

5. After you finish editing the table, select Save from the File menu to save the Migration Table. Make sure that you save it with a name that clearly identifies the source, target and GPOs being migrated.

Resetting default GPOs

It is generally not recommended to edit or modify the Default Domain Policy or the Default Domain Controller Policy, but if you ever need to restore them back to their original state, you can do so with the Dcgpofix.exe command. The syntax for this command is the following:

```
Dcgpofix [/ignoreschema] [/target: {Domain | DC | Both }
```

Without the /ignoreschema switch, dcgpofix works only if the domain controller is the same level of operating system as the domain schema version.

Delegating Group Policy management

By default, members of the Domain Admins and Enterprise Admins groups have full permissions to manage Group Policy. However, you can delegate permissions on specific GPOs or OUs to non-administrators to manage. The permissions you can delegate are these:

- Permissions on a GPO
- Permissions to link a GPO
- Permissions to generate Group Policy modeling data
- Permissions to generate Group Policy results
- Permissions on a WMI filter

All these permissions are delegated in the GPMC. The steps are similar for each set of permissions, so start with granting delegated permissions on a GPO:

1. Expand the console tree of the GPMC and navigate to the Group Policy Objects container of the domain for which you want to delegate permissions.

2. Select the GPO you want to delegate and click the Delegation tab in the details pane (see Figure 6-18).

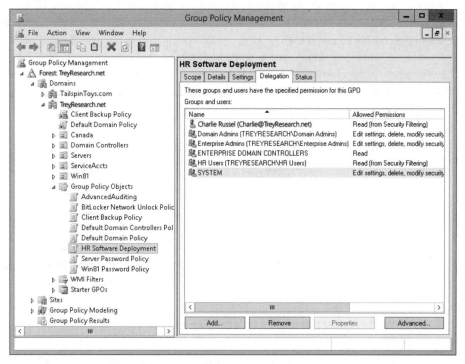

FIGURE 6-18 The Delegation tab of the GPMC

3. Click Add to open the Select User, Computer Or Group dialog box; enter the user or group to whom you want to delegate permissions.

4. Click OK and then select the Permissions from the drop-down list in the Add Group Or User dialog box (see Figure 6-19).

FIGURE 6-19 The Add Group Or User dialog box

5. Click OK; the user is added to the Delegation list.

You can delegate permissions to create GPOs in the domain by either adding the users to the Group Policy Creator Owners security group, or adding the user or group to the Delegation tab as described previously for individual GPOs.

You can delegate permissions to Link GPOs, to Perform Group Policy Modeling Analyses, or to Read Group Policy Results Data to a site, domain, or OU by selecting the site, domain, or OU in the console tree and then clicking the Delegation tab in the details pane. Select the permission you want to delegate and then click Add to add the user or group. You can restrict the delegation to the specific container or include child containers.

> ### *Thought experiment*
> #### Creating a comprehensive GPO management policy
>
> In this thought experiment, apply what you've learned about this objective. You can find answers to these questions in the "Answers" section at the end of this chapter.
>
> You are the network administrator for TreyResearch.net. The Engineering group works out of a separate campus with its own support staff who are not currently members of the Domain Admins group. You need to create a comprehensive GPO management policy that enable the Engineering support staff to manage Group Policy for Engineering while also ensuring that you can quickly recover if they make a change that has unanticipated consequences.
>
> **1.** What changes do you need to make to allow Engineering support staff to manage the Group Policy?
>
> **2.** How can you ensure that you can quickly recover if there are problems with a GPO?

Objective summary

- Back up GPOs to provide an easy recovery scenario.
- Use Import Settings to copy the settings from a backed-up GPO to a new or existing GPO.
- Copy GPOs within the domain or across domain boundaries.
- Use Migration Tables to copy or import GPOs from another domain.
- Reset the Default Domain Policy or the Default Domain Controller Policy to return to an as-installed condition for these critical GPOs.
- Use the Delegation tab in GPMC to delegate authority to edit GPOs.

Objective review

1. After thorough troubleshooting of problems with the behavior of client computers in the TreyResearch.net domain, you determine that the Default Domain Policy has significant issues and the best way to correct the problems is to restore the default GPO. What command should you use?

   A. Invoke-GPO | New-GPO -Name "Default Domain Policy"

   B. New-GPO -Name "Default Domain Policy" -StarterGPOName *<startername>*

   C. Dcgpofix /ignoreschema /target Domain

   D. Dcgpofix /ignoreschema /target DC

2. You need to restore the Client Backup GPO from the most recent backup. What command should you use?

   A. Restore-GPO -Name "Client Backup GPO"

   B. Restore-GPO -All -Path \\Server\BackupGPOs

   C. Import-GPO -BackupGpoName "Client Backup GPO" -TargetName "Restored Client Backup GPO" -Path \\Server\BackupGPOs

   D. Restore-GPO -Name "Client Backup GPO" -Path \\Server\BackupGPOs

3. You want to copy the settings from the TreyResearch.net "Client Backup GPO" to the "ClientBackupGPO" in the TailspinToys.com domain. What command should you use?

   A. Use the GPMC's Restore From Backup command to restore the GPO in the TailspinToys.com domain, specifying the Migration Table.

   B. Use the GPMC's Restore From Backup command to restore the GPO from the TreyResearch.net domain.

   C. Use the GPMC's Copy command to copy the "Client Backup GPO" from the TreyResearch.net domain and then paste the GPO into the TailspinToys.com domain.

   D. Use the GPMC's Import Settings command to import the settings from the most recent backup of the "Client Backup GPO" from the TreyResearch.net domain into the "ClientBackupGPO" in the TailspinToys.com domain, specifying the Migration Table.

Objective 6.4: Configure Group Policy Preferences

Group Policy Preferences (GPPs) is a set of CSEs to Group Policy that enable preference settings on domain-joined computers. Unlike policy settings, preference settings can be altered by the user, but provide a starting point for configuration. You use the GPMC to set preference items and you can do specific targeting to configure settings appropriate to the user or group. There are both Computer Configuration and User Configuration preference settings.

Configuring Windows settings

You can set Group Policy Preferences with two different sets of settings: Windows settings and Control Panel settings. Windows settings are detailed in Table 6-2.

TABLE 6-2 Windows settings

Extension	Action
Applications extension	Configures settings for applications
Drive Maps extension	Creates, deletes, replaces, or updates mapped drives; configures the visibility of all drives
Environment extension	Creates, deletes, replaces, or updates environment variables
Files extension	Copies, modifies the attributes of, replaces, or deletes files
Folders extension	Creates, deletes, replaces, or updates folders
Ini Files extension	Adds, replaces, or deletes sections or properties in configuration settings (.ini) or setup information (.inf) files
Network Shares extension	Creates, deletes, replaces, or updates shares
Registry extension	Copies registry settings and applies them to other computers; creates, replaces, or deletes registry settings
Shortcuts extension	Creates, deletes, replaces, or updates shortcuts

In the following sections, you will learn more about printer preferences, network drive mapping preferences, custom registry settings, and file and folder deployment preferences. I will also use the Group Policy Printer preference to detail how item-level targeting works because I expect item-level targeting to definitely be a part of this exam, even though it's not explicitly identified in the objective as a separate item.

Configuring printers

The Group Policy Printers extension is used to configure local, shared, and TCP/IP printers without having to create and maintain logon scripts. You can create, replace, update, and delete printers. Printers can be set in either the Computer mode or the User mode of Group

Policy. To create a Printer preference for users in the Canada OU, create a Preferences GPO, link it to the Canada OU, and then set the preferences in that GPO. Follow these steps:

1. Open the GPMC and locate the Canada OU in the console tree.

2. Right-click the Canada OU and select Create A GPO In This Domain, And Link It Here.

3. In the New GPO dialog box, enter **Canada Preferences** in the Name box and click OK.

4. Right-click the Canada Preferences GPO link and select Edit from the menu.

5. Expand the User Configuration node and click Printers in the Preferences/Control Panel Settings container, as shown in Figure 6-20.

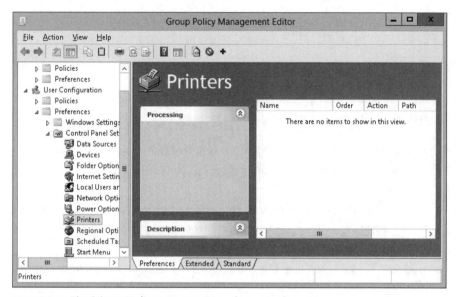

FIGURE 6-20 The Printer Preferences container of User Configuration

6. Right-click Printers, select New, and then select Shared Printer. The New Shared Printer Properties dialog box displays (see Figure 6-21).

7. Select Replace as the Action and enter the path to the shared printer in the Share Path box.

8. Specify whether this printer is to be the default and whether that default setting should apply only if there isn't a local printer present.

9. Click OK; the new preference settings will be propagated to the linked OU.

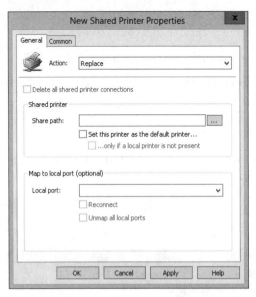

FIGURE 6-21 The New Shared Printer Properties dialog box

When you use preferences to map a printer, you have four choices for an action, as follows:

- **Create** Creates a new local printer. If a local printer with the same name already exists, it makes no changes.

- **Delete** Removes a local printer of the same name if it exists without removing the printer driver. No action is taken if the printer doesn't exist.

- **Replace** Combines the actions of Delete and Create.

- **Update** Similar to Replace, but also updates the settings defined for the printer.

Configuring item-level targeting

Before you go any further to cover other preference items, let's cover item-level targeting, introduced in Windows Server 2012 and Windows 8. You can use item-level targeting to narrow the scope of preference items to only certain computers or users within the overall scope of the GPO.

The targeting items that you can configure and use are these:

- Battery Present
- Computer Name
- CPU Speed
- Date Match
- Disk Space
- Domain
- Environment Variable
- File Match

- IP Address Range

- Language

- LDAP Query

- MAC Address Range

- MSI Query

- Network Connection

- Operating System

- Organizational Unit

- PCMCIA Present

- Portable Computer

- Processing Mode

- RAM

- Registry Match

- Security Group

- Site

- Terminal Session

- Time Range

- User

- WMI Query

To use item-level targeting, select the Item-Level Targeting check box on the Common tab of the preference setting, as shown in Figure 6-22.

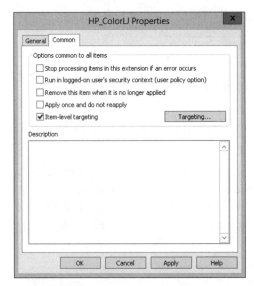

FIGURE 6-22 The Common tab of the HP_ColorLJ Properties dialog box

To see how it works, restrict the Printer preference created previously to apply only to Terminal Sessions that are not displaying on computers with a battery. To do that, follow these steps:

1. Open the GPMC and locate the Canada OU in the console tree.

2. Right-click the Canada Preferences GPO link and select Edit from the menu.

3. Expand the User Configuration node and click Printers in the Preferences/Control Panel Settings container.

4. Double-click the Printer preference that you created to open the Properties dialog box for it.

5. Click the Common tab, select the Item-Level Targeting check box, and click Targeting to open the Targeting Editor dialog box (see Figure 6-23).

FIGURE 6-23 The Targeting Editor dialog box

6. Click New Item and scroll your mouse down to Terminal Session to add The Terminal Session Is Any to the targeting query.

7. Select Remote Desktop Services from the Type Or Protocol drop-down list and leave the Parameter value set to Any (see Figure 6-24).

8. At this point, you could add additional parameters or reverse the logic by clicking Item Options and choosing Is Not. Or you could add additional targeting items and combine them with Remote Desktop Services in any combination of AND or OR logical statements. You have to restrict this to computers that don't have a battery, so continue by clicking Item Options and selecting AND.

9. Click New Item and select Battery Present.

10. Click Item Options and select Is Not. The targeting query should now look like Figure 6-25.

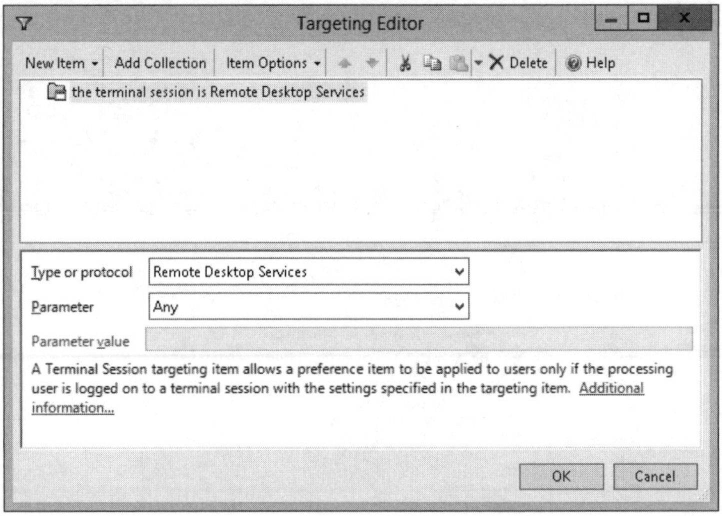

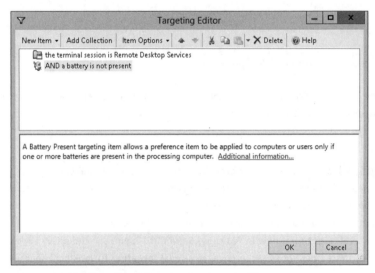

FIGURE 6-24 The Targeting Editor showing a condition

FIGURE 6-25 The Targeting Editor showing two conditions

11. Click OK to close the Targeting Editor and OK again to close the Properties dialog box.

12. Exit the Group Policy Management Editor, and the revised preference is enabled.

13. To see the settings in GPMC, click the Settings tab of the Canada Preferences GPO link, as shown in Figure 6-26.

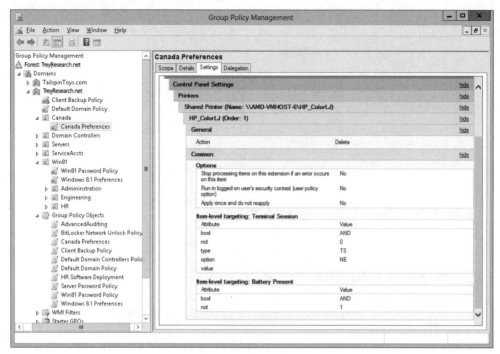

FIGURE 6-26 The Canada Preferences GPO Settings tab

You can use the Targeting Editor to create item-specific targeting to ensure that a specific preference item applies only to the users or computers that it is appropriate for.

EXAM TIP

Item-level targeting is an obvious way for exam writers to ask detailed questions that require you to clearly understand what the targeting options are and how to implement them. The combination of possible options means you need to clearly think through the logic of the question to make sure you choose the answer that correctly matches that logic. Given that item-level targeting is new in Windows Server 2012, you can definitely expect there to be one or more questions that require item-level targeting to satisfactorily meet the question criteria.

Configuring network drive mappings

Preference settings for network drive mappings enable you to set standard drive maps for groups of users or computers. When combined with item-level targeting, you can also ensure that the maps aren't enabled when a covered laptop or mobile device is off the domain network. To create or replace a drive map that maps the S drive to the Software share on server trey-dc-02 when a computer is on the 192.168.10/24 domain network, follow these steps:

1. Open the GPMC and navigate to the Group Policy Objects container for the TreyResearch.net domain.

2. Right-click the Group Policy Objects container and select New. In the Name box, enter **Drive Preference** and click OK.

3. Right-click the TreyResearch.net domain in the console tree and select Link An Existing GPO. Select Drive Preference from the list of Group Policy Objects and click OK.

4. Right-click Drive Preference and select Edit to open the Group Policy Management Editor.

5. Expand the User Configuration container and select Drive Maps from the Preferences/Windows Settings container.

6. Right-click and select New and then Mapped Drive to open the New Drive Properties dialog box,

7. Select Create from the Action drop-down list, and enter **\\trey-dc-02\software** in the Location box.

8. Select Reconnect and enter **Software Distribution Point** in the Label As box.

9. Select S from the Use drop-down list in the Drive Letter section, as shown in Figure 6-27.

FIGURE 6-27 The New Drive Properties dialog box

10. Click the Common tab and select Item-Level Targeting.

11. Click Targeting to open the Targeting Editor.

12. Click New Item and select IP Address Range from the drop-down list.

13. Enter **192.168.10.1** in the Between box and **192.168.10.254** in the And box, as shown in Figure 6-28.

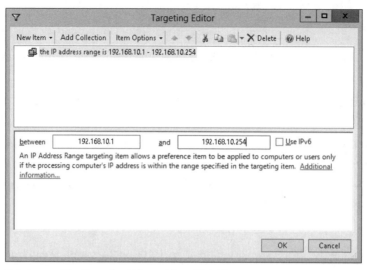

FIGURE 6-28 The Targeting Editor with an IP Address range target

14. Click OK to close the Targeting Editor and OK again to close the New Drive Properties dialog box.

EXAM TIP

Item-level targeting for IP Address Range targets doesn't support IPv6 addresses in Windows Server 2012 and Windows 8. Support was added in Windows Server 2012 R2 and Windows 8.1.

Configuring file deployment

The Group Policy File preference extension enables you to use Group Policy to do the following:

- Copy a file or files in one folder to another while configuring the attributes of those files
- Delete a file or files in one folder, replacing them with copies from a source folder
- Modify the attributes of one or more files in a folder
- Modify the attributes of, replace, or delete all the files in a folder that have a specified extension
- Modify the attributes of, replace, or delete all the files in a folder

The actions available with the File preference extension are these:

- **Create** Copies a file or files from a source location to a target location if the file or files don't already exist and configures the attributes of the target files.
- **Delete** Removes a file or files from a single folder.

- **Replace**   Combines the actions of Delete and Create. It overwrites any files that already exist at the target location or copies ones that don't exist. Sets the attributes of the files at the target location.
- **Update**   Modifies attributes of existing file or files, changing only those attributes specified in the Group Policy Preference. If a file doesn't exist at the target location, the file is copied from the source location.

The settings that can be configured for files include these:

- **Source file(s)**   The source location, which can be a UNC path, or a local or mapped drive path from the perspective of the client. Variables and wildcards are accepted.
- **Destination file**   The target location for the file if creating, replacing, or updating a single file. It can be a UNC path, or a local or mapped drive path from the perspective of the client. It can have the same file name as the source file, or can change the name of the target file.
- **Destination folder**   The target location for the file or files. This can be a UNC path, or a local or mapped drive path from the perspective of the client. This option is available only if the Source File(s) options includes wildcards.
- **Delete file(s)**   The target file path from the perspective of the client. Wildcards are accepted.
- **Suppress errors on individual file actions**   If selected, individual errors are ignored, and the rest of the actions continue.
- **Attributes**   Configures the file system attributes for target files. By default, the Archive attribute is selected.

Configuring folder deployment

The Folder preference GPO extension allows you to create, modify, or remove a folder on a client computer. With this extension, you can do the following:

- Create or modify a folder and then configure its attributes
- Delete a folder and its contents, or delete it only if it is empty
- Delete all the files in folder without deleting the folder
- Delete all the files in a folder without deleting subfolders

The actions available with the Folder preference extension are these:

- **Create**   Creates a new folder if the folder doesn't exist, setting the attributes of the folder.
- **Delete**   Removes a folder if it exists or the files within the folder.
- **Replace**   Combines the actions of Delete and Create, replacing any existing files or subfolders if they were included. It overwrites any existing folder and re-creates it with the specified attributes, or creates a new folder if it doesn't exist.
- **Update**   Modifies an existing folder without deleting it and re-creating it. It does not overwrite existing settings except those explicitly set in the preference, but creates a new folder if the folder doesn't exist.

Configuring custom registry settings

The Group Policy Registry preference extension enables you to manipulate registry settings for computers (HKLM) or Users (HKLU). With this extension, you can do the following:

- Copy registry settings from a source computer and apply them to target computers
- Create, replace, or delete an individual registry value
- Create an empty key, delete a key, or delete all values and subkeys in a key
- Create collections of Registry preference items in the GPMC and apply the collections to multiple registry items
- Create collections in the GPMC based on the registry of a source computer

You can use the Registry Wizard to create multiple registry items by following these steps:

1. Open the GPMC and right-click the GPO you want to add Registry preference items to.

2. Select Edit to open the Group Policy Management Editor. Expand the Computer Configuration or User Configuration container and select Registry from the Preferences/Windows Settings container.

3. Right-click Registry and select New and then Registry Wizard to open the Registry Browser. If the settings you want to copy are on the local computer, click Next. If they're on a different computer, enter the computer name in the Another Computer box (or use the Browse button to locate it) and then click Next.

4. On the Select Any Registry Item By Checking Its Check Box To The Left page of the Registry Browser (see Figure 6-29), expand the registry hive where the settings you want to copy are located and select the check box for the folder that contains the settings.

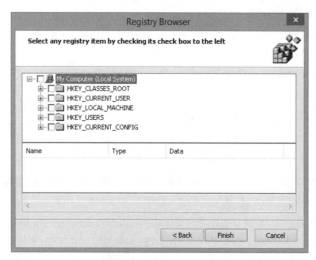

FIGURE 6-29 The Registry Browser

5. After you select the registry entries you want to make part of this preference, click Finish. The values are added to the Registry Wizard Values folder, as shown in Figure 6-30.

6. Add any additional items you want and then close the Group Policy Management Editor to return to the GPMC.

You can also create collections of registry settings by selecting New and then Collection Item in the Group Policy Management Editor. Collections can contain other collections, or items added individually or by using the Registry Wizard.

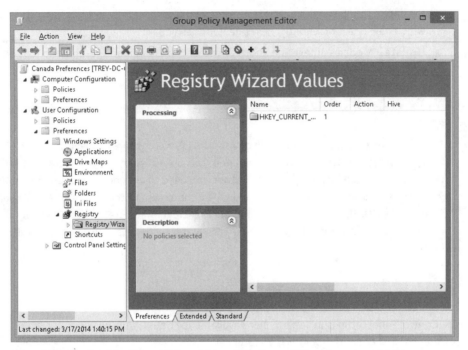

FIGURE 6-30 The Registry Wizard Values folder of the Group Policy Management Editor

Configuring shortcut deployment

The Shortcut preference extension enables you to deploy standard shortcuts to users and computers. Shortcuts can be deployed in either the Computer mode or the User mode of Group Policy. The Shortcut preference GPO extension allows you to create, modify, or remove a shortcut on a client computer. Shortcuts that include drive mappings can only be made in the User mode of Group Policy. Shortcuts can point to:

- **URL** A webpage, website or other location that can be addressed with a URL, such as an FTP site.

- **File system object**   A Windows path, including a file, folder, share or computer. If the path includes a mapped drive, it is only available in User mode.
- **Shell object**   An object within the Windows shell, such as a printer, desktop or Control Panel item. Can also be any file system object.

The actions available with the Shortcut preference extension are these:

- **Create**   Creates a shortcut if the shortcut doesn't already exist.
- **Delete**   Removes a shortcut if it exists.
- **Replace**   Combines the actions of Delete and Create, replacing an existing shortcut with a new one, or creating a new one if it doesn't exist.
- **Update**   Modifies an existing shortcut without deleting it and re-creating it. It does not overwrite existing settings except those explicitly set in the preference, but creates a new shortcut if the shortcut doesn't exist.

EXAM TIP

By default, variables in the Target path of a shortcut preference are resolved by Group Policy before it is created, replaced or updated. This is usually not what was intended and can lead to a compelling, but incorrect, answer. You need to use unresolved variable syntax for variables to allow them to be resolved in the environment of the user or computer. So, for example, %USERNAME% will resolve to the user creating the preference. This likely was not what was intended. Instead, use %<USERNAME>% to cause the username of the logged on user to be used.

Configuring Control Panel settings

The Control Panel settings in Table 6-3 are available for both Computer Configuration preferences and User Configuration preferences.

TABLE 6-3 Control Panel settings

Extension	Action
Data Sources extension	Creates, deletes, replaces, or updates Open Database Connectivity (ODBC) data source names
Devices extension	Enables or disables hardware devices or classes of devices
Folder Options extension	Configures folder options Creates, deletes, replaces, or updates Open With associations for file name extensions Creates, deletes, replaces, or updates file name extensions associated with a type of files
Internet Settings extension	Modifies user-configurable Internet settings
Local Users and Groups extension	Creates, deletes, replaces, or updates local users and groups

Extension	Action
Network Options extension	Creates, deletes, replaces, or updates virtual private networking (VPN) or dial-up networking connections
Power Options extension	Creates, deletes, replaces, or updates power schemes; or modifies power options
Printers extension	Creates, deletes, replaces, or updates TCP/IP, shared, and local printer connections
Regional Options extension	Modifies regional options
Scheduled Tasks extension	Creates, deletes, replaces, or updates scheduled or immediate tasks
Services extension	Modifies services
Start Menu extension	Modifies Start menu options

Configuring power options

A typical Control Panel setting uses the Power Options preference extension. Using this extension, you can create a new domain power plan and deploy it to selected users and computers by using Group Policy Preferences. The four actions for the preference extension are:

- **Create**   Creates a new power plan configuration. If an existing power plan has the same name, the plan isn't changed.

- **Delete**   Removes a power plan of the same name; it does not remove built-in power plans.

- **Replace**   Deletes and then re-creates a power plan. If the named power plan exists, it overwrites all existing settings for the plan. If the plan doesn't exist, it creates it.

- **Update**   Updates an existing plan without removing settings that aren't part of the defined preference item. If the plan doesn't exist, it creates it.

You can create a power plan preference in either the Computer Configuration container or the User Configuration container. User power plans process after computer power plans, and users who are local administrators or Power Users can change their power settings in Control Panel. Power plan preferences are subject to item-level targeting.

Configuring Internet Explorer settings

You can set Internet Explorer (IE) settings by using the Internet Settings Group Policy preference extension. To set preferences, follow these steps:

1. Open the GPMC and right-click the GPO for which you want to set IE preferences.

2. Select Edit from the menu to open the Group Policy Management Editor.

3. Expand the User Configuration container and select the Preferences/Control Panel Settings/Internet Settings node.

4. Right-click Internet Settings and select the version of IE for which you want to create settings. Select Internet Explorer 10 for both Internet Explorer 10 and Internet Explorer 11.

5. Use the New Internet Explorer 10 Properties dialog box to configure options for IE 10 and IE 11. For example, you can set a default home page and have IE always starting on that home page (see Figure 6-31).

FIGURE 6-31 The New Internet Explorer 10 Properties dialog box

6. After you make all the settings changes, click OK to close the dialog box. Exit the Group Policy Management Editor to return to the GPMC.

Thought experiment

Using Group Policy Preferences

In this thought experiment, apply what you've learned about this objective. You can find answers to these questions in the "Answers" section at the end of this chapter.

You are the network administrator for TreyResearch.net. You want to provide new users with a consistent experience that provides them access to resources to facilitate their transition. You opt to use Group Policy Preferences to provide them with that experience during their first 90 days with the company.

1. One of the most important resources is an electronic New Employee Handbook that is regularly updated with new content. How can you ensure that employees have access to the latest version?

2. How could you ensure that the preference is only applied to employees during their initial 90 probationary period?

3. There are several intranet web sites that have employee related resources, offers and forms. A consistent feedback from new employees is that they don't know where to find all of these resources, which are on multiple, unconnected sites. How can you make it easier for them to find what they need?

Objective summary

- Use Group Policy Preferences to configure Windows Settings and Control Panel settings.
- Use item-level targeting to provide fine-grained control of which users or computers the preference targets.
- Group Policy Preferences have four actions: Create, Delete, Replace and Update.
- The Replace action is a combination of Delete and Create; it removes any existing settings.
- The Update action leaves the existing Windows or Control Panel settings in place and changes only the specific settings in the preference item.
- Some preferences, such as Drive Mappings, are applied only during a Synchronous Group Policy update. Over slow links, they typically are not processed.
- Use Group Policy Preferences to deploy standardized template files to all computers covered by the GPO.

Objective review

1. You want to provide all users in the Training Department with the same default printer. It should not delete any existing printers. How can you do that?

    A. Create a GPO linked to the Training OU and specify a Printer preference with the Replace action.

    B. Create a GPO linked to the Training OU and specify a Printer preference with the Create action.

    C. Create a GPO linked to the Training OU and specify a Printer preference with the Update action.

    D. Create a GPO linked to the Training Department security group and specify a Printer preference with the Create action.

2. You need to provide a default power plan for all laptop users running Windows 8. The plan should be applied only to laptop users. How can you do that?

    A. Create a GPO linked to the Win8 OU and specify a User Configuration Power Options preference with the Create action. Specify item-level targeting of a Battery Present.

    B. Create a preference linked to the Win8 OU and specify a Computer Configuration Power Options GPP with the Create action. Specify item-level targeting of a Portable Computer.

    C. Create a preference linked to the Win8 OU and specify a User Configuration Power Options GPP with the Update action. Specify item-level targeting of a Portable Computer.

    D. Create a GPO linked to the Win8 OU and specify a Computer Configuration Power Options preference with the Update action. Specify item-level targeting of a Battery Present.

3. You need to ensure that all domain computers currently on the local network are using a special version of the Hosts file. You create a network share of \\server\ConfigFiles that has Read permissions for Everyone. You configure a Hosts GPO and link it to the Domain. What settings do you need to add to the GPO?

   A. Configure the Computer Configuration Files preference to have a source file of \\server\ConfigFiles\hosts and a target of C:\Windows\System32\Drivers\Etc\Hosts. Set the attributes of the file to read-only and set the IP Address item-level targeting of the local network.

   B. Configure the User Configuration Files preference to have a source file of \\server\ConfigFiles\hosts and a target of C:\Windows\System32\Drivers\Etc\Hosts. Set the attributes of the file to read-only and set the IP Address item-level targeting of the local network.

   C. Configure the Computer Configuration Files preference to have a source file of \\server\ConfigFiles\hosts and a target of C:\Windows\System32\Drivers\Etc\Hosts. Set the attributes of the file to read-only and set the Domain item-level targeting of the target domain.

   D. Configure the User Configuration Files preference to have a source file of \\server\ConfigFiles\hosts and a target of C:\Windows\System32\Drivers\Etc\Hosts. Set the attributes of the file to read-only and set the Domain item-level targeting of the target domain.

Answers

This section contains the solutions to the thought experiments and answers to the lesson review questions in this chapter.

Objective 6.1: Thought experiment

1. The Administrative Template for mapping drives is never run when Group Policy is running asynchronously. By forcing a slow connection to always run asynchronously, you block the drive map from happening on any slow link.

2. There are several settings that could improve the policy, including these:

   - Configure Direct Access Connections As A Fast Network Connection
   - Configure Drive Maps Preference Extension Policy Processing
   - Configure Group Policy Slow Link Detection

3. This Group Policy setting applies only to Windows 8 and later, Windows Server 2012 and later, and Windows RT. Any users still running Windows 7 aren't affected by this policy.

Objective 6.1: Review

1. **Correct answer:** C

   A. **Incorrect:** In Merge mode, some settings from users' normal GPOs are still visible.

   B. **Incorrect:** In Merge mode, some settings from users' normal GPOs are still visible. Also, when you use Loopback mode, you use the Computer Configuration container, not the User Configuration container.

   C. **Correct:** In Replace mode, all the settings come from the Computer Configuration container.

   D. **Incorrect:** Replace mode is correct, but configuration settings can only be done in the Computer container, not in the User container when running in Loopback mode.

2. **Correct answer:** D

   A. **Incorrect:** The correct verb is Invoke.

   B. **Incorrect:** The correct verb is Invoke.

   C. **Incorrect:** You need to specify the computer name, the Computer parameter, and Computer for the Target parameter.

   D. **Correct:** The -Computer parameter points to the correct computer to force the GPO update, and the Target mode is set to Computer.

3. **Correct answer:** A

    A. **Correct:** Blocking inheritance at the OU enables you to set separate policies on the OU, but by enforcing the Domain Password Policy, it will pass through.

    B. **Incorrect:** Blocking inheritance at the domain won't allow you to set separate policies on the OU, and the requirement is for the Default Domain Policy to be used.

    C. **Incorrect**. Blocking inheritance at the domain won't allow you to set separate policies on the OU.

    D. **Incorrect:** You need to block inheritance at the OU level to allow you to use separate policies.

Objective 6.2: Thought experiment

1. Roaming Profiles don't meet the needs. Forcing a Roaming Profile to a remote computer is not the best experience for the user, and it doesn't recognize the partial personal use nature of that remote computer.

2. Folder redirection can be used to meet the needs. You have to not redirect Music, Pictures, and Video folders to meet the backup and data storage requirements, especially because these are areas in which users are more likely to use the remote computer for personal storage, and you don't want their entire MP3 collection on your server. You have to redirect AppData to ensure that corporate templates are available.

3. Rather than folder redirection, you can also implement User folders on a corporate server and direct users to save to that folder for company documents. It has limitations, however, because it requires user education and will inevitably miss some documents. Also, if DirectAccess goes down for any reason, items can't be saved to the corporate servers.

   Another possibility is OneDrive for Business. After all computers are moved to Windows 8.1 and Office 365, OneDrive gives them a secure storage solution that is well integrated into Windows and Microsoft Office.

4. User Configuration/Policies/Windows Settings/Folder Redirection. Don't redirect the Music, Videos or Pictures folders, but do redirect AppDataRoaming and Documents.

Objective 6.2: Review

1. **Correct answers:** A, C, E, G

   A. **Correct:** You need to create a policy for the HR software distribution or use an existing HR-specific GPO.

   B. **Incorrect:** The software is to go only to the HR department, not company-wide.

   C. **Correct:** You need a software distribution point, and users in HR need Read privileges on that distribution point.

   D. **Incorrect:** Choose Publish for software packages that are optional.

   E. **Correct:** Choose Assign for mandatory software packages.

   F. **Incorrect:** Always use a UNC as the package location. The package location is from the perspective of the client, not the server.

   G. **Correct:** Always use a UNC as the package location. The package location is from the perspective of the client, not the server.

2. **Correct answer:** D

   A. **Incorrect:** Set-GPPermission doesn't limit the GPO to the HR users.

   B. **Incorrect:** This would link the GPO to the Domain level, not the OU level.

   C. **Incorrect:** Property filters limit the view of settings, but don't block their use.

   D. **Correct:** You can use security filters to limit the policy to only those users who are part of a security group.

3. **Correct answer:** C

   A. **Incorrect**. The problem is consistent versions of the templates (and computers read Group Policy when they start up, anyway).

   B. **Incorrect:** The problem is consistent versions of the templates (and user policies are updated at logon, regardless).

   C. **Correct:** By configuring a central store, all users of GPMC and GPEdit automatically read that store on SYSVOL.

   D. **Incorrect:** There is no special value to a share of policies, regardless of which computer on which it is located.

Objective 6.3: Thought experiment

1. In the GPMC, configure the Engineering OU to block inheritance, which enables Engineering to maintain its own policies, while you can still set any critical policies to Enforced so that they are propagated to Engineering. Next, create a new GPO for Engineering and link it to the OU. Then delegate permissions on that GPO to the Engineering Support security group and give them Edit Settings permissions. What you don't

want to do is make them Domain Admins, which would give them the permissions they need, but would have all sorts of security implications in other areas of the company.

2. You need to set a regular GPO backup for the Engineering OU GPOs. (Actually, you should be doing this for the entire domain.) Use the Backup-GPO cmdlet as part of a regularly scheduled task and use a Group Managed Service Account to run the task. (See Chapter 5, "Configure and manage Active Directory," for details on Group Managed Service Accounts.) Make sure that the GPOs are backed up to a location that is available only to Domain Admins. If you need to recover a GPO to its previous state, you can use the Restore-GPO cmdlet, or use the GPMC and restore by selecting Manage Backups from the context menu of the Group Policy Objects container.

Objective 6.3: Review

1. **Correct answer:** C

   A. **Incorrect:** You can't use Windows PowerShell to restore the default GPOs.

   B. **Incorrect:** You can't use Windows PowerShell to restore the default GPOs.

   C. **Correct:** This command restores the Default Domain Policy, even if the schema doesn't match.

   D. **Incorrect:** This command restores the Default Domain Controller Policy, but does not restore the Default Domain Policy.

2. **Correct answer:** D

   A. **Incorrect:** The Restore-GPO command requires a path to the GPO to be restored.

   B. **Incorrect:** This restores all GPOs in the domain.

   C. **Incorrect:** This imports the GPO to a new GPO, but leaves the original GPO intact.

   D. **Correct:** This is the correct command line to restore the most recent backup version of the GPO.

3. **Correct answer:** D

   A. **Incorrect:** You can't restore a backup across domain boundaries; you need to import the backup.

   B. **Incorrect:** This restores the backup to the original domain.

   C. **Incorrect:** This copies everything, not just the settings, and does not bring the settings into the correct GPO, even with a Migration Table.

   D. **Correct:** This is the correct procedure for importing just the settings from the backup of the source GPO to the target GPO.

Objective 6.4: Thought experiment

1. Use a File preference with the Replace option to place this document in the user's Documents\HR folder. By using replace, it will automatically replace the file with the latest version.

2. One way to accomplish this would be to use item-level targeting preferences with an Item of User Is A Member Of The Security Group and place all probationary employees in the security group. When they pass their probationary period, they come out of the security group and the preference item setting no longer applies.

3. There are at least two ways to accomplish this, but think of other ways too. One is to use URL shortcut preferences to the individual websites. This, however, requires managing individual shortcuts. Another possibility is to create an Intranet Resources folder that is deployed to their desktop via a Folder deployment preference. Then you simply add the URL shortcuts to the source folder for the Group Policy Preference. You'll want to use the Update or Create option, not Replace. Users are quite likely to add their own shortcuts to the folder as they discover items they use.

Objective 6.4: Review

1. **Correct answer:** C

    A. **Incorrect:** Using the Replace action deletes any current settings for printers with the same name.

    B. **Incorrect:** This would work if the printer didn't yet exist, but would not set the printer as the default if it already existed.

    C. **Correct:** This would create the printer if it didn't exist and would modify it to make it the default if it did.

    D. **Incorrect:** You can't link a GPO to a security group; you can use a security filter to a GPO.

2. **Correct answer:** D

    A. **Incorrect:** This needs to be a Computer Configuration item so it is enforced during startup.

    B. **Incorrect:** The Portable Computer item-level targeting checks to see only whether a computer is docked or undocked.

    C. **Incorrect:** This needs to be a Computer Configuration item so that it is enforced during startup, and Portable Computer item-level targeting checks to see only whether a computer is docked or undocked.

    D. **Correct:** This sets the power options for the computer based on it having a battery, which is a good way to target laptop users.

3. **Correct answer:** A

   A. **Correct:** The domain linking ensures that all domain computers are targeted and the setting is in the Computer Configuration, ensuring that it happens whether the user logs on as a domain user or local user. And the IP Address targeting ensures that it is enforced only on the local network.

   B. **Incorrect:** With the User Configuration, this will not work if the user logs on locally.

   C. **Incorrect:** Domain item targeting causes the file to be enforced even when the computer is not on the local network.

   D. **Incorrect:** With the User Configuration, this will not work if the user logs on locally. Domain item targeting causes the file to be enforced even when the computer is not on the local network.

Index

A

D

About the author

A chemist by education, an electrician by trade, a UNIX sysadmin and Oracle DBA because he raised his hand when he should have known better, an IT Director and consultant by default, and a writer by choice, **CHARLIE RUSSEL** is a founding Microsoft STEP speaker and the author of more than two dozen computer books on operating systems and enterprise environments. His recent books include *Windows Small Business Server 2011 Administrator's Companion* (Microsoft Press), *Microsoft Windows Server 2008 Administrator's Companion* (Microsoft Press), and *Oracle DBA Scripting Quick Reference* (Prentice-Hall PTR).

From technical overviews to drilldowns on special topics, get *free* ebooks from Microsoft Press at:

www.microsoftvirtualacademy.com/ebooks

Download your free ebooks in PDF, EPUB, and/or Mobi for Kindle formats.

Look for other great resources at Microsoft Virtual Academy, where you can learn new skills and help advance your career with free Microsoft training delivered by experts.

Microsoft Press

Now that you've read the book...

Tell us what you think!

Was it useful?
Did it teach you what you wanted to learn?
Was there room for improvement?

Let us know at http://aka.ms/tellpress

Your feedback goes directly to the staff at Microsoft Press,
and we read every one of your responses. Thanks in advance!